THE UNITED NATIONS:
POLICY AND
FINANCING
ALTERNATIVES

———

*Innovative Proposals
by Visionary Leaders*

———

EDITORS:

HARLAN CLEVELAND
HAZEL HENDERSON
INGE KAUL

ORDERING INFORMATION

This book may be ordered from the primary distributor:

> BookCrafters
> 1-800-879-4214,

or from:

> Apex Press
> 777 United Nations Plaza, Suite 3C
> New York, New York 10017
> Tel.: 1-800-316-2739 or 212-972-9877,

or from:

> The Global Commission to Fund the United Nations
> *(see address below)*

Copyright ©1995 Elsevier Science Ltd.

No part of this publication may be reproduced, stored in a retrieval system or transmitted in any form or by any means, electronic, electrostatic, magnetic tape, mechanical, photocopying, recording or other-wise, without permission in writing from the copyright holder.

This edition of *The United Nations: Policy and Financing Alternatives,* edited by Harlan Cleveland, Hazel Henderson and Inge Kaul, is published by arrangement with Elsevier Science Ltd. (Butterworth-Heinemann Imprint), The Boulevard, Langford Lane, Kidlington 0X5 1GB, England.

Publisher's Cataloging in Publication

The United Nations: policy and financing alternatives / edited by Harlan Cleveland, Hazel Henderson and Inge Kaul. – [American ed.]
    p. cm.
    Includes bibliogaphical references.

    1. United Nations – Finance. I. Cleveland, Harlan. II. Henderson, Hazel, 1933- III. Kaul, Inge.
JX1997.8.F5U75 1996   341.23'3
                       QBI95-20815

ISBN 0-9659589-0-5

Published by:
The Global Commission to Fund the United Nations
1511 K Street NW, Suite 1120, Washington, D.C. 20005
Tel.: 202-639-9460   Fax: 202-639-9459

Printed and bound in the U.S.A.

THE UNITED NATIONS:
POLICY AND FINANCING
ALTERNATIVES

Edited by: Harlan Cleveland, Hazel Henderson and Inge Kaul

*The editors wish to thank the Global Commission to Fund the United Nations
for its assistance in preparing this volume and publishing this second printing.*

INTRODUCTION TO THE U.S. EDITION

By Hazel Henderson

This report, the first from the Global Commission to Fund the United Nations, was released on the first official day of the United Nations World Summit on Social Development, in Copenhagen, Denmark (March 6, 1995), as a Special Issue of the British-based journal of forecasting, *Futures*, published by Elsevier Scientific Limited. The report was titled, *The United Nations at Fifty: Policy and Financing Alternatives.* Some two thousand copies were made available to the world's journalists covering the Summit with generous assistance from the Jessie Smith Noyes Foundation of New York, U.S.A.

The report broke open the debate about innovative alternatives for restructuring and financing United Nations functions – supplementing the current dues system. The report has been widely reviewed and is being used in many universities and schools as a text in curricula on world affairs. The Commissioners, Advisors, and associates of the Global Commission to Fund the U.N. contributed the papers in the report, while Harlan Cleveland, and Inge Kaul, and I donated our time as co-editors. We are grateful to Colin R. Blackman, the editor of *Futures*, for his helpful editorial suggestions.

Heads of state and leaders of delegations in Copenhagen were obliged to address the issues in the report: including innovative financing proposals; currency exchange fees (targeted toward the 90% of such trading which is speculative); fees for communications satellite "parking spaces" in crowded low earth orbits; small levies on air transport and ocean shipping; for all commercial, for-profit uses of global common heritage resources – oceans, atmosphere, Antarctica, and space, as well as the newest global commons, information highways and the "financial cyberspace" they have spawned.

Journalists in Copenhagen who read the report asked delegates and heads of state alike whether they favored such user fees and royalties and in the case of abuse of such global commons, whether they favored fines and taxes on, for example, pollution, toxic dumping in oceans, and arms sales.

The Commission views the United Nations as an indispensable world convenor of all nations as well as provider of a host of services to "We the Peoples," from small pox eradication to cooperative standard setting with the private sector and civil society in many important global services from air travel, ocean shipping, accounting protocols, and monetary stability, to allocating radio and other communications band widths, agreements on human rights, employee safety, and environmental protection – as well as peace keeping and development. There seems no reason that those who benefit commercially from these global services should not pay fairly for them. In the area of peace-keeping, the proposal for a United Nations Security Agency (UNSIA) could raise funds for a stable U.N. conflict-resolution, rapid-response capability. The

UNSIA would sell insurance to countries seeking security protection. Using commercial insurance industry risk assessors, UNSIA would set "premiums" based on the risk level and types of peace operation that nations requested. This arrangement would permit nations to reduce military spending, gain more security, and fund civilian sectors. UNSIA is assessed in this report and since it was first proposed in 1993 the proposal has gathered much high-level support, including from Nobel Laureates, Dr. Oscar Arias, Dr. John Polanyi, and other major personalities and civil society organizations.

The Global Commission to Fund the United Nations is an example of the civil society functioning at a high level of responsibility. The Commission reports directly to the international media, the world's decision makers, and the civil society. This new edition of its first report became more crucial during 1995 as the debate over the future of the U.N. expanded and, unfortunately, became politicized in the U.S.A. The confused public debate over globalization processes and painful social and economic restructuring in the U.S.A. caught the U.N. in unfair, uninformed, and often irrational political crossfires. This historic report will continue to be a lightning rod and a goad to fresh thinking and social innovation for the rest of this decade and into the 21st Century.

Hazel Henderson, Co-editor
St. Augustine, Florida
December, 1995

THE UNITED NATIONS: ITS FUTURE IS ITS FUNDING

Harlan Cleveland

Who pays for 'international relations'? And how much? Readers who have had a surfeit of mystery stories, readers who find fictional plots too decipherable, readers yearning for more complicated puzzles, are hereby invited to think hard about the modern matrix mystery called 'financing the international system'.

What do 'international relations' cost? The calculation cannot be based on the expense accounts of the scattering of diplomats around the world, let alone those concentrated in New York or Geneva or other international watering holes.

You would surely have to add in all the intelligence agents clustered in Washington, Brussels, Istanbul, Cairo, Tokyo and the many other places where well known people gather, and who are assumed, because they are gathered with maximum media attention, to have some higher wisdom highly priced in the international market for secret information. And you would have to count the many agents of less impressive yet even more international networks of merchants, shipowners, airlines, insurance underwriters, currency speculators—and militant religionists and terrorist conspirators.

Then you would have to widen the net to count the world's military establishments, and the puffery of the arms suppliers whose business it is to make sure that the world's arms races are never quite swift enough. Better add in, too, the growing army of volunteer peacemakers who cluster around those who brandish the biggest weapons.

You could widen the net further to include all the trade negotiators, the exporters and importers, the protectionist lobbies and free-trade advocates, the business firms that span the globe with their internal transactions, and the miracle workers in information technology who make possible a truly global trade in things, money, culture, ideas and information, more and more of it bounced off orbiters in the sky.

You should certainly count the cost of exchanging more than a trillion dollars (ie $1 000 000 000 000) each day across the world's increasingly porous boundaries. And you can't leave out the costs of migration—the costs that were too heavy to bear where the migrants came from, the costs of holding some of them in semi-permanent

Harlan Cleveland was an official of the United Nations Relief and Rehabilitation Administration (1946—48) and the US Marshall Plan (1948—52). He served as Assistant Secretary of State for International Organization Affairs in the Kennedy Administration, and as US Ambassador to NATO under Presidents Johnson and Nixon. He is currently President of the World Academy of Art and Science and may be contacted at 1235 Yale Place #802, Minneapolis, MN 55403, USA (Tel: +1 612 339 3589; fax: +1 612 339 6230).

'camps', the costs of their transition in leaky boats and across leaky frontiers, the costs of proving they belong somewhere else, the costs of their resettlement wherever compassionate new neighbours welcome them to a new 'home'.

As they say in Hawaii, where everybody is in a 'minority', the world is now 'all mix up'. In such a world there is no way to count the costs—and values—of wars and rumours of wars, the costs of preparing for war then preparing for peace, the costs of international criminals and international police to pursue them, the costs of disease and dislocation and disasters natural and human-made, the costs of cultural diversity pursued to the limit, the cost of electronic networks and their impact on local cultures that can isolate themselves only by intentional ignorance or desperate acts of collective suicide or immolation.

Nor should we forget one of the biggest costs of all: the consequences of what humans now know and may yet discover—the knowledge that has made us the first generation in human history to learn that what we humans consciously do, or refrain by conscious decisions from doing, has become the biggest variable in the health of our human environment. We are still conducting, in Roger Revelle's memorable metaphor, a giant geophysical experiment, the outcome of which we cannot guess.

How to finance international functions?

The aggregate costs of international relations are thus incalculable. What can be calculated, calibrated, judged, and acted on are the costs of doing something international about the human choices and chances in 'world affairs'.

Until recently most national governments, and most scholars of their own nations' 'international relations', have been preoccupied with (and appalled by) what it would cost their national taxpayers to take seriously the undisputed United Nations mandate, half a century ago,

To take effective collective measures for the prevention and removal of threats to the peace...;
   To develop friendly relations among nations based on respect for the principle of equal rights and self-determination of peoples...;
   To achieve international cooperation in solving international problems of an economic, social, cultural, or humanitarian character, and in promoting and encouraging respect for human rights and for fundamental freedoms for all without distinction as to race, sex, language, or religion; and
   To be a center for harmonizing the actions of nations in the attainment of these common ends.

In the United Nations itself, the debate has mostly been not about what was needed to do this job, but about how some lesser 'burden' should be shared. In the wider community, what the US Declaration of Independence called the 'general opinion of mankind', most people have latterly yawned at that debate, correctly judging the amounts of money at stake to be marginal in relation to the really important issues requiring attention—such as a new chance for freer trade, the progress on the US budget deficit, a scandal of public corruption in Tokyo, growing unemployment in Western Europe, Eastern Europe's reform-generated depression, turbulence and uncertainty in the former Soviet Union, most of Africa's slough of despond, the extraordinary turn of events in South Africa, the precarious potential of peace in the Middle East, the surprising success of India in producing food and computer software, the sudden surge of productivity and consumption in China and its East Asian neighbours—and the disturbing yet exciting sideshows in Sri Lanka, Somalia, Bosnia-Herzegovina, Haiti and Iraq.

In the midst of these and other perils and possibilities is the global system summarized in the durable Charter of the United Nations, a multipurpose club that has grown in 50 years from 51 to 184 member-states (including hundreds of culturally conscious 'nations') and from 2.6 billion to 5.7 billion human beings, with more affluent people and more families in poverty, by any reasonable measure, than when the Charter's original signatories were calling for 'social progress and better standards of life in larger freedom'.

Judging from recent experience, we will all be relying more and more—for peacekeeping and peaceful settlement, for the promotion of fairness in the human family, and for fostering human development—on the United Nations. Financing the UN is no longer an issue to be ignored, bypassed, or swept aside by the excitement of 'world affairs'. It is high time we looked hard at how best to finance a widening range of international functions that grows more obviously necessary with every passing year.

This is why the editor of *Futures*, and the editors of this volume, thought that now would be a special moment to take stock of this neglected subject, and serve up a menu of the best thinking now available on the subject. The 'Social Summit', to be held in Copenhagen in spring 1995, provides a good occasion to bring UN funding to the world stage where it now belongs.

Funding crises

In the past, even those international programmes widely agreed to be essential have been plagued by chronic funding crises.

This chronic plague was not clearly foreseen 50 years ago. The dominant idea at this time was that the UN General Assembly would be like a kind of legislature in a parliamentary system. Dean Rusk, who as a young public servant worked closely with some of the original architects of the Charter (and who later became US Secretary of State during most of the 1960s), called the new system 'parliamentary diplomacy'.

But the legislative analogy turned out to be flawed when applied to a committee of sovereign states. In a genuine legislature, clashing interests are fought out bloodlessly and some form of majority decides for all. A committee of sovereign states does not act that way.

In the early 1960s the Soviets defaulted on their assessed United Nations dues—as a mark of displeasure with the inconvenient success of the UN's big peacekeeping operation in the former Belgian Congo (now Zaire), and with Secretary General Dag Hammarskold's leadership role in that policy. The instinct of the US officials dealing with this issue was to enforce Article 19 of the Charter, where the message seemed crystal clear:

A member of the United Nations which is in arrears in the payment of its financial contributions to the Organization shall have no vote in the General Assembly if the amount of its arrears equals or exceeds the amount of the contributions due from it for the preceding two full years . . .

US officials, arguing from the legislative analogy, thought that a parliamentary body, even an international one, could be relied on to defend its own power to tax a member-state. As it happened, I was then the person in the US State Department responsible for making that judgment. I guessed wrong. Most members of the General Assembly scampered away from dunning a superpower for overdue bills.

Later, after a couple of turns of the political wheel in Washington, DC, the USA also defaulted with impunity on the Charter obligation to pay its dues—an obligation that supposedly has the force of US law under the treaty power of the US constitution.

Tax proposals

Buying a world of peaceful change should be much less expensive than the threat or use of force. There are plenty of international systems and transnational transactions which depend for their viability on a managed peace. The stake they share in a world peaceful enough to make possible their transporting, communicating and transacting should be reflected in the prices we all pay for such services.

The recommendations of several international commissions that have studied the shortcomings of the international system, including the *North—South Report* by the group chaired by former West German Chancellor Willy Brandt and *Our Common Future*, the report of the World Commission on Environment and Development chaired by Prime Minister Gro Harlem Brundtland of Norway, have included the suggestion that international taxation is part of the solution. One of the earliest, an Aspen Institute consensus report on *The Planetary Bargain* (1975) advocated an international development tax. We described the idea this way:

Rather than trying to pump life back into the worn-out policy of year-to-year decisions by individual governments on how much to appropriate and to whom it should go, what's needed is a flow of funds for development which are generated *automatically* under *international control* . . . The idea of international taxation (on ships for the use of international waters, on international air travel, on passports, on international tele-communications, on ocean fisheries) is a hardy perennial, but we believe it should be treated as an idea whose time has come.

The most recent international group to address the issue is the Commission on Global Governance co-chaired by Prime Minister Ingvar Carlsson of Sweden and Sir Shridath Ramphal of Guyana, formerly a long-serving Secretary General of the Commonwealth. Its report, *Towards the Global Neighborhood*, approaches this whole question rather cautiously: a carbon tax might be introduced 'gradually'; charges for the use of common global resources are endorsed in general terms; an international tax on foreign exchange transactions should be 'explored'.

One idea that has fortunately not picked up any steam would link development funding to the creation of special drawing rights (SDRs) by the International Monetary Fund. But SDRs are supposed to be a device for creating monetary stability and should therefore be created at irregular intervals, at moments when more international liquidity is needed. Such a system could starve international development (or whatever other function was to be supported by such money creation) whenever, as frequently happened in the 1970s and 1980s, world liquidity did not justify the creation of more international money.

This objection does not apply to the idea of taxing all currency exchange transactions, an idea which has been around for three decades. It was recently mentioned (with reservations) by the Commission on Global Governance. It would be a small charge on each foreign currency exchange transaction, intended partly for revenue and partly to discourage international currency speculation. The market is now so huge (more than $1 trillion a day) that the tax rate could be, indeed would have to be, so tiny that it would not likely be perceived by current speculators as a major disincentive. But even a tiny tax on a huge volume of daily transactions could readily raise large 'automatic' revenues for such UN programmes as peacekeeping and development assistance.

As a matter of common sense, fund raising for international functions should bear most heavily on those activities which benefit most from a peaceful and predictable world environment. Travel, transport, communication and international transactions are the obvious candidates. As a frequent international traveller and communicator, I see no reason why I should not pay a tithe of my passport fee, a fraction of the price of my airline ticket, or an override on my bill for telephoning, faxing or sending data across international frontiers, to help fund the privilege of moving myself and my thoughts around in a world which will become much more unfair, much more turbulent, and much more dangerous if the international system doesn't 'work'.

Another easily understood device is a tax on the use of a part of the Global Commons. Rent for a parking stall in geosynchronous orbit; licensing fees for the exploitation of resources in the deep ocean, on the seabed, and on the continental margin; an easement for work in Antarctica; payments for the international transfer of genetic resources; fees for transborder data flows and especially on international financial transactions; a tax on the deliberate emission of 'controlled substances' (CFCs, CO_2, methane etc), intended as a disincentive (like tobacco and alcohol taxes) as well as a revenue measure—the list is limited only by the human imagination.

Catching a wave

Over the years, a good deal of thinking has been done, mostly below the surface of public attention, on this whole subject. Much of this thinking is reflected in the pages of this issue. It will clearly be necessary to develop international income streams that do not depend on annual soul searching by half a hundred governments. A good many suggestions, not all of them consistent with each other, are laid on the table in the articles that follow.

No national government or major international leader has yet persuasively espoused a comprehensive plan for financing the international functions that are bound to grow in the years ahead. Yet 'peace in our time', and 'sustainable development', will both crucially depend on major international financial innovations. Whoever first 'catches a wave' on this subject will make an unforgettable contribution to a workable system of peaceful change.

NEW MARKETS AND NEW COMMONS

Opportunities in the global casino

Hazel Henderson

The United Nations is well positioned for the global changes of the information age now engulfing nation-states. The UN role and tasks—as global norm setter, broker, networker, convenor, and peacekeeper—are ideally suited to today's world of linked 'infostructures' and distributed power, influence and knowledge typified by the emerging global civil society. The UN can serve all these emerging infostructures—and be compensated by fostering debates and convening parties to design the needed agreements for operating the emerging 'electronic commons', including today's global financial casino. Technological, social and economic contexts for this new global agenda are described together with some market opportunities in new public/private partnerships to serve the global commons.

Currency speculation and the inability of the global securities and financial industry to address the mounting risks to all players is a classic example of how events and technology render economic textbooks obsolete. Economic theory is highly articulated concerning markets and various market failures. But economics has consistently overlooked the commons and their allocations theories—except when commons can be owned as property. Today, most governance and allocation issues perplexing human societies involve the global commons. Interestingly, today's now-integrated, 24-hour global casino is transforming itself from a classic free market place of win–lose competition to a new form of electronic commons, where each 'rational actor's' self-interested behaviour can endanger the entire system—unless rapid cooperative, collective action is taken. Recent examples

Hazel Henderson is an international development policy analyst and forecaster, a Fellow of the World Business Academy, and a member of the Global Commission to Fund the UN. She may be contacted at PO Box 5190, St Augustine, FL 32085-5190, USA (Tel: +1 904 829 3140; fax: +1 904 826 0325).

illustrate the vulnerability of tightly interlinked global financial systems operating without overall rules, such as Germany's Herstatt Bank failure and the US savings and loan crisis. Both these episodes were addressed by cooperative agreements and government intervention. The more recent losses by banks and corporations in derivatives and hedging strategies raise concerns that the process of risk reduction for individual players increases risks in the whole financial system which will require new global rules. Even otherwise free market economists, including Fred Bergsten, Jeffrey Sachs and Lawrence Summers, are urging the formation of a 'GATT for investment and finance'.[1] Clearly, the UN has a key role in fostering such innovations.

Today, information technology innovations have created a global financial casino where as much as $1 trillion of 'virtual securities' (*derivatives* of underlying real stocks, bonds, commodities and currencies) are traded each day—bringing new uncertainties such as raids on the dollar, sterling and other major currencies, and scenarios of financial collapse. Worried central bankers and national politicians, trying to stave off such scenarios, are left with failing textbook economic remedies to support their domestic economies and currencies (such as raising interest rates or buying efforts). These national players, handicapped by eroding national sovereignty, manoeuvre painfully towards the *social innovation* needed to match the advance of the global casino's computer and satellite-based *technological innovation*.[2] The UN in its preeminent role as global norm setter, broker, networker and convenor is well suited to fostering such social innovations in the new electronic commons.

In today's financial markets, bankers, brokers, bond and currency traders themselves—along with growing numbers of finance ministers, parliamentarians and regulators—see the need for new rules to create more orderly capital and currency markets. Such new market regimes can inspire confidence, such as the 'circuit breakers' introduced on Wall Street after the 1987 stock market crash, which now dampen the effects of program trading. Finance ministers acknowledge the loss of domestic controls as well as diminished tax revenues which came with the financial deregulation of the 1980s. Bond markets more concerned with inflation than unemployment limit 'pump-priming' projects and jobs while reducing options for social safety nets. Some central banks have even tried to join the derivative trading game—on occasions with heavy losses. Only global agreements on capital investment, currency exchange stabilization and restructuring the IMF, World Bank and the World Trade Organization (WTO) can address today's paradoxes so well described by Jeffrey Sachs in *The Economist*.[3] However, his prescriptions for closing 'the big holes [that] remain in the legal fabric [which] may yet threaten global economic systems', fall far short of addressing the dilemma of national governments squeezed between currency speculators and bond traders on the one hand and the perils of domestic protests of IMF structural adjustments, on the other. Sachs assumes 'in 1994 the world is closer than ever before to the global *cooperative* [emphasis added] free market arrangements championed 50 years ago by the visionaries who met at Bretton Woods'. However, cooperative agreements do not emerge automatically from free markets and must be designed by human rather than invisible hands.

The social innovation lag

The 300-year evolution of Western industrial societies involved a continuous lag between technological innovations and the social innovations needed to accommodate their societal assimilation. From the spinning jenny and the steam engine, to the automobile and computer, such technologies have always outpaced and eventually called forth responding social innovations: double-entry book keeping and accounting protocols, national currencies, and central banks, standardization of rail gauges, highway signs and electrical fixtures. The computer industry, now automating service sectors worldwide, underpins today's global casino. The UN—itself a major social innovation—is well suited to development of the legal infrastructure of this electronic commons. Computer industries are still in their competitive, market expansion phase—facing many paradoxes of technological evolution often experienced at this stage of the innovation cycle, eg incompatibility and mismatches between software, operating systems, etc. This diversity of design—originally a competitive advantage to individual firms—begins to hinder further market expansion into more system-wide applications. The other major paradox is joblessness, poverty, and thus loss of consumer purchasing power. Market competition (or in game theory terms, win–lose strategies) begins to disorder social structures and also *limits* market penetration. Incompatibility often leads to chaotic conditions, for example, in the early railroads and multiplicity of bank-issued currencies, or the separate development in the 1970s of a dozen or so different machine-readable product code systems. Paradoxically, textbook market theory inhibits the social innovation response which could distribute the fruits of technological productivity more widely via new tax policies *and* widen market penetration. Such social innovations are seen as 'interference in free markets'. In France, Minitel terminals were distributed freely by government—achieving much more rapid acceptance of computers than in the USA. In France, there is also a widening debate about shortening work weeks to reduce rising unemployment.[4] Systems approaches view the win–lose market framework as simply entering a transitional phase whereby cooperation (ie win–win strategies) could expand opportunities for all, as well as by standardizing a regulatory regime, now at the global level, as I have detailed elsewhere.[5]

Today, it is not surprising that social efforts are still lagging in the control of the rate and direction of technological innovation. Western societies are still unsuccessful in channelling these now powerfully institutionalized technological drives toward systemic, social and ecological goals. Social inventions arise in response, such as the US Office of Technology Assessment, founded in 1974 on whose original Advisory Council I served until 1980. Nowhere is this widening lag in social innovation more visible than in the growing gap between the explosion of computerized global financial trading (over 90% of which is speculation) and the so-far feeble efforts of finance ministers, bankers and international bodies, such as the Bank for International Settlements (BIS) and the International Monetary Fund (IMF), to create the needed regulatory regime. This new regulatory framework is now essential and must be global and as 'real-time' as the markets themselves. Minimally, it should resemble the functioning of the Securities and Exchange Commission (SEC) which regulates Wall Street in the USA. Other similar capital market regulations in other countries will need to be harmonized into a single 'Global SEC'. Many *ad hoc* efforts are occurring behind closed doors in studies under way at the IMF, the BIS, at meetings of the G-7, and in academe, such as the 'Rethinking Bretton Woods Symposium' at the American University, in June 1994.[6] Even Bankers Trust chairman, Charles Sanford, envisioned the restructuring consequences of global information networks which can now bypass banks—allowing entrepreneurs seeking capital simply to upload their business plans on to the Internet.[7] Similarly, I have predicted that financial TV channels will offer 'The Venture Capital Show', 'The Initial Public Offering Show', etc, complete with 800 numbers to complement existing electronic trading systems, such as Instinet, AutEx and Reuters. National legislators can only respond to global speculation, hedging and derivatives with ineffective domestic legislation. Market responses are equally suboptimal, such as increasing the contracting out of hedging and risk-management activities to banks (including Bankers Trust and Tokai Bank Europe) or private consulting firms such as Emcor Risk Management Consulting, USA, the largest player.[8] This outsourcing is driven by the complexity and costs of the computer programs and 'rocket science' experts in such hedging strategies—now beyond the capabilities of most company treasurers. Such outsourcing creates even greater risk to the system as a whole since the few providers of such services may lead to a *de facto* 'cartelization' of them.

Thus, today's looming global financial crises have deep systemic roots based in the paradigms which underlie industrialism and still drive the so-called post-industrial information age. No wonder traditional banking and financial leaders are unable to transcend their competitive models to visualize needed social innovations. Only new paradigms—beyond reductionism, the Puritan ethic and nationalistic competition—can allow social innovation to catch up with rampant technological innovation, whether in computerized hedge programs and global financial markets or the globalization of today's arms markets and industries. Such new paradigms need to extend beyond individualistic economic textbook models of maximizing self-interest as 'rational' behaviour and global competitiveness of such actors in a 'level global playing field' of few rules and 'free trade'. Regulation is opposed by equating free enterprise technological evolution as 'natural as ecosystems', while invoking chaos theory and system dynamics to 'prove' that regulatory intervention to deal with rising poverty and joblessness is too unpredictable. It remains to be seen whether today's chaotic global financial casino and other new technological domains in cyberspace will be even more unpredictable without some regulatory intervention. It is never a matter of *either* rules and regulations *or* freedom and markets. In human societies rules for interaction are fundamental—it is only a matter of who, what, when, why, where, and how we choose to regulate ourselves. The invisible hand is our own.

Today's abstracted world trade/global competitiveness model has alienated financial markets from the real economy of 'Main Street' (where actual people in real factories produce real shoes or build real houses and grow real food). Thus, the global casino is now spinning into cyberspace—divorced from any understanding of the whole picture: human societies with people working, cooperating and competing, while interacting within webs of other species and ecosystems in a fragile, ever-changing biosphere. Thus, the needed paradigm shifts are towards systems and chaos theory and other interdisciplinary, dynamic change models, informed by psychological re-integration to overcome the pervasive fear/scarcity-based strategies of economics. They are now *conditions* for the shift of our financial systems from pervasive GNP-based, 'trickle-down' economic growth typified still in the Bretton Woods institutions to diversified, decentralized 'trickle-up', sustainable development—which restores incentives to mutual aid, cooperative informal sectors, and the development of agreements and rules or managing global commons.

These paradigm shifts begin with rethinking scarcity, abundance, needs and satisfaction, and lead inevitably to wholesale redefinitions of money, wealth, work, productivity, efficiency and progress. A prerequisite of this new worldview is the understanding that money isn't scarce, and that its apparent scarcity is itself a major social regulatory mechanism—a social innovation, which, when functioning well, provides a beneficial circulatory system for wider human exchange and purchasing power beyond face-to-face barter. As Boulding noted in 1968,[9] there are three basic kinds of human interactions: (1) *threat*, based on fear; (2) *exchange*, barter and reciprocity; and (3) *love*, based on gifts, altruism, and more comprehensive, long-term value systems.

Many of the operating principles derived from industrial paradigms remain unexamined: technological innovation is widely encouraged and subsidized; social innovation is suspect (as 'planning') and occurs only after crises, such as the Great Depression. The UN itself emerged only after the experience of two ghastly world wars. National societies are assumed to be divided up into a private sector (market competition) and a public sector (government and non-profits) with a 'Berlin Wall' inhibiting interaction (buttressed by anti-trust laws). Government is enjoined from 'competing' with private sector business. Much creativity and inventiveness is dammed up behind such rigid definitions and restrictive institutions which operationalize the competitive nation-state-based industrial paradigm now moving towards its logical conclusion—global economic warfare. In pre-industrial and traditional societies, most land and natural resources were held communally, for example, 'the commons'—the village green (as the common grazing land of feudal England was known). Garrett Hardin, in 'The tragedy of the commons', pointed out the problem that occurred when individuals could maximize their self-interest by putting more of their sheep to feed on the commons—leading to overgrazing that destroyed the commons for all.[10] Hardin failed to dispel the confusion among economists between the commons as 'property' and the commons as 'closed systems' which are accessed collectively[11] (see *Figure 1*). Either communities could agree on rules to access fairly the commons—or it could be enclosed as private or group property and plots could be traded in a market. In either case, issues of equity and freedom always have to be adjudicated, while the poor and powerless tend to be denied fair access. The world's oceans, the air we breathe, the planet's biodiversity, are all also commons—not property. They can only be managed with agreed rules to prevent exploitation. This is now true for the emerging electronic commons. The concept of private property, as I have detailed elsewhere[12] is derived from the Latin word *privare*: all those goods, lands, and resources that individuals wished to *withhold* from the community and to *deprive* common usage.

Today, commons are still widely evident in traditional agricultural societies and many developing countries. Indeed, the march of industrialism has involved the enclosure of commons begun by force in 17th-century Britain when peasants were driven off common lands by the Enclosure Acts as described by Karl Polanyi in *The Great Transformation*.[13] Today, market forces seek to enclose such declining commons as ocean fish stocks (by arbitrarily allocating property rights to fisheries) and biodiversity (by continually encroaching on natural habitats and by patenting life forms and species)—thus shortchanging future generations via current market discount rates. Such pre-empting of commons and simply declaring them as 'common property' or 'markets' by fiat, denies due process to indigenous people who have fostered such resources and biodiversity for generations. Markets are the focus of economic textbooks, since economics arose as an epistemological justification for early capitalism and industrialization. Commons are still barely examined, even in much more recent 'green' economics texts, except as common

	Economists	Futurists/systems
	Markets Private sector • Individual decisions • Competition • Invisible hand • Anti-trust	**Open systems** • Divisible resources • Win–lose rules • (Adam Smith's rules)
	Commons Public sector... • Property of all • Monopoly under regulation • Consortia	**Closed systems** • Indivisible resources • Win–win rules • Cooperation • Agreements

Note: One must remember that all such schematizations are, at best, approximations and often culturally arbitrary

Figure 1. Differing views of markets and commons.

property.[14] The global electronic commons of finance, computer and other communications networks are still widely viewed as 'markets'.

From a systems viewpoint, 'markets' are merely open systems with abundant resources that can be used individually and competitively, while commons are closed systems, where resources are used indivisibly, such as national parks, air, oceans, satellite orbits, and the earth's electromagnetic spectrum (see Figure 1). From the economic textbooks' standpoint, these commons conceived as 'common property' can only be rationally managed if *owned* by somebody. Thus economists rely on private ownership and property rights schemes as 'market-based regulations' (eg taxes and subsidies) leading them, for example, to lobby governments to set up such 'markets' as those in the US Clean Air Act of 1991 allowing polluting companies to sell and trade their 'licenses to pollute' the common air to other companies. The rhetoric used borders on schizophrenia, ie markets *v* 'command and control' (a straw man in the post-communist world) and a false dichotomy, since such pollution 'markets' are *set up* by new regulations and require costly monitoring and enforcement of total emission levels. Needless to say, many local citizen-groups point out that these polluting companies did not 'buy' the air and have no right to sell a common resource such as air, which is a condition of *survival* and protected as a human *right* along with liberty and the pursuit of happiness (for example, in the US and others' constitutions). Today's issues of markets-*v*-commons (and regulations) still concern equity, accountability, democratic access to public assets and essential services. Debates on the information superhighway typify the now bankrupt 'public *v* private/market *v* regulation' polarization. Even Wall Street analysts schizophrenically characterize the cut-throat and still privatizing telecommunications sectors as 'balkanized and fragmented' and 'needing national standardization' in order to develop further. This state of affairs typifies the myriad players in the global casino—banking, brokerage and insurance services which are now merging, *ad hoc* groups such as the Paris Club, as well as the International Organization of Securities Commissions (IOSCO), the BIS and its 1988 Basle Accords, the Committee on Inter-Bank Netting Schemes, etc.[15] These public and private sector actors in today's global casino can be convened with the help of the UN to create broader agreements on currency regimes at a new 'Bretton Woods' conference, as many groups, including the Volcker Commission, are now proposing.

More systemic theoretical frameworks can help reconceptualize today's great globalizations and the restructuring processes which they engender—the globalization of industrialism and technology, of finance and information, of work and migration, of human effects on the biosphere, of the arms race, and the emergence of global consumption and culture.[16] Concepts that provide the context for the rise of information societies and the eclipse of industrialism and its now dysfunctional economic paradigm include:

(1) The shift from human progress as equated with quantitative GNP growth (to more complex qualitative goals of quality of life and sustainable development), requiring new scorecards such as the Human Development Index (HDI) of the United Nations Development Programme, and my Country Futures Indicators (CFI) and its first version for the USA—the Calvert-Henderson Quality-of-Life Indicators. The reclassification of the 'economy' beyond textbook public-*v*-private sectors and market-*v*-regulations is necessary as well as expanding the mapping of productive sectors to include the unpaid, informal economy and the undergirding of productivity by nature, as well as the rise of the global civil society.

(2) A systems view of markets as open systems and commons as closed systems (see Figure 1) to clarify policy options and new strategies. Economic textbooks need to reflect systems theory and teach how to recognize when markets saturate (ie all niches are filled), and they turn into commons. A sure sign of the need to reorganize a market from win−lose competition to broader win−win rules for all players is the pervasive appearance of cutthroat competitiveness, ie lose−lose, such as today's competitive global economic warfare or conflicts over the earth's cluttered electromagnetic spectrum, or increasing global arms sales which make no one more secure.[17] Most institutions geared to meeting today's needs and those of future sustainable development will require restructuring and cooperative linking in networks and consortia of *both* public and private actors and institutions. There will be as many new types of enterprise charters, providing new incomes and jobs as human imagination can devise: from joint stock companies and employee stock ownership plans, worker-owned enterprises, non-profit institutions, private/government corporations (such as the World Bank and INTELSAT) and new UN agencies, such as the proposed Development Security Council, to community development banks, cooperatives, and networks of cooperating small businesses, such as those in Italy and Denmark (see Figure 2).

Break-up of the global money cartel

Today we see the rise of non-money, information economies (local, regional, and global networks for barter, counter-trade, reciprocity and mutual aid) wherever macroeconomic management is failing in societies.[18] In G-7 countries, Russia and Eastern Europe—all challenged by the global casino—people are creating their own local information societies of mutual aid on the Internet and other networks where users are increasing by 25% per month. Businesses in high unemployment and poverty areas are issuing discount coupons and other scrip, just as cities all over the USA did during the Great Depression of the 1930s. In the 1990s' information age,

New markets	New commons
• Telecom services	• Space, Earth systems science
• Desert greening	• Electromagnetic spectrum
• Pollution control	• Oceans, water resources
• Renewable energy	• Atmosphere, ozone layer
• Recycling, eco-resource management	• Security, peace keeping
• 'Caring' sector (day care, counselling, rehabilitation, nursing)	• Forests
• Infrastructure (extending transport, telecommunications, etc)	• Health
• Eco-restoration, bio-remediation	• Global economy
• Peacekeeping risk-assessment services	• Global electronic commons

Figure 2. Exploring the evolving global playing field.

democracy is now sweeping the planet as people everywhere can see on satellite TV how politics, economics, money and cultural traditions interact to control human affairs from the global to the local level. A global civil society made up of millions of citizens groups now linking electronically is challenging both governments and corporations—as a third 'independent sector'. New demands include reducing working weeks to 30 hours so as to share the fruits of automation, of for guaranteed incomes for all citizens so as to maintain purchasing power.[19] Many in governments and at the local level are realizing the implications of the global information age: money and information are now equivalent—if you have the one, you can get the other. In fact, information is often *more* valuable. Today, money often *follows* information (and sometimes *misinformation*) and markets are no longer so 'efficient'. Indeed, psychology and game theory now often explain markets better than economics, as the latest Nobel awards in economics attest.

Thus, the global money monopoly is breaking up, even as its casino becomes more unstable with bouncing currencies, derivatives and increasing volatility. Socially innovative governments can now go around the money monopoly and conduct sophisticated barter and counter-trade deals directly (as do corporations) using computer-based trading systems similar to those that Chicago's commodity traders use. Indeed, one-quarter of all world trade is already done this way, according to industry estimates. Thus, the 'need to earn foreign exchange', which hung over governments like a sword of Damocles, can now be lifted and the IMF must face up to this new game which it can never control. Complicated four-, five-, and six-way trading deals between multiple partners can be executed with almost the ease of money. Computers keep the audit trails of who promised to 'pay' for which commodity in exchange for what other commodity on what dates—which is what money is and does anyway.

Today, calls for democratizing and restructuring the World Bank, the IMF and the WTO, as well as opening up the still private BIS, have grown out of new evidence of the irrelevance of structural adjustments[20] and the failure of the economic approaches in the United Nations Third Development Decade. These demands culminated in the 1994 clashes in Madrid between developing and industrial countries over fairness and special drawing rights (SDRs) to the global, grassroots campaigns, 'Fifty years is enough', actually to shut down the World Bank. Protests will become more strident as more people see that money is not in short supply and that credits and liquidity often follow politics and could be made available more widely and equitably—not just to governments to shore up alliances and pander to bond traders and other special interests. Democratic reformers seek wider access to credit for private groups, local enterprises, villages, and many other NGOs and communities for 'trickle-up' development. Such campaigns will persist until the political assumptions of the Bretton Woods institutions are teased out of their economic models and their relationships with governments, banks, securities traders, stock exchanges and bond holders are made clearer.

Local information commons as safety nets

As the crises swamping macroeconomic management become more evident worldwide, people at the local grass roots are rediscovering the oldest, most reliable safety net—the non-money, information economy. Over half of the total world production, consumption, exchange, investments and savings are conducted outside the money economy—even in industrial countries (for example, some 89 million American men and women volunteer an average five hours each week, saving taxpayers millions in social programmes). No wonder World Bank and other development projects have failed, since they overlooked these non-money sectors. Meanwhile, many OECD countries face 11% average unemployment rates while economic 'shock treatment' still roils Eastern Europe and Russia, and debt problems worsen in 'developing' countries.

Independent, urban money systems have always flourished whenever central governments mismanaged national affairs. Such alternative currencies which fostered local employment are catalogued in *Depression Scrip of the United States* (1984), documenting the hundreds of US cities and others in Canada and Mexico which recovered from 1930s' unemployment by issuing their own money. Most economic textbooks excoriate such informal local economies as backward or inefficient and ignore the rich history of such information-based alternatives to central banks and national currencies. Earlier examples were based on the theories of economist Silvio Gesell and included the city of Worgl in Austria and the Channel Islands of Jersey and Guernsey off the southern coast of Britain. All three became enclaves of prosperity and survived botched national policies of the period. Today, Jersey and Guernsey still survive as examples of how independent, local credit and money systems can maintain full employment, public services and low inflation. Economists and bankers, after fighting such local initiatives, may need to rely on them today to stabilize spluttering national economies.

Today, ordinary people are not sitting idle hoping that macroeconomic managers can help them. Local communities see the confusion at the top and are not waiting. In Russia, as the rouble declined, barter and flea markets become pragmatic substitutes. Oil flows from Kiev, Ukraine, to Hungary to purchase trucks, while Russian engineers design power plants in exchange for Chinese coal. The big lesson of the information age is being learned: information can substitute for scarce money. Information networks operate barter systems in the USA worth $7.6 billion per year. The number of US companies engaged in barter services has increased from 100 in 1974 to 600 in 1993.[21] These barter companies, according to *AT WORK* newsletter, range from the Barter Corporation, a trade exchange network in the Chicago area, to Ron Charter of Costa Mesa, California, which exchanges recycled appliances and sports equipment for Green Card credits good towards payment for goods and services at more than 200 participating businesses in Orange County. Some of these exchanges are for education and healthcare for employees. Goods bartered range from trucks, office furniture and carpeting to clothing, travel, hotel rooms, dental and optician services. At the local level, barter clubs now keep track of credit, investment and exchange transactions. These information networks function like commodity exchanges, just as payments unions and trade agreements do for governments. These non-money and scrip-based economies are leading indicators signalling the decline of macroeconomic management.

Such decentralized, local ingenuity still alarms bankers and central monetary authorities. Such local 'currencies' and *ad hoc* alternative economies in the past have been stamped out by governments as being illegal or tax dodges. Yet whenever local producers and consumers are faced with hyperinflating national currencies or jobless economic growth policies, they resort to such pragmatic ways of clearing local markets, creating employment, and fostering community well-being. These new local information societies are not only attempts to create safety nets and home-grown economies, but are a resurgance of kinship systems. Thus they are understood better from anthropological and cultural perspectives than as 'economic' or merely financial/currency systems (an excessively reductionist view). These local information societies are rooted in the informal economy and derive from traditional societies and their systems of reciprocity, mutual aid and self-reliance, and based on attempts to re-knit community bonds, work and relationships.[22] Now that information has become the world's primary currency, both on international computer trading screens and in local PC-networks and exchange clubs, people are at last beginning to understand money itself.[23] The implications of the new global information currency are shattering all our former assumptions about central banks, money, credit, liquidity and trade. This fast moving information has end-run fiscal and monetary tools, and calls into question how deficits should be calculated and the role of other macroeconomic management models, statistical apparatus, and conventional measures of progress such as money-denominated gross national product (GNP) and gross domestic product (GDP).[24]

New markets to *serve* both global and local commons

The UN itself is best positioned to serve this new global information age. The UN is now the world's *de facto* 'superpower'—being called on daily to assume even larger burdens of peacekeeping from Bosnia and Somalia to Cambodia, Cyprus and El Salvador. Yet member-countries making these demands include the richest G-7 countries, and they are collectively in arrears by almost a billion dollars in paying their dues to the UN. Secretary General Boutros Boutros-Ghali has noted in *Agenda for Peace* (1993) and *Agenda for Development* (1994) that a strengthened UN, which can meet the new burdens, requires more secure and predictable financing. The UN Charter mandates these dues. Logically, it should impose penalties on arrears and be able to collect taxes, for example, on arms trading and currency speculation, such as those proposed in this issue, which could yield sufficient revenue to fund all the UN programmes from peacekeeping to health, education, children's and humanitarian aid.[25] Issues of restructuring the UN for greater accountability are crucial to its new role. The UN, acting as a convenor and broker, can continue its vital service to the international community by assisting in organizing global commons—thus fostering the formation of new markets to *serve, not control* them. Markets, as the Chinese and others know, are good servants but bad masters, and social markets are emerging in most OECD countries.

Industrialism, now worldwide, is about labour *saving*—resulting in worldwide jobless economic growth, corporate downsizing and automation. At the same time, deficit-strapped governments are unable to continue serving as employers of last resort (via military spending, public works, jobs and welfare). Only rebalancing tax codes towards neutrality between labour and capital can stem wasteful and often irrational capital investments and reduce the heavy burden of payroll taxes. Globally, capital markets can be made more efficient by shifting taxes on to resource depletion, inefficiency, waste and pollution while reducing income and payroll taxes (calibrated to meet each country's tax code differentials between labour and capital). Such a tax formula could correct prices (by internalizing social and environmental costs) and run economies with a leaner mixture of resources, energy and capital, and a richer mixture of employment. Globally, taxation of currency speculation (collected automatically by all governments as proposed in the 1970s by James Tobin and discussed in this issue by David Felix) is winning much support. This tax should be less than the 0.5% originally proposed, since the volume of speculation is now so huge. Some currency traders are comfortable with a tax of 0.003% or less—even though their trades often involve spreads of only a few basis points.

There are few good arguments against the UN being able to issue its own bonds. The $700 billion of socially responsible investment demonstrates that many globally concerned investors and bond traders could make a viable market in such UN bonds. This would recognize that the UN has become a mature global institution which provides its 186 member-countries with indispensable services. Unfortunately, a high-level Advisory Group on UN financing convened by the Ford Foundation in 1993, representing many players in the now dying global financial order (including former central bankers Paul Volcker of the USA and Karl Otto Pohl of Germany's Bundesbank), rejected many such pragmatic new UN funding mechanisms. Nevertheless, the debate about democratizing the global financial system in the information age has been joined. Social innovations to enhance UN functions and provide secure financing were debated at the UN World Summit on Social Development in Copenhagen, March 1995.

Many new markets and new commons will provide opportunities in the emerging global playing field (see Figure 2). For example, a new public/private agency, the United Nations Security Insurance Agency (UNSIA) could provide a substantial source of revenue for peacekeeping and peacemaking while providing to member-states more security for less money.[26] Initial calculations suggest that this new UNSIA (a newly organized global commons) could eventually cut countries' defence budgets by as much as 50%; provide enormous new markets for subcontracting insurance companies; and allow former defence budgets to be redirected towards investments in health and education—now recognized, at last, by economists to be keys to development. New agreements can raise the floor under this global playing field by building on the girders already in place, such as the *Agenda 21* treaties and other UN agreements, so that we can build a win–win world where the *most ethical* companies and countries can prosper—together with the growing global civil society.

Notes and references

1. See, for example, *The Economist*, 8 October 1994, pages 85–86; and *The Economist*, 'Beyond Bretton Woods', 1 October 1994, pages 23–27,
2. Hazel Henderson, 'Social innovation and citizen movements', *Futures*, 25(3), April 1993, page 322.
3. *The Economist, op cit*, reference 1.
4. *New York Times*, 22 November 1993, page A-1.

5. Hazel Henderson, *Politics of the Solar Age* (Indianapolis, IN, Knowledge Systems, 1988), chapter 4, page 85.
6. Jo Marie Griesgraber (editor), *Rethinking Bretton Woods* (Washington, DC, Center of Concern, 1994).
7. *The Economist*, 26 March 1994.
8. *The Economist*, 1 October 1994, page 96.
9. K E Boulding, *Beyond Economics* (Ann Arbor, MI, University of Michigan Press, 1968).
10. Garrett Hardin, 'The tragedy of the commons', *Science*, 13 December 1968, page 1243.
11. See for example, Frederico Aguilera-Klink, 'Some notes on the misuse of classical writings in economics on the subject of common property', *Ecological Economics*, April 1994, pages 221–228.
12. Henderson, *op cit*, reference 5.
13. Karl Polanyi, *The Great Transformation* (Boston, MA, Beacon Press, 1944).
14. Hazel Henderson, *Paradigms in Progress* (Indianapolis, IN, Knowledge Systems, 1991), chapter 3, pages 97–100.
15. Richard N Cooper, Stephany Griffith-Jones, Peter B Kenen, John Williamson *et al*, *The Pursuit of Reform* (Editor, Jan Joost Teunissen), (The Hague, November 1993), Forum on Debt and Development (FONDAD), (Fax: 31-70-346-3939).
16. Henderson, *op cit*, reference 4.
17. Hazel Henderson, 'Riding the tiger of change', *Future Research Quarterly*, 1986.
18. Henderson, *op cit*, reference 14, chapter 5, page 111.
19. Hazel Henderson, 'Changing faces of work', The 4th Lowell Hallewick/Personnel Decisions Inc Lecture, University of Minnesota, 13 April 1994.
20. *The Economist*, 'How poor are the poor', quoting Elliott Berg, 1 October 1994.
21. *At Work*, 2(6), November–December 1993.
22. See for example, Lewis Hyde, *The Gift* (New York, Vintage, 1979); Vandana Shiva, *Staying Alive* (Led Books, London, and Atlantic Highlands, NJ, 1989); also A Salins, *Stone Age Economics* (Chicago, Aldine Publishing Co, 1972); and Polanyi, *op cit*, reference 13.
23. Hazel Henderson, 'Information; the world's new currency isn't scarce', *World Business Academy Perspectives* (San Francisco, Berrett-Koehler, Fall 1994).
24. Henderson, *op cit*, reference 14, chapter 6.
25. *Human Development Report* (New York, United Nations Development Programme, 1994).
26. Alan F Kay and Hazel Henderson, Policy Department, 'United Nations Security Insurance Agency (UNSIA)', available on request from Center for Sustainable Development and Alternative World Futures, PO Box 5190, St Augustine, FL 32085-5190, USA.

WHERE IS GLOBALIZATION TAKING US?

Why we need a new 'Bretton Woods'

Morris Miller

While globalization brings global increases in income in the aggregate, it also threatens to leave much of humankind in conditions of absolute poverty and to widen the gap between rich and poor. These trends are likely to be accentuated with the advent of the information/knowledge economy, the increasing power of multinationals, and the growing severity of environmental constraints. This article sketches these trends and then addresses the question: what are the necessary conditions for the attainment of a growing global economy with equity and acceptable environmental standards? It then tackles the issue of the prospects for these conditions to be realized under the prevailing global economic/financial system.

The history of man is a graveyard of great cultures that came to catastrophic ends because of their incapacity for planned, rational, voluntary reaction to challenge.

Erich Fromm

Powerful dialectical forces are at work as the world economy undergoes a structural transformation, one that promises hope and opportunity and the other that threatens a future of despair and breakdown. The lifting of the enormous psychological, social and financial burdens of the Cold War and the tantalizing promise of scientific/technological innovations symbolized by the computer chip and fibre optics encourage hope and opportunity; the despair and the traumatic fear of slow or cataclysmic breakdown stem from the symptoms of global crisis, or rather of three overlapping and mutually reinforcing crises, if we differentiate the interrelated

Professor Morris Miller has worked internationally for the World Bank as Executive Director (1982–85) and as staff senior economist (1964–74). He is presently Adjunct Professor for the Faculty of Administration at the University of Ottawa, 136 Jean-Jaques-Lussier, PO Box 450 STN A, Ottawa, Ontario, Canada K1N 6N5 (Tel: +1 613 564 2452; fax: +1 613 564 6518).

aspects of trade and capital flows—the debt crisis, of equity—the poverty crisis; and of ecology—the environment/energy crisis.[1]

Heeding the lesson of the shepherd boy parable, there are, admittedly, good grounds to be cautious about crying 'crisis!'. One could argue that there has been a continuing increase in aggregate global income even when the 'decade of the miserable 1980s' is included, and that even the trend in average *real* annual per capita income in both the low-income and middle-income developing countries has been positive—albeit very modest—when the period considered spans the five post-war decades. Furthermore, taking these countries as a group, average longevity has risen to 63 years from 46 only a generation before, adult literacy has increased over the same period from about 20% to 60%, and key morbidity rates have fallen dramatically.[2]

Conventional thinking about the global economic process—that is to say establishment-supportive economic theory—attributes this growth in incomes and related benefits in large part to the beneficence of trade. On this view one can cite the rise in the world's GDP of almost all countries that has accompanied the rise in the value of trade, with trade leading the way.[3] There has, indeed, been an intensification of the interdependence of nations through trade and capital flows that goes well beyond that of previous eras. It follows, therefore, the argument goes, that there is a causal link between global growth and the nature, scale and scope of the trends of international trade and capital flows and their underlying productive and exchange relationships, a process that is loosely labelled as 'globalization' as a short-hand term for an ever increasing degree of economic/financial interdependence. By this line of reasoning, the phenomenon of globalization has been one of the main factors playing a role in determining the speed and shaping the pattern of global growth and bears a large measure of responsibility for the positive attributes of this growth—and for the negative ones.

At the outset it is important to note that the positive trends attributed to globalization have been very unevenly distributed and have been erratic from year to year. Furthermore, the circumstances of the periods when the correlation of trade and growth has been *universally* positive include such factors as steady-hand statesman-like leadership that has underpinned the stability of key currencies, kept *real* interest rates low and stable, induced a fairer sharing of the rising incomes through measures improving market access and the terms of trade for the poorer trading partners, and such.[4] In the course of recent history, that is, dating back a few decades, such favourable periods of growth *with equity* have been the exception rather than the rule, while, at the same time, the spread and speed of globalization have accelerated steadily. Thus, relying on a simplistic cause-and-effect relationship that is supported by a limited set of upbeat numbers is a recipe for delusion about the benefits, stability and sustainability of our present global system with its distribution of incomes and powers. In any case, these numbers tell us little or nothing about the potential for a better life that is *not* being realized under the present order of things, that is, about the shortfall between 'what-is' and 'what-might-be'. We, therefore, have to ask: where is globalization taking us?

A few examples of troubling trends sketched in broad-brush fashion should suffice to make the point that there is good cause for concern, especially as several key trends appear to be deeply embedded within the global social/economic/financial system and can, therefore, be regarded as *systemic*.

The gap between rich and poor is widening with immiserization remaining persistent and widespread

The statistical picture as set out in the World Bank's *1994 Social Indicators of Development* and *1994 World Tables* reveals that the 'low-income developing countries' enjoyed an annual average rate of increase in GDP of 7.2% in 1992 and that their per capita incomes have grown since 1975 at a respectable rate of 3.6%. This has been heralded as a great achievement especially when contrasted with the rate of growth of the 'high-income group of countries' that had an average GDP growth in 1992 of 1.7% and barely averaged over 2% per capita income growth over the period since 1975. These numbers would suggest that over the past two decades the incomes of the average person have been rising and that the income gap between rich and poor has been narrowing. However, when account is taken of the *absolute* numbers, the inferences to be drawn from this comparison are not encouraging.

Percentage changes are deceptive when the base numbers differ widely, as they do in this case: the low-income countries in 1992 had an average annual per capita income of less than $400 while the high-income countries enjoyed an average annual per capita income level of almost $22 000—or more than 50 times higher![5] With contrasts as great as these numbers indicate it should hardly be surprising that the percentage rates of change of the poorer countries would be higher than those of the richer ones. Comparing per capita income averages on a country-by-country basis obscures two related facts: (1) the drop has been much greater for the poorest and most vulnerable segment of their societies; and (2) one in five persons living on this planet—or over 1 billion persons—are existing in conditions of 'absolute poverty' (roughly identified by an income level of less than $1 per day) and are thus unable to feed, clothe and house themselves in a manner that can sustain health and human dignity, or cannot provide educational opportunities for themselves and their children of a quality commensurate with current, let alone, future needs. The picture is bleak to a point of obscenity when four out of ten of those living in the developing countries are considered to be malnourished and functionally illiterate.[6] This has profound implications for their nation's hope of ever escaping from a state of technological and scientific backwardness that, in turn, leads to perpetual economic/financial dependency with all that that state of affairs implies.

Lest it be thought that this is a contrast between the industrialized countries and the developing ones, it should be noted that the North too has its own figurative South. The industrialized countries have not been spared the impact of this distributional trend: in the USA, for example, over the two decades from 1969 to 1989, the *real* income of the poorest fifth of wage earners declined by about 25% while the richest 1% managed to increase their after-tax incomes by well over 50%. The income gap has been widening to a degree and at a speed which is bound to have broad societal implications as reflected, in the first instance, in a significant global increase in violence in the form of both crime and civil unrest. In both the industrialized and developing countries, the numbers of those now engaged in criminal activities and drug-related activities are now large enough to justify the characterization of the present situation as a 'social and cultural crisis'.[7]

The nature of technology is changing rapidly, widening the educational/informational gap and increasing the unemployment rate

Almost all the industrialized countries and a few of the developing ones are well embarked on what has been aptly labelled 'the third industrial revolution' or 'the information age', and some are already in the midst of what Professor Robert Heilbroner has called a 'transformational boom' and Professor Peter Drucker has labelled as 'The age of social transformation'.[8] Rapid changes are stressful enough, but when the spearheading technologies are 'high-tech', labour-saving and involve extremely mobile intangible assets, the social impact is magnified. Unable to keep up with the rapidly and profoundly changing nature of technology, most developing countries are falling further and further behind the industrialized nations in the acquisition and deployment of these technologies that are opening the way to new modes of production, distribution and, in effect, new modes of economic and social life.

One of the most significant implications is the *structural* shift towards production and distributional activities that require a well trained and well educated labour force and, *pari passu*, there is a reduced need for the unskilled and the semi-skilled members of the labour force who make up the larger proportion of the working population. This is reflected in the widening of the wages gap between the well educated/skilled and the unskilled, and in the much higher levels of unemployment with a rate of youth unemployment that is much higher yet. In the case of Europe, for example, the forecast for 1994 is that it will be as high as 12% with over half of those unemployed having been out of work for more than a year. This situation has prompted the observation that 'the surplus of gifted, skilled, undervalued and unwanted human beings is the Achilles' heel of this emerging system'.[9]

In the developing countries—where the picture is bleaker still—one of the key factors contributing to this troubling employment trend is the high rate of population growth, a rate much higher (over 2%) than that in the industrialized countries (0.7%). On the basis of present trends, world population will almost double by the middle of the next century with over 90% of that increase occurring in the developing countries—and particularly in their cities.[10] Given the rate of population increase and the consequent annual flow of new entrants into the labour force, and given the phenomenon of what has been labelled 'jobless growth' with its implication of a continuing high overall rate of unemployment and of underemployment, there is a spreading recognition that the rise in unemployment is *structural* rather than simply cyclical. This has tempted establishment-supporting commentators to regard a high rate of unemployment as 'the natural rate'—or, euphemistically, 'the equilibrium rate', a view that has provoked Professor William Vickrey, a former President of the American Economic Association, to assert that '"the natural rate" of unemployment (justifying an historically high rate) is one of the most vicious euphemisms ever coined'.[11]

The concern goes beyond the employment issue to focus as well on the decline in the real levels of wages and salaries, and on the 'social wage', that is, the benefits every citizen enjoys as entitlements through the spending undertaken by their respective governments for education, health and programmes related to 'social welfare'. In the name of 'fiscal responsibility' and in the cause of 'debt reduction' the amount of funding and the nature of social programme spending—that now comprises about 25% of the budgetary expenditures of the industrialized countries—is under great pressure.[12] Much of that pressure, vigorously supported by politically powerful multinational corporations, is rationalized as part of the price to be paid for the benefits derived from the process of 'globalization'.

This political/cultural assault on welfare systems has had its counterpart with regard to the volume and nature of the flow of aid ('official development assistance' or ODA) from the industrialized countries to the developing ones. The volume of ODA has not increased over the past decade *in real terms,* and the part devoted directly to poverty eradication programmes and projects has not increased beyond 10% of total ODA, while a larger percentage has shifted to what is called 'policy lending' or 'structural adjustment lending' (SAL) that calls for a host of 'belt-tightening' measures. It should, therefore, come as no surprise that the global underclass has been growing in numbers and displaying increasing levels of stress.

The pressure on the environment is increasing, exacerbated by spreading poverty and the debt overhang

Since 'poverty is', as India's former Prime Minister, Mrs Indira Gandhi, observed, 'the greatest polluter', the stress is reflected not only in human misery but also in environmental deterioration. Under the circumstances, the poor are unable to concern themselves with undertaking the kind of research that would enable them to pursue *new patterns* of development that are environmentally more desirable and that hinge on much greater reliance on environmentally benign sources of energy and radically different ways of using energy.[13] Even if they had the funds and talent—and those they do not have—their political leaders find it difficult to be concerned about a distant tomorrow when today's needs press so heavily on their people, pressure that is accentuated by the overhanging debt burden that has more than doubled since 1982 and is still absorbing, on average, about one-third of their foreign exchange earnings.[14] Weighed down by the debt burden, their economies are being 'cannibalized' as they eat into their capital base and become even less able to compete. And with this downward-depressing dynamic comes an enervating loss of hope and the onset of despair and social unrest.

With the exceptions of the newly industrializing countries (NICs) and China, almost all developing countries are finding themselves less and less able to compete in world markets for both primary and manufactured higher value-added products. Leaving to one side the conventional trade obstacles of tariff and non-tariff barriers, the primary commodity exports of the developing countries have been losing markets to substitutes (fibre optics for copper, nylon for jute, aspartame for sugar, etc). But perhaps the more formidable competition comes from the products that are subsidized by the governments of the industrialized countries. When the estimated annual total of agricultural subsidies in the industrialized countries is about $300 billion, the impact on the exports of the developing countries is devastating. They find themselves unable to compete in the subsidies contest and lack the flexibility to shift production to take advantage of market opportunities beyond their limited domestic ones.

Under these circumstances, as the tax base shrinks or fails to expand rapidly enough, the financial burden that has to be imposed on the formal sectors of the economy becomes heavier. This results in strong incentives for producers and distributors to operate in the tax-evading 'informal sector' which is now estimated by the International Labour Organization to account for as much as 35% of the GDP of many developing countries. And so a vicious circle begins: with this reduced ability to finance their education, health and infrastructure programmes and projects, these governments become less and less able to find the financial and other resources that are necessary to change the economic and sociopolitical structure so as to raise the productivity of the economy; this, in turn, puts more pressure on the formal sector, etc. The victims most severely affected by this 'vicious cycle' process are those at the bottom of the income and power scales, largely women and, in particular, peasant women.

The capacity of developing countries to compete is decreasing and that of the large multinational companies is increasing with particularly distressing socioeconomic-political consequences for developing countries

But with these changes in the economic and sociopolitical structure, the power of labour *vis-à-vis* indigenous and foreign capital is also weakened—and this is especially so in the developing countries that have exceptionally high rates of unemployment and underemployment. This unequal contest has the effect of weakening the bargaining power of the host country *vis-à-vis* the foreign investors, especially if—as is likely—the bargaining is with the larger of the 35 000 multinational companies that might be seeking to invest in their country.

The comparative financial strength of the multinationals can be gleaned from the 'fact' (an estimate by *The Economist*) that 300 of the largest companies control about one-quarter of the world's $20 trillion stock of productive assets, and 600 of the biggest with annual sales above $1 billion account for more than a fifth of the world's total value-added in manufacturing and agriculture.[15] The largest 20 have total sales that exceed the total of the gross domestic output (GDP) of 80 of the poorest developing countries.[16] These organizations are not simply atomistic economic agents searching out profitable opportunities. Their size in terms of capital and sales networks confers enormous power. They can shape markets and production relationships. Since 1983 the amount of annual flows of private international investment has grown four times as fast as global output, and this resurgence of private international capital flows has been largely due to multinational companies that annually account for over $150 billion of the flow. In a cover story of the 14 May 1990 issue of *Business Week*, entitled 'The stateless corporation: today's giants that are really leaping boundaries', the authors note one of the implications of this estimated annual capital flow being undertaken by multinational corporations as they invest abroad:

There has been a reversal of roles between government and corporation [with] governments acting as if they are fully sovereign within their own borders on economic policy, [while] stateless corporations have increasingly learned to shape national climates by offering technology, jobs and capital.

The economically weaker countries have little hope of controlling such investments so as to capture their putative benefits.

In this regard it is relevant to note that almost all the multinationals have a well earned reputation as fierce opponents of organized labour and, as a corollary, they display a strong preference for countries where they can engage in non-unionized low-wage production with accompanying low safety, environmental and social standards. In non-democratic developing countries they need only make common cause—'splitting the spoils', so to speak—with the elites of the countries in which they invest to ensure that these conditions are maintained.

'Offshore' international financial flows are large and growing rapidly—and the rate of increase, composition and volatility of these flows has been increasingly beyond governmental control

The global integration of financial markets on a large scale can be dated back to

1963 with the launch of the first Eurobond issues totalling $164 million. Financial innovations that were made possible by new technologies gave a tremendous boost to the volumes of capital handled by the fledgling markets bringing their annual compound rate of growth to more than 36%. As the volume increased, the pressure mounted for the easing and then the removal of restrictions applied to cross-border financial flows, so that by 1994 the daily flow through the foreign exchange (forex) centres around the world exceeded $1 trillion, or the rough equivalent of the foreign exchange holdings of all the central banks of the major industrialized nations.[17] Given the relative size and nature of these flows with their impact on the volatility of exchange and interest rates, the issue of control of these offshore financial activities has emerged recurrently as a priority item on the agenda of meetings of the G-7.

The lack of ability to dampen the fluctuations had long ago become worrisome. A minor concern related to the injury inflicted by the speculative and volatile attributes of many of these capital flows on the developing countries that generally lack adequate financial resources to take hedging measures against the turbulent financial waves and to 'roll with the punches', so to speak, by being policy-flexible. By early 1994 there was a perceptible rise in the level of concern with the focus placed on the business of derivatives that are estimated to be outstanding in the amount of about $16 trillion.[18] The size and volatility have provoked a Congressional committee hearing and prompted *The Economist* to devote the cover and lead editorial of the 14–20 May 1994 issue to the theme, 'Your financial future', and to ask what the fuss is all about. The reasons given are that:

the industry is new, global and already very big: the telephone number figures for the supposed value of outstanding derivatives. (. . . $16 billion+) make the eyes spin . . . Lastly, there are fears that derivatives fuel financial-market uncertainty by multiplying the leverage, or debt-based buying power, of hedge funds and other speculators—an uncertainty that could, if things went wrong, threaten the whole of the world financial system.[19]

The risk-engendered fear of playing with such large financial stakes has spread beyond the derivatives business that many regard as being only a part and a symptom of the broader phenomena of high and gyrating interest and of sharp and wide fluctuations in exchange rates. This anxiety is combined with concern about the low proportion of the capital flows being channelled towards productive purposes and the high concentration of this flow that is intra-multinational companies and directed to a very limited number of countries.

The questionable nature and composition of the capital flowing through financial markets arise from the 'fact' (again, a 'best guess' estimate by *The Economist*) that only about 5% is for the financing of trade and less than 15% for investment. *The Wall Street Journal* (in its 18 September 1992 issue) has ventured to state that 'less than 10% of this staggering sum has anything to do with trade in goods and services'. It would seem that the remaining 80+% of the ebb and flow is attributable to speculative and/or 'money-laundering' motives that are in large measure beyond the bounds of serving any beneficent social purpose, and which revalidates John Maynard Keynes's references to the 'casino society'.[20] Capital movements, it seems, have only a weak, tenuous connection to societal objectives; major financial decisions are made without reference as to whether the projects being financed are or are not 'productive' in the broadest social sense of that term.

All this has been accentuated by the failed attempts to achieve coordinated financial policies among the larger industrialized countries, especially the Group of 7 (G-7).[21] This failure has raised the issue of leadership and prompted some critical questions about both the *will* and the *capability* of these countries to control—or even significantly and consistently to influence—global capital movements so as to

- dampen the extreme volatility of exchange rates and realign them to conform to underlying and sustainable realities, and in the process also to dampen the volatility of *real* interest rates and lower them from their historically high and unsustainable levels; and
- ensure that the rapid rise in the rate of global foreign investment gets directed in a manner that promotes the kind of growth in poorer countries that is shared widely, environmentally acceptable, and responsive to democratic control—in a phrase, subject to policies that raise social, labour and environmental standards.[22]

The evidence points to a negative response to both these questions with regard to both objectives.

The challenge

The optimists/rationalizers, as supporters of the prevailing system, have always been with us. The ranks of the doomsters ebb and swell, but of late it is not surprising to find that their voices have tended to become more frequent and strident as they focus on the downside aspects of the globalization process. 'What lies ahead', a reviewer wrote in commenting on Paul Kennedy's best-selling book, *Preparing for the Twenty-first Century*, 'are famine, endemic poverty and malnutrition, irreversible environmental damage, mass migrations, regional wars, disease—and no solutions'.[23] Before solutions can be offered with any hope of being considered, let alone acted on, there is a need for the recognition of the need for *significant* policy and institutional changes at the level of international governance so as to arrest and reverse the deplorable and dangerous trends that are global in scope.

The countervoices that dismiss the warnings and pleas point to the 'successful' cases, the economies of South-east Asia and China that are enjoying rapid rates of growth. Because a few developing countries have done rather well during the past few decades, there is a tendency to ascribe the current plight of the other developing countries—and that includes most of them—to inappropriate institutional arrangements and misguided policies, that is, their wounds have been largely self-inflicted; the extent and dynamic of poverty are therefore, *not* attributable to *systemic* failure. Their refrain runs as follows: 'all would be well if the poverty-stricken developing countries were to rely more on the operations of "market forces" by removing the severe constraints placed on private initiatives of an entrepreneurial nature and by reducing government involvement'.

However, a convincing case could also be made that exceptional circumstances played a role, as, for example, the infusion of enormous amounts of US capital due to the Korean and Vietnamese wars and later of Japanese capital, especially by multinational corporations. Furthermore, the growth has been very unevenly distributed. But, in any case, even if each developing nation 'corrected' these institutional policy and cultural faults by 'structural adjustment', only a few of them could hope to reverse these deplorable trends *so long as the international milieu remains essentially the same*. This school of thought thus puts the spotlight on the weak points and unwelcome trends of the present global economy *as a system* and calls for measures that go beyond the objective of *restoration* of the debtor nations to that nebulous concept called 'creditworthiness'. After all, recovery can hardly suffice as a goal of policy when it implies a return to a global economic system that contained within itself the seeds that germinated these unwelcome social, financial, environmental and other trends. This broader objective implies the use of resources *in a different way* and *for different purposes,* in a phrase, changes that are *systemic* in their nature and scope that would, in effect, harness the dynamic of the globalization process to achieve a more productive global economy in which there is both much greater fairness and sensitivity to the maintenance and then enhancement of social/cultural/environmental quality.

Necessary conditions for attaining the objectives

The world community has long tolerated desperate poverty and extremes of income distribution, conditions that *should* not be acceptable on grounds of justice or fairness. Thus, hard-headed realists would expect and accept a significant degree of change only if such changes were indicated on *non-compassionate* grounds, that is, if they could be expected to work to the advantage of the stronger parties in trade and other relationships. On this non-compassionate basis it is possible to identify the minimal changes that are *necessary—but not necessarily sufficient—*for achieving the desired objectives.

The international economic scene is far from a level playing field. Economic and financial power being what it is, the rules of the game are tilted against the developing countries *as a group.* A 'hands-off, leave-it-to-the market' approach would bring into play a series of developments that are especially unfavourable for the great majority of developing countries, such as, (1) secularly deteriorating terms of trade for those developing country economies greatly dependent on the export of primary commodities, (2) the persistence of high protectionist barriers of these industrialized economies that, interestingly enough, have remained higher for imports from the developing countries than from other industrialized countries, (3) historically and unsustainably high and volatile *real* interest rates on capital borrowed from abroad, and (4) exchange rates that fluctuate widely and wildly—as they have ever since 1970 when President Nixon closed the 'gold-window' that had, until then, enabled bankers and individuals to exchange gold for their US paper dollars, and, thereby, effectively terminating the 1944 Bretton Woods agreement.

If the economies of developing countries are to get back on to a growth path that is desirable in terms of both pace and pattern, 'correcting' all these unfavourable factors is a *necessary* condition—but, as noted, they are by no means *sufficient,* since the developing countries have a role to play in terms of establishing effective honest administrations and adopting 'appropriate' policies. It may suffice to focus discussion on the issues of the level and volatility of interest rates, of exchange rate volatility, and of capital transfers that are key preconditions for attaining and maintaining the desired objective of global growth with equity and improvement of social and environmental standards.

Lowering real interest rates to the historic range of 1% or less and dampening the volatility of exchange rates

Either or both of these financial objectives is likely to prove difficult to achieve on a sustained basis. In the early 1980s nominal interest rates reached historically unprecedented heights of over 20% and in the range of 10% in real terms. This rise, known as 'the Volcker shock' (after the then-chairman of the US Federal Reserve System), was a primary factor in precipitating the actions of Mexico and Brazil that brought on the debt crisis panic of 1982. The rate was unsustainably high and bears comparison with the global average real long-term rate of interest that ranged for decades in the neighbourhood of 0.3%. The basis for taking the historic level of 1% or less as the desired and sustainable level for Third World borrowing is simply that at an early stage of development the funds borrowed for development purposes cannot be expected to earn a higher rate of return in *financial* terms but may, nonetheless, yield a high *socioeconomic* rate.[24]

Lowering real interest rates calls for an international cooperative effort with the US in the linchpin role by virtue of the size of its economy and its importance in world trade and capital flows and, therefore, of its impact on the supply and demand for capital that, in the final analysis, determines the price of capital or the real rate of interest. Japan, the EU and, to a lesser extent, others have a role to play in this process since any action by one to set interest rates could be offset or nullified by the actions of others. It is this interdependence that has necessitated the periodic meetings of finance ministers and their presidents and prime ministers that has now become ritualized as summitry and, as noted, shown meagre results.

This low success rate should occasion no surprise. There is, after all, little hope of lowering interest rates without action taken to arrest the decline in world savings. These fell, in aggregate terms, from 26% (as a ratio to GNP) in the early 1970s to about 20% by the end of the 1980s, and have continued to decline as all the major industrialized countries, with the exception of Japan and Germany, have been sliding on the downward course.[25] The chief culprit has been the US economy, which has had a low rate of savings and remains heavily dependent on foreign-generated savings. Necessity will undoubtedly force changes to bring real interest rates back to their historically low levels. The big question is whether the 'necessity' is forced by cataclysmic events or by deliberate steps taken with forethought so as to anticipate the inevitable, and make the adjustment a soft one.

Increasing financial flows to developing countries

With few exceptions the developing countries must contend with serious financial gaps. The critical question is whether those gaps are bridgeable under any reasonable scenario that could be envisaged. On that score, the prospects are grim. The basis for this pessimistic judgment is evident when one looks at the gap between estimates of the minimum amount of capital required and—if one judges by the past record—the likelihood of such sums being forthcoming on commercial and on concessional terms.

The questions to ask and to answer are:

• How much foreign capital is 'needed' for growth and for environmental programmes assuming, as seems likely, that 'internal savings will account for the lion's share of investment'?[26]
• Where is the foreign capital to come from?

How much capital inflow do developing countries need? With due regard to the conceptual and methodological reservations associated with modelling exercises, they do provide a useful, though rough, guide. One such exercise—as set out in the *1994 Human Development Report*—yields an estimate of the amount of capital required to wipe out the worst forms of poverty in the world: an *additional* $30–40 billion per year.[27] This assumes an approach that is sharply focused on programmes that tackle the most onerous features of poverty. This could be complemented by programmes to finance the research and diffusion of stand-alone energy technologies (solar, wind, biomass etc) that would enable those living beyond the reach of electricity grid networks—that is where the poorest of the poor are to be found—to be more productive and to live better in terms of housing with cheap and easy access to lighting, cooking, water and sanitation facilities.

Beyond the poverty-focused programme, modellers have made estimates of capital requirements based on various assumptions. Assuming the objective is to achieve an annual 2% increase in per capita incomes in the low- and middle-income developing countries and that about one-fifth of the needed investment would need to be supplied from foreign sources, the estimates of the *additional* annual *net* capital inflows required have ranged from about $60 billion to about $125 billion. When the capital needs of the former Soviet republics and the Eastern European countries are also included, another $60–90 billion would need to be added.[28] If the additional capital required annually to implement the minimal targets of UNCED's *Agenda 21* is factored into the calculation, the estimates rise yet again by orders of magnitude ranging from $100 billion to $300 billion annually over the next 20 years.[29] Thus, the annual tally runs from $250 billion to $500 billion, or about three to six times the current flow of ODA. Private capital flows could not be expected to increase sufficiently to meet this gap either in its total volume, let alone its sectoral and geographic distribution that has, up until now, been narrowly focused on a few developing countries.

What are the likely and possible sources of capital? The main financial burden must rest on the countries themselves but the gap between what they can be expected to generate from their own internal savings would need to be filled by the governments and private investors of the richer industrialized and oil-exporting countries that can carry that burden or, as the case may be, seize that opportunity for profitable investment. It is clear that the largest part of the capital transfer must take the form of interest-free or low-interest grants and loans through substantially augmented ODA programmes, but ODA channelled through both multilateral and bilateral aid programmes has remained relatively constant in real terms over the past few years. Its importance can be gauged by the fact that these ODA funds accounted in 1990 for about half the total capital inflows to developing countries.

There are strident voices raised in favour of dependence on private capital flows. The volume has, indeed, increased in the past few years with syndicated credits and bond issues amounting to about $16 billion in 1991, but over three-quarters of this flow went to just four Asian countries. A similarly narrow concentration applies to private direct investment flows that had jumped threefold since 1986, from less than $10 billion to over $30 billion. A recent report of the International Finance Corporation (IFC), notes that private investment to the developing countries 'has climbed back to the high point reached in the late 1970s, while public investment remains at a 10-year low'.[30] The catch is that only six of the developing countries—those with the largest markets—accounted for more than half this total, and much of this flow has been intra-multinational firms and a reflow of 'flight capital' that has been returning home on very financially attractive terms through transactions labelled as 'debt–equity swaps'.

In relation to the magnitude of the need, the amounts involved in these private investment flows are not impressive, especially considering their limited geographic coverage.[31] Nor can much be expected from the private bankers who have had their fingers burnt and are not likely to be forgetting or forgiving for quite a while. The bleak prospects of securing capital from the traditional sources has prompted an outpouring of suggestions regarding innovative approaches to securing the needed additional funds. The most popular suggestion has been some form of a 'Global Marshall Plan'.[32] In addition, funding proposals have included ideas such as taxing, fining and extracting royalties on commercial operations utilizing and polluting the 'global commons' (principally the upper atmosphere, the high seas, Antarctica and areas not under any one nation's jurisdiction), taxing the trillion dollar per day volume of foreign exchange transactions handled by forex centres at rates so low they would not be a deterrent and yet yield exceptionally large sums, and issuing SDRs through the IMF.[33] Then, of course, there are the 'peace dividend' proposals that would divert a stipulated percentage of disarmament 'savings' to development and environmental programmes.

In more detail, the search for further funding has given rise to the following proposals:

- a global carbon tax on the users of fossil fuels, which at $50 per ton of carbon emission would yield annually in the US alone about $28 billion if 10% of the revenues were allocated to environmental programmes;
- issue by the IMF of a substantial amount (say, $50 billion over three years) of SDRs with a bias in its distribution towards needy developing countries rather than in accordance with quota entitlements which would favour the industrialized nations;[34]
- debt-for-nature swaps which can, in some cases, provide a measure of financial relief that can be directed towards the funding for establishing and maintaining nature reserves, parks and related environmental programmes such as the environmentally beneficial forestry policies and practices that help maintain the tropical rain forests that play an important role in absorbing CO_2;
- payment of 'rent' by the developed industrialized countries for their past and current *disproportionately* heavy use of the 'global commons' as waste disposal bins, that is, payment to compensate for their *unfair* share of use of the oceans and upper atmosphere;[35]
- levying taxes on the international transfers of money between money centres dealing in foreign exchange that now amounts to over $1 trillion per day. It is estimated that a rate of 3/100th of 1% (the Walker tax proposal) would yield enough to finance all UN operations, including peacekeeping and a rate of 0.5% (the Tobin tax proposal) would yield about $1500 billion a year—or more than 25 times the present level of ODA![36]

It is envisaged that these rents, royalties and taxes secured from the *commercial* exploitation of the deep oceans and the upper atmosphere would be paid into some sort of newly established 'development/environment fund'. The enforcement of these measures of assessment and collection could not be left to an *ad hoc* administrative arrangement. It would need an institutional basis with some empowerment mandate and long tenure not only to secure and allocate funds but also to do so on the basis of a 'global structural adjustment programme'. The negotiations for the establishment of the institutions and its mode of operations would be akin to the process that secured the Bretton Woods agreement of 1944 that put in place a global system of rewards and penalties designed to secure adherence to agreed rules governing trade and capital movements and gave birth to the 'Bretton Woods twins'—the World Bank and the International Monetary Fund. Today, the rules of any such agreement would be extended to ensure guidelines/adherence to norms of fairness and environmental 'good behaviour'.

The 'new Bretton Woods' as concept and reality

The policy makers of the major industrialized nations have only recently begun to show serious signs of worry about the implications of the growing immiserization, polarization, volatility and fragility of the prevailing global system. Their concern, in the first instance, has focused on the large size and speculative nature of 'offshore' financial movements that are now beyond control. Voices had been raised before, notably by Raoul Presbisch, Henry Kissinger and President Mitterand, among others.[37] At the outset of the 1990s, the tinge of anxiety was reflected in the call by the former US Secretary of the Treasury, Nicholas Brady, for the establishment of a special commission to focus on this issue. Gerald Corrigan, former head of the Federal Reserve Bank of New York, and others such as New York financier, Felix Rohatyn, also echoed the same refrain.

More recently, a knowledgeable commentator, Fred Bergsten, the Director of the Washington-based Institute for International Economics, has noted that under the pressure of global stress there has emerged 'a more collective tripolar management (that has tried but not succeeded in) putting together a stable system, (but has succeeded in) avoiding crisis and total breakdown'. This has prompted him to suggest that: 'we need to get back to the global negotiations on a new world monetary system, as well as on trade, international investment, and policy coordination . . . [recognizing that] *systemic reform* takes a long time'.[38] (emphasis added)

In another recent publication (co-authored with Robert Reich, now the US Labor Secretary), he went on to advocate a 'GATT for Investment (under) new tripolar management (that) would round out a three-pronged agenda for the '90s that must address the issue of how to maintain a stable economy in the 21st century'.[39] More recently still, the concern about the prevailing state of affairs has given rise to a report prepared by a group of prestigious international bankers led by Paul Volcker under the auspices of the Bretton Woods Commission in which governmental action is advocated 'to overhaul the world monetary system'.[40]

The recognition by members of the establishment of the need to *overhaul the system* is perhaps more significant than the specifics of their proposals. In effect, the calls are for change in the prevailing global 'rules of the game' for trade and capital movements, but the nature and degree of change that is implied is very dependent on the objectives that are sought:

- Is the intention limited to the avoidance of a possible catastrophic breakdown of the economic/financial system and the attainment of the nebulous phrase, 'return of debtors' creditworthiness' or 'recovery'?
- Or does it go beyond this to envisage the creation of conditions that are conducive not only to faster global growth in real per capita incomes, or well-being as measured in terms of national averages, but also to a more equitable sharing of this growth and to a pattern of growth that is compatible with standards of environmental quality, locally and globally, that would enable such growth to be sustained over the long term?

Attaining the former objective implies acceptance of the very system that incubated the present debt, poverty and environmental crises. If, however, the objective is to attain a state of affairs commensurate with high growth, equity and environmental standards, the call is for the establishment of a global set of institutions and rules analogous to what was achieved at the conference held in Bretton Woods, New

Hampshire, in 1944 but going beyond the scope of that agreement to include more than rules with respect to trade and capital flows and beyond its limited number of participants. If the call for a 'new Bretton Woods' is to have any resonance, that is, sufficient popular appeal to make its way in the face of vested interests and inertial forces, it must be broad enough in its participation, its objectives, and its institutional modalities to inspire support. In a phrase, it must be sufficiently imaginative and bold to be commensurate with the challenge of the 1990s and the 21st century.

The challenge is profoundly different from that of the 1930s and the early 1940s which brought about the first Bretton Woods agreement. There are, however, valuable lessons to be learnt from the experience of drafting and operating the original Bretton Woods agreement that emerged out of the collapse of the international system as epitomized in the agonies of the Great Depression and World War II. In terms of trade and income growth and stability—but much less so in terms of equity and environmental concerns—the global economic/financial system operated reasonably well for a quarter of a century when its 'rules' held sway: the global flows of trade increased over this period by 250% and incomes by 150%, with developing countries growing on average at a much faster rate than the industrialized ones.

After the collapse of the Bretton Woods agreement in 1970—for reasons that are politically understandable but not excusable for a nation playing a *global* leadership role[41]—there was no longer an adequate control mechanism in place to prevent the chain of events that led to the subsequent volatility of exchange rates and interest rates and to the enormous pile-up of an unsustainable mountain of debt, since the countries that went on a borrowing and lending binge in the 1970s were likely to have been brought up short by the Bretton Woods reins. Those who call for 'rules' such as those that held sway for a quarter century from 1945 until 1970 are, however, proposing changes in scope and modalities and, possibly institutional arrangements that can avoid the weaknesses and mistakes and be appropriate for today's conditions with their dynamic troubling trends.

The world has long lived with indecision, inefficiency and inequity. Few advocates of a new Bretton Woods would be moved to urge changes on that account, but they make common cause in feeling that, as a matter of pragmatism, the present arrangements are unsustainable both environmentally, socially and politically.

The necessary policy and institutional changes will be made by volitional decisions in a controlled and orderly way or they will be made by *force majeure*, that is, in an uncontrolled and precipitous manner. Should the changes come about in the second manner, the solution or outcome is likely to be a retreat from the 40-year-old trend towards interdependence to autocratic policies as each of the industrialized countries endeavours to minimize the damage to itself by adopting 'beggar-thy-neighbour' policies. The possibility of the last outcome gives the problem and the approach to finding a solution an element of urgency.

The process of institutional change at the level of global governance has already begun but needs to be accelerated and to be led with an overarching conceptual vision that sets out the multifaceted objectives. This needs to be combined with a down-to-earth sense of how to drive and steer the process through the political reefs in the face of powerful cross-currents of conflicting ideas and headwinds of vested interests in the *status quo*. This is a situation that calls for leadership at every level of governance to provide what economists refer to as 'the collective public good', namely, the establishment and maintenance of a global milieu that is characterized by the rule of law, acceptable modes of behaviour in commerce and everyday activities, and other attributes of a desirable world in terms of stability, fairness and openness.[42]

The most economically powerful nations have been judged to be failing the test of global leadership that assumes the basic responsibility of leadership is not only to avoid cataclysmic breakdown but to go beyond that to promote that 'public good', that is, to create and/or maintain a global milieu or system congenial for achieving the desired objective of a world that is growing with equity and with high social, political and environmental standards. This is a formidable challenge at the best of times, but especially so in this time of transformation or megachange. The appreciation of the dire consequences of not rising to the challenge can, perhaps, be a forcing mechanism. The fear of mutual peril might have more persuasive power than the appeals to teamwork and the appeal of a humane and prosperous world for *all* its current and future inhabitants that, for the first time in history, human ingenuity has made a realizable dream.

Notes and references

1. The 'energy crisis' that was so worrisome in the 1970s appears to have faded as a problem, let alone as a crisis. But, in fact, there is a strong element of truth in the concept of an energy crisis when it is subsumed within the concept of the global environmental crisis. Energy is needed for development and the source or form of energy used is the critical factor. Since some forms of environment-damaging energy such as fossil fuels are the principal sources in the industrialized world, as the so-called developing countries proceed to industrialize they will likely to be following along the same path. The crisis is, therefore, of a dual nature and can be treated as an 'environment/energy crisis'. For a fuller discussion of this theme, see M Miller, *Debt and the Environment: Converging Crises* (New York, UN Publications, 1992).
2. The picture is spelt out statistically in various publications of which the most complete and authoritative are the annual editions of the UN's *Human Development Report* and the World Bank's *Social Indicators of Development* and *Trends in Developing Countries*. The IMF's *World Economic Outlook* is a source for some of the relevant statistics pertaining to their economies, as, for example, the 1993 edition states that the per capita growth of developing countries in 1992 was 2.75%.
3. Over the quarter century from 1945 to 1970—the 'normal' period when the Bretton Woods agreement prevailed—global income rose by about 150% while trade rose by over 250%. For the most recent period, the World Bank's *World Tables, 1994* provides estimated income as follows: (in *current* US$) from 1982 to 1992 the total global GDP rose from about $3500 trillion to about $4800 trillion (or an increase of almost 38%), the low-income countries from about $900 trillion to almost $1200 trillion (a one-third rise), the middle-income countries, from about $2500 trillion to $3500 trillion (less than a one-third rise), and the high-income countries from $7900 trillion to $18 600 trillion (or more than doubling); (in *constant* US$) over the same period average per capita incomes rose globally from $2600 to $4200, the low-income countries from about $340 to almost $400 (an increase of one-sixth), the middle-income countries from about $2200 to $2400 (an increase of less than one-tenth), and the high-income countries, from less than $11 000 to almost $22 000 (a doubling).
4. For a fuller treatment of this relationship, see Arthur MacEwan, 'Globalization and stagnation', *Monthly Review*, April 1994. He notes that 'when globalization has been associated with rapid growth that growth has had historically specific causes and cannot be attributed to globalization *per se* . . . that when it generates inequality it tends to undermine growth . . . and when globalization has been most effective as a foundation for economic growth, a firm institutional basis for stability has existed'. (pages 1–15)
5. Taking *all* the developing countries as a group, that is, including also the 'middle-income countries' that have had average annual per capita incomes of about $2500 rather than just the 'low-income developing countries', their per capita income level in 1992 was only about 1/8th of that prevailing in the industrialized countries, but the annual average percentage change since 1975 was a barely perceptible improvement of 0.3%. The 'low-income countries' are those with average per capita incomes of $675 or less; the 'lower middle-income countries', $676 to $2695; the 'upper middle-income countries', $2696 to $8355; the 'high-income countries', $8356 and more. The countries included in each category as of 1992 GNP per capita statistical records compiled by the

World Bank can be found in *Global Economic Prospects and the Developing Countries—1994* (Washington, DC, World Bank, 1944), pages 88 and 89.

6. The trends in the key indicators of 'the human condition' are graphically documented in the annual editions of the UN's *Human Development Report*, the World Bank's annual *Atlas*, and the World Bank's annual *Social Indicators of Development* (Baltimore, MD, The Johns Hopkins University Press). To put this in graphic terms—leaving aside tragedies due to natural calamities and war—about 20 million persons per year or 40 000 per day or 1700 per hour are dying from *preventable* diseases that are related to poverty. And, of those children who survive, about 100 million are being denied any educational opportunities and hundreds of millions more are being denied access to adequate school facilities and well trained teachers.

7. As an example of the nature of the deteriorating societal scene that is close to home it might suffice to note the rise of violence in the world's largest economy: in a recent issue (15 May 1994) of *The New York Times*, a columnist, Anthony Lewis, cited Senator Bradley's call to Americans 'to join in a national rebellion against violence', noting in this connection that 'violence in America is so pervasive we most often take it for granted, like background noise'—and the statistics bear this out. According to a study by John Dilulio of Princeton University, the basic crime rate in the USA, that is property and violent crimes per 100 000 people, has risen more than threefold over the past 30 years (from 190 to about 600) and the prison population—over half of whom have been serving time for violent crimes—tripled over the past 15 years. He estimated that from 1987 to 1990 the lifetime costs borne by Americans for violent crimes alone amounted to about $180 billion. In his column Mr Lewis went on to comment that 'a national rebellion against violence would be a terrific reaction by this great culture to a critical challenge, [but] at the moment there is no evidence that it is about to happen'.

8. Heilbroner's term is used in his article entitled 'Anti-depression economics, *The Atlantic Monthly*, April 1993, page 103, and Drucker's is the title of an article in the same journal's issue of November 1994, pages 53–93.

9. R Barnet and J Cavanagh, *Global Dreams: Imperial Corporations and the New World Order* (New York, Random House, 1994), page 425.

10. Almost 50 of the developing countries have a rate of increase of over 3%. The UN's statisticians project that the current world's population of about 5.6 billion will probably continue to increase to reach about 10 billion by 2050 and level off by 2150 at less than 12 billion.

11. 'Today's task for economists', *Challenge*, March/April 1993, page 10. Vickery expressed his views in this manner: 'The Phillips curve, relating the evolution of inflation to the level of unemployment, has been added to the economists' tools of analysis with its "non-inflation-accelerating rate of unemployment" or NIARU . . . [but] in one of the most vicious euphemisms ever coined, this NAIRU has been termed the "natural" rate of unemployment in some quarters'. In this sentiment he joins another famous economist, John Maynard Keynes, who observed in the mid-1930s in his *General Theory of Employment, Income and Money* that 'the outstanding faults of the economic society in which we live is its failure to provide for full employment and its arbitrary and inequitable distribution of wealth and incomes'.

12. According to a 1990 OECD study the range of spending for social welfare and health programmes runs from Japan (11.6%) to Sweden (33.9%) with Canada and the USA both under 20%. If education is included the European average rises to about a third of their budgetary expenditure totals.

13. For example, an encouraging precedent is provided by the experience of the Consultative Group on International Agricultural Research (CGIAR) that contributed to the development of new wheat, rice and other varieties of food by more effectively using the available research funds. To focus research funds on the energy/environment connection in an analogous organizational manner, that is, on the feasibility of establishing a CGIE²R might seem an appropriate initiative. After all, funds are already available for research in a dispersed manner in dozens of underfunded organizations. For a fuller discussion of the proposal for the CGIE²R project see, M Miller, *The Energy/Environment Connection: Overcoming Institutional Obstacles to 'Doing the Right Thing'* (Washington, DC, World Bank/EDI Energy Series Working Paper, 1989).

14. The developing country debt issue is off the front pages, but is still alive. The total debt owed by these countries to their official and private banking creditors has more than doubled in the past decade, amounting to more than $1700 billion by the end of 1992. And it is still going up—by over 5% in 1992. For the relevant statistics, see *World Debt Tables, 1992–93* (Washington, DC, World Bank, 1993), especially page 15. The tone of the document is that the situation is under control and that only a few distressing pockets of troublesome debt remain, principally in African countries, that is, the *crisis* nature of the situation as a *global issue* is over. This reflects a common view held in the donor countries.

15. 'A survey of multinationals', *The Economist*, 27 March 1993, pages 5–6; and 'Come back multi-nationals . . . [that] seemed fated to succeed colonial powers as the bogeyman . . .', 26 November 1988, page 73. It is estimated by the UN that the multinational companies account for the direct employment of about 65 million persons or 3% of the global labour force. Their network has created

jobs outside their host countries. US multinationals are estimated to account for more than 6 million jobs abroad, of which about one-third are in developing countries. By 1986 the amount of foreign direct investment made by multinational companies exceeded $50 billion, a fivefold increase since 1970. It has continued to increase. But the flow was not one way: between 1980 and 1988 the flow of foreign direct investment *into* the US economy amounted to over $250 billion (at 1980 prices) or over $40 billion per year, much of it accounted for by multinationals—DeAnne Julius, *Global Companies and Public Policy* (London, RIIA/Pinter, 1990), cited in *The Economist*, 23 June 1990. The article notes that 'foreign direct investment has already reduced the freedom of governments to determine their own economic policy'. (page 67)

16. *The Global Corporation: and Nation-states: Do Companies of Countries Compete?* (Washington, DC, National Planning Association, 1993), page 5. See also Barnet and Cavanagh, *op cit*, reference 9, *passim*. They point out that 'a relatively few companies with world-wide connections dominate the four intersecting webs of global commercial activity on which the new world economy largely rests: the Global Cultural Bazaar, the Global Shopping Mall, the Global Workplace, and the Global Financial Network'. (page 15)

17. See Bank for International Settlements, *Recent Innovations in International Banking* (Basle, BIS, 1986), page 149, and *passim*; RC Smith, *The Global Bankers* (New York, EP Dutton, 1989) especially the chapter entitled 'The globalization of capital markets' in which he writes that 'the cutting edge of globalization has been the Euromarkets—those loosely organized, virtually unregulated, over-the-counter global markets . . .'.

18. *The Economist*, 14–20 May 1994 (page 15), provides a succinct definition of derivatives that it characterizes as 'a fast-growing and arcane business—futures, options and other financial instruments whose values are partly based on (derived from, hence the name) the price of bonds, equities and other assets'. The editorial quotes a congressman's characterization of the business of the trade in derivatives and related financial instruments of futures and options as 'the wild card of international finance'.

19. The journal's editorial judges this fear to be 'overdone' with the underlying reason being that 'in general, financial systems are self-correcting', and the conclusion being that 'derivative misfortune-tellers are wrong'. *Ibid*, pages 14–15.

20. 'Traders put a daily net turnover in foreign exchange (including derivative products like futures, options and swaps) at about $900 billion, only about $50 billion or so less than the total foreign-currency reserves of all IMF members . . . [and] more than a third higher since April 1989 and double the previous survey's figure for 1986 . . . Less than 5% relates to underlying trade flows . . . another 10% representing capital movements'. 'The last of the good times (for the principal participants of the world's foreign-exchange market)?', *The Economist*, 15 August 1992, page 61. In late August 1992 the concerted intervention of the central banks of all major economies into foreign exchange markets failed to arrest the decline of the US dollar. Summitry as a means of achieving cooperation has occasionally succeeded, but if judged on the basis of results, this process has fallen far short of expectations and, on the whole, merits a failing grade.

21. Although the range and frequency of the volatility of capital movements and especially of foreign exchange relationships began to rise appreciably in the period when the Bretton Woods agreement was no longer operative, that is, in the early 1970s and thereafter, it was only in the mid-1980s that the concern was acute enough to precipitate the first of the *ad hoc* 'summitry' meetings when the US Treasury Secretary, James Baker, invited the leaders and finance ministers of the seven largest industrialized nations known as the Group of Seven to the Plaza Hotel in New York. These meetings became ritualized, even though on an *ad hoc* basis, and some members of the group came to regard themselves as 'the board of directors of the international economy'. But the meetings became little more than symbolic events with not much to show for all the posturing beyond the publicized communiqué as real-world events went their own way seldom, if ever, affected by the pronouncements. Paul Krugman, 'International adjustments 1985–90: what have we learned?: A review of an IIE Conference', *International Economic Insights* (Washington, DC, Institute for International Economics, November/December 1990), has made a pertinent comment in connection with one 'success' of the G-7: 'in retrospect, *the apparent success of the G-7 at enforcing target zones* after the Louvre meeting (of February 1987) appears to have been something of a fluke: the G-7's actions had a major effect only because the market expected them to, not *because they were powerful in their own right, (thus) meaningful monetary reform on a global scale remains to be achieved*'.

22. For example, under the banner of the Coalition for Justice in the Maquiladoras, a group of religious, labour, women and other organizations in Mexico, and the USA has issued a code of conduct for US corporations operating in Mexico. For a fuller discussion on this and other initiatives, see the article by Jeremy Brecher, 'After NAFTA: global village or global pillage?, in the 6 December 1993 issue of *The Nation*. There are international precedents such as the European Community's 'social charter' and the UN's proposed code of conduct for transnational corporations. It is an open question whether such regulatory codes could be passed and be implemented/enforced effectively in an

interdependent global economy in which the multinational corporations play a powerful political role both in their own and in the host countries where they invest and operate. Both routes can be considered as they are not mutually exclusive. They may, in fact, be mutually reinforcing and, therefore, this applies to both levels of governance.

23. Robert Dowling, *Business Week*, 15 March 1993, in his review of *Preparing for the Twenty-first Century* (New York, Random House, 1993) paraphrases the prognosis set forth in the book if we remain on the present trajectory.

24. The concept of external economies and diseconomies is a key one in what is called 'welfare economics' and is of special importance at all stages of a nation's development, but especially so for nations in their earlier stages of development. The reason for this is simply that there is a long gestation period from initial investment to the time for the financial pay-off and, accordingly, there is bound to be a low *financial* rate of return on capital borrowed for development programmes and projects having to do with building basic infrastructure from roads to research facilities, and for education and health purposes and all that goes into making a viable productive community. Yet, if a society is to develop economically it has no choice but to invest in such programmes and projects and to judge these programmes and projects by the socioeconomic rate of return. Furthermore, capital-intensive programmes and projects often have benefits that are not measurable and cannot be counted in any cash register; even where they could be so counted, there are benefits that are *external* to the programme or projects though *internal* for society.

25. See BB Aghevil and JM Boughton, 'National saving and the world economy: why have savings rates declined since the early 1970s?', *Finance and Development*, June 1990, pages 2–5; AL Bovenberg, 'Why has US personal saving declined?', *Finance and Development*, June 1990, pages 10–11; and JJ Polak, 'The decline of world savings', *Economic Insights* (Washington, DC, Institute for International Economics, September/October 1990), pages 18–19.

26. Susan Collins in 'Capital flows to developing countries: implications from the economies in transition', *Proceedings of the Annual Conference on Development Economics 1992* (Washington, DC, World Bank) writes that 'it may be a mistake to focus on the role of international capital flows to developing countries. Arguments for the view that too much attention has been paid to the availability of external capital point out that internal, not external, savings will account for the lion's share of investment. This view is supported by a wealth of recent and historical country experience (and Paul Krugman argues that "international capital markets as an engine of growth have been oversold"). [However] at the same time, the magnitude of capital inflows in relation to total income or investment in a given economy may understate the role of that capital in development [since] foreign direct investment may lead to a transfer of technology and the acquisition of new skills with important positive spillover to other sectors'. (page 351) The paper contains a wealth of statistics on the theme of capital flows both to developing countries and to Eastern Europe, the so-called economies in transition.

27. The objective set in a ten-year timeframe would be to eliminate severe malnutrition, reduce moderate malnutrition and adult illiteracy by half, provide safe sanitation and drinking water and supply primary healthcare for all, provide every child with a primary education and family-planning services for all willing couples. These would be elements in a World Social Charter. The funds would be derived from a commitment by the developing countries to increase the budgetary allocation to these programmes from the prevailing average of 13% to 20%, and from donor countries the commitment would be to raise the percentage of their aid that goes to programmes and projects addressing poverty and related basic needs from the prevailing 7% to 20%. By this 20:20 formula the developing countries would provide three-quarters of the new money needed to make this proposed initiative a reality.

28. The Institute of International Economics has estimated $1500 billion per year would be needed over ten years to catch up to US per capita income levels, and that the inflow forecasted would be between $30 billion and $90 billion per year. A Munich-based economic forecasting institute, IFO, has estimated that the annual capital needs of Eastern Europe is between $75 billion and $100 billion and of the former Soviet republics and Russia, between $180 and $235. Assuming these countries manage to provide a little less than four-fifths of their capital requirements from internal sources, the estimated gap ranges from about $60 billion to $90 billion per year.

29. For a breakdown of the estimates see, M Miller, *The Energy/Environment Connection: Overcoming the Institutional Obstacles to 'Doing the Right Thing'* (Washington, DC, World Bank/EDI Working Paper, 1990); and 'Getting grounded at Rio', *Ecodecision*, Montreal, April 1992. The carbon emission reduction programme alone runs into hundreds of billions of dollars with one estimate for a 40% reduction estimated at $300 billion per year and $400 billion to achieve a 60% reduction target.

30. Guy Pfefferman and Andreas Madrassy, *Trends in Private Investment in Developing Countries 1993: Statistics for 1970–91*. From 1986 to 1991 the amount of foreign direct investment climbed from less than $10 billion to approach $30 billion. The six countries that received the most are Argentina, Brazil, China, Malaysia, Mexico and Thailand.

31. As a means of attracting more of the global pool of available inevitable capital to the Third World, an initiative of a guarantee nature has been established by the World Bank, namely, the billion-dollar Multilateral Investment Guarantee Agency (MIGA). MIGA is designed to reduce the political risks for private investors. Another initiative is the Emerging Markets Growth Fund (EMGF) which has been set up by the International Finance Corporation to facilitate private capital flows by offering diversified portfolios of investment opportunities in Third World enterprises. While helpful, these initiatives are modest: MIGA may contribute to a slight resurgence of foreign private investment flows to the developing countries; the EMGF is targeted to raise $50 million, a minuscule amount in relation to the need. There is little prospect for a substantial capital flow breakthrough as a result of either of these initiatives, but they are, of course, welcome on the basis of the idea that every little bit counts. John Williamson, a fellow of the Institute for International Economics (IIE), has suggested that the World Bank could augment the flow of private capital through offering guarantees in cofinancing arrangements, these guarantees being phased out as the Bank raises its lending levels and is in need of the newly authorized capital. *Voluntary Approaches to Debt Relief* (Washington, DC, Institute for International Economics, September 1988), pages 33–38.

32. See, for example, Philip Shabecoff, in an article 'A "Marshall Plan" for the environment', *The New York Times*, 3 May 1990. The same idea has also been put forward under various labels with the necessary funding being raised through such means as the issue of environmental mutual funds, tax-free environmental bonds, environmental flow-through shares, environmental capital venture funds, an emergency environmental fund, and such. A 'Global Environment Facility' has been set up and is operational, but with funding far far short of the scale of the Marshall Plan.

33. R Dobell and T Parson, 'A World Development Fund', *Policy Options Politiques*, 12, 1988, have suggested the establishment of a World Atmosphere Fund to be financed in part from the auctioning of pollution-emission permits, a proposal that is already incorporated in the seabed mining provisions of the UN Convention on the Law of the Sea. The Brandt Commission reports of 1980 and 1983 put forward a similar proposal to establish a World Development Fund that would collect and administer the incomes generated by such royalties and taxes. There is treatment of this theme in the Brundtland Commission report, *Our Common Future* (Oxford, Oxford University Press, 1987), in a chapter entitled 'Managing the commons'.

34. The issue of SDRs by the IMF was approved in the early 1970s to meet a special situation, each country having an entitlement according to its quota. Proposals have been put forward to issue SDRs to developing countries on a basis that would break from the conventional allocation by quotas so as to make the developing countries the main recipients.

35. Any such form of payment to developing countries could be construed as a bribe and, therefore, morally troublesome. D Helm and D Pearce have noted that the practice 'can easily turn the morality of the polluter-pays principle upside down [to become] the victim-pays principle'. They have predicted, in this connection, that 'the issue of "side payments" will dominate the 1992 United Nations Environment Conference in Brazil'. 'Assessment: economic policy towards the environment', *Oxford Review of Economic Policy*, 6(1), 1990). See also D Dasgupta, 'The environment as a commodity', in the same issue.

36. Martin Walker, a former chief of the US bureau of *The Guardian*, set out his proposal in 'Global taxation: paying for peace', *World Policy Journal*, Fall 1993, pages 7–12; and Tobin's proposal is set out in the 1991 *UN Human Development Report*.

37. For a long list of such voices, see M Miller, 'The chorus calling', *Coping is not Enough! The International Debt Crisis and the Roles of the World Bank and the IMF* (Homewood, IL, Dow Jones-Irwin Inc, 1988), pages 151–155. The substance and tone of these warnings of the early 1980s can be gleaned from one quote: 'The biggest politico-economic challenge to statesmen is to integrate national policies into a global perspective, to resolve the discordance between the international economy and the political system based on the national state . . . In [today's] circumstances the international economic system operates—if at all—as crisis management. The risk is, of course, that some day crisis management may be inadequate. The world will then face a disaster its lack of foresight has made inevitable . . . My major point is that the world needs new arrangements . . . The spirit that produced Bretton Woods reflected the realization that in the long run the national welfare can only be safeguarded within the framework of the global welfare'.

   Henry Kissinger, in a lecture reprinted on the op-ed page of the 22 November 1984 issue of *The Washington Post*, under the suggestive heading: 'It's time to change the rules of the game'.

38. 'A new Big Three to manage the world economy', *Challenge*, November–December 1990.

39. Bergsten, *Ibid*, page 24; Robert Reich, 'Commentary on "Globalization and the Nation-state"', *Review '90, Outlook '91*, (Ottawa, North-South Institute, 1991), page 21: 'Among the most important new issues is direct investment . . . Some sort of agreement on appropriate strategies, on inducements and even on appropriate steps when a nation wants to thwart investment, is desperately needed'.

40. As reported in *The Wall Street Journal*, 9 May 1994. This group report finds it unacceptable that 'there has been no reliable long-term global approach to coordinating policy, stabilizing market

expectations, and preventing extreme volatility and misalignments among the key currencies'. It advocates 'a more formal system for managing exchange rates' that would, in the words of the *WSJ* commentary, 'require countries to relinquish some of their economic sovereignty and put international considerations above domestic political concerns'. The journal item's author concludes that 'world leaders aren't likely to embrace such a plan, no matter what the advantages'.

41. In the late 1960s and early 1970s, under the pressure of financing the expensive Vietnam War, US policy makers had to choose between adhering to the obligations their country had assumed under the Bretton Woods agreement—by reining in the inflationary forces through the imposition of tough fiscal and monetary policy measures—or breaking the agreement. They effectively chose the latter course of action by 'closing the gold window' in 1969 to private individual and in 1970 to central banks. Leadership—and how to ensure *benign* far-sighted leadership—is thus a key issue that would need to be faced to avoid a repetition of this painful experience.

42. 'Public goods' or 'collective goods' are defined as 'that class of goods (or services) like public works where exclusion of consumers may be impossible, but in any event consumption of the goods by one consuming unit—short of some level approaching congestion—does not exhaust the availability for others'. Professor CP Kindleberger of MIT provided this succinct definition in his presidential address to the American Economic Association annual meeting on 29 December 1985 (reprinted in 'International public goods without international government', *The American Economic Review*, March 1986). He points out that public goods are typically underproduced since its voluntary provision 'is plagued by the free rider'. In the international sphere the list would include: 'an open trading system, well-defined property rights, standards of weights and measures that may include international money, or fixed exchange rates, and the like'. In *Governments and Corporations in a Shrinking World: Trade and Innovation Policies in the United States, Europe and Japan* (New York, Council of Foreign Relations Press, 1990), Dr Sylvia Ostry, former Director of the OECD's Economics Department, argues her case on the basis of the premise that the primary 'international public good' of the multilateral trading system is stability and that greater harmonization or coordination of trade policies among the major economies will increase global stability and, thereby, global welfare.

FINANCING THE UNITED NATIONS' OPERATIONS

A frustrating nightmare

Emilio J Cárdenas, R Carlos Sersale di Cerisano and Oscar A Avalle

The financing of the United Nations, one way or another, has been under constant evaluation and discussion since its early years. The organization has been forced by some of its member-states to live in a sort of permanent financial emergency which does not allow its effective operation. Unless full compliance with financial responsibilities by all member-states becomes a reality, the potential of the organization will always be restricted. Ensuring an adequate financial basis for the organization in today's open world has thus become a question of commitment and self-respect. The United Nations can obviously do no more than its members will allow it to do.

In a recent address to the General Assembly, the Secretary of the United Nations stated that the present financial situation of the organization is 'precarious'.[1] That is, as we see below, quite an understatement. For too long, member-states have delayed payments or withheld contributions for 'reasons of principles'. As a result, the organization has been forced to live with a permanent cash-flow crisis.

The financial problems of the United Nations, however, seem to conceal a much deeper question, ie how deeply, in fact, are its member-states committed to the goals and work of the organization?

A few weeks ago, the Australian Minister of Foreign Affairs, Mr Gareth Evans,[2]

Ambassador Emilio J Cárdenas is the Permanent Representative of Argentina to the United Nations. Mr R Carlos Sersale di Cerisano and Mr Oscar A Avalle are senior diplomatic officers of Argentina posted to the Permanent Mission of Argentina to the United Nations in New York.

pointed out that 'there is no use talking about reintegrating the United Nations, or reshaping its responsibilities, unless the resources are there to carry out these responsibilities. And the central responsibility of member-states in this respect is to set to right the organization's current financial problems'. Indeed it is.

According to the Secretary General,[3] 'at the end of August 1994, the organization had debts exceeding 1.7 billion US dollars'. Such amount 'included about US$1 billion due to some seventy member-states for troop and equipment contributions to the peacekeeping missions. At the same time, the United Nations owed US$400 million to its vendors and suppliers. It also owed all member-states a total of US$325 million for budgetary surpluses in prior years, amounts which should have been returned to member-states'.

The United Nations, Dr Boutros Boutros-Ghali reminded, needs about US$400 million per month to meet its present ongoing costs. As of 31 August 1994—while member-states owed to the United Nations some US$3.2 billion for assessments levied but unpaid—it nevertheless had only US$375 million in cash balances.[4]

The situation, from a financial standpoint is, no doubt, very serious. *Figure 1* is clear and self-explanatory. Unless the member-states restore a sound financial basis for the organization, its effectiveness will always be a question mark.

Unfortunately, under the circumstances, to be able to continue operating, the United Nations has been forced to delay its reimbursements to peacekeeping missions' troop-contributing member-states. Arrears in this type of reimbursements have now reached a US$1 billion level. It can, thus, be argued that those member-states that continue supplying troops and equipment to the various United Nations peacekeeping operations are, in fact, financing those others who, instead, do fall behind.

On the other hand, the United Nations has depleted its cash reserves. The Secretary General has just informed that at present, there is 'virtually no cash in the Peace-Keeping Reserve Fund' and that 'the Working Capital Fund—set up in 1945—is less than one month's requirement of the regular budget, and is today virtually depleted'.[5]

Without the necessary resources, the United Nations cannot be capable of effectively performing its duties. 'This problem', stated the Secretary General, confirming the above, 'has now assumed a proportion which undermines the effectiveness of the organization as a whole. It imperils the capability of the United Nations to perform the very functions for which it was created. It therefore needs to

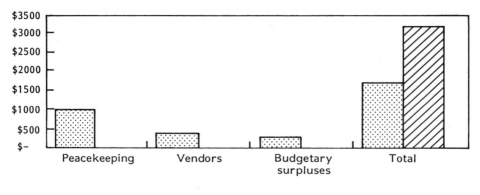

Figure 1.   UN financial position as of 31 August 1994.

be treated as an urgent political question'. He is definitely right.

As the financial shortcomings of the organization are jeopardizing the chances of the United Nations performing the difficult tasks the world community has entrusted to it, there is, therefore, a lot at stake in trying satisfactorily to restructure its present financial position.

An old problem

The financial problems of the United Nations, nevertheless, are certainly not new. The financing of the United Nations, one way or another, has been under constant evaluation and discussion since its early years, in fact for most of its life.[6] Every five years or so, a major effort to try to improve the financial health of the United Nations has been launched, but with limited success.

Such exercises have often occurred in the midst of a crisis attributable to member-states refusing to pay on time moneys that they legally owe to the organization. It could even be argued that some sort of a 'power game' may be identified, since certain member-states have frequently attempted to obtain political benefits from 'helping' the United Nations to solve the very crisis they themselves had provoked.

Back in 1954, when the organization was still young, a Staff Study by the US Senate Subcommittee on the United Nations Charter[7] stated:

Financing the United Nations is somewhat like the job of providing for an unusually large and disparate family on a very modest income. Some worthy projects may have to be sidetracked; a portion of the funds available may be wasted; it is difficult to get each member of the family to accept his share of responsibility; and there will be a constant concern over whether both ends will meet.

It is often said that the veto is the greatest single problem facing the United Nations. But money is the lifeblood of any organization. And the financial problems the United Nations has encountered—although less spectacular—have proven almost as difficult and, in some ways, even more complex than the veto.

Those words are applicable to today's United Nations. As stated then by the Subcommittee: 'From the day of its creation, the United Nations has been riding the horns of a fiscal dilemma'. Up to now, it has not been able to solve it. In fact, the rapidly expanding mandate of the United Nations seems to have compounded financial difficulties.

The provisions of the Charter

The United Nations Charter deals with the financial matters in three different articles—17, 18 and 19. Under article 17, the General Assembly is in charge of considering and approving the organization's budget. It states that 'the expenses of the Organization shall be borne by the member as apportioned by the General Assembly'. As pointed out, this means that the purse strings of the United Nations are placed squarely in the hands of the General Assembly.

Under article 18 of the United Nations Charter, however, all decisions on important questions are to be made by obtaining a two-thirds majority. Budgetary questions are, *inter alia*, singled out as matters of importance, thus requiring such qualified majority.

Article 19, in turn, specifies that a member-state which is in arrears in the payment of its financial contribution to the organization shall have no vote in the

General Assembly, if the amount of its arrears equals or exceeds the amount of the contributions due from it for the preceding two full years. At its fifth session, the General Assembly adopted the following criteria, to interpret such provision:

Contributions and advances shall be considered as due and payable in full within thirty days of the receipt of the communication of the Secretary General referred to in the regulation 5.3 above, or as of the first day of the financial year to which they relate, whichever is later. As of January 1 of the following financial year, the unpaid balance of such contributions and advances shall be considered to be one year in arrears.

Under the current interpretation,[8] such regulation is understood to mean that no member is in arrears, within the terms of article 19, unless its arrears equal or exceed the amount of the contributions due for the preceding two full years, not counting, however, the current year.

For all practical purposes, this interpretation unacceptably stretches the criteria contained in the Charter. It is time to revisit said criteria, with the view of providing a stricter interpretation and thus less room for late payments.

Financial situation of the United Nations system in the area of economic cooperation for development

In his report on An Agenda for Development,[9] the Secretary General indicates not only that 'Development is a fundamental Human Right', but that at the same time, 'development is the most secure basis for peace'.

In this regard the United Nations has been mandated by its Charter to 'achieve international co-operation in solving international problems of an economic, social, cultural or humanitarian character, and in promoting and respecting human rights and fundamental freedoms for all without distinction as to race, sex, language, or religion'.[10]

The United Nations constitutes also a unique forum in which all member-states are able to undertake—from a political and conceptual perspective—macroeconomic policy discussion, related to the global future of economic growth and development.

In this regard and although the United Nations activities in the area of economic cooperation for development, in comparison to other financial institutions, could be considered rather modest (see *Figure 2*), the contribution of the United Nations in the field of economic cooperation for development should be analysed from a qualitative point of view.

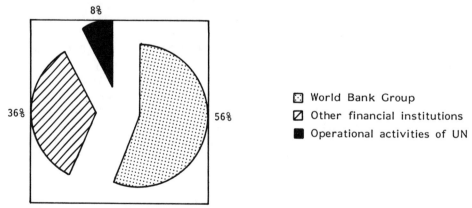

Figure 2.   Resources commitments of multi financial institutions, 1993.

There is a widely shared belief that the UN system must be strengthened to put into practice the growing commitments undertaken by the international community in the old and new issues of its economic agenda. National governments, international agencies and civil populations recognize that the experience and knowledge gained over the past 50 years place the UN system in a pivotal position to meet the new political and economic challenges of a rapidly changing and increasingly interdependent world.

Almost certainly, the restructuring of a system constructed to meet a different set of problems will initiate a period of uncertainty and confusion. However, in a system which depends critically on its human resources, renewed leadership must not come at the expense of the loyalty and commitment of those responsible for guaranteeing the UN's future effectiveness. That said, the process of strengthening the UN raises many difficult problems.

A possible entry into this discussion is through the distinction between institutional strengthening and financial strengthening. By the former is implied the introduction of new, or the enhancing of existing, capabilities required by the UN system to enable it better to carry out its mandate. Important differences have already emerged between those, on the one hand, seeking modernization through better leadership, governance and efficiency, and on the other those who wish to preserve and build on the UN's traditional commitment to impartiality, fairness, pluralism and cooperation. In the absence of an ideal combination of these institutional characteristics, required changes will reflect continual debate and compromise between those responsible for the well-being of the UN system.

By financial strengthening is implied both the acquisition of adequate and predictable resources to carry out mandated activities to the highest standards, and the most efficient distribution of those resources to the various components which comprise the UN system. The changing responsibilities facing the UN have again produced a certain polarization between those emphasizing the need to expand the financial base and those seeking to use existing resources more effectively.

In practice, institutional and financial strengthening are intimately connected. However, discussion to date has largely assumed that agreement on building institutional capabilities will be matched by required changes in financial matters. This is too simple an assumption. The kind of multilateral funding required by the UN system is vulnerable to economic and political pressures independent of the functioning of the system itself.

The UN system in the economic field has traditionally been funded on a multilateral basis. This reinforces the UN's status as a vehicle of international cooperation while providing a certain amount of flexibility to member-states in the support that they extend. However, the economics of multilateral financing introduce a number of difficult problems.

On the one hand, the voluntary nature of its funding can generate an underfunding problem as free-riding by some donors places a growing burden on more generous contributors. On the other hand, changing the voluntary nature of these contributions might create some difficulties in establishing an appropriate multilateral decision-making process over the distribution of funds, requiring a complex managerial structure which not only divorces the donors from the recipients of funds but introduces possible inefficiencies and misuse of resources.

These problems have particular bearing on the economic programmes organized through the UN. Creating a stronger development institution has been identified in the Nordic UN Project as central to the changing role of the UN and given broad shape in a series of documents discussing the required changes.

The existing programmes (in particular UNDP, UNICEF, UNFPA AND WFP) have been funded by voluntary multilateral contributions allocated in accordance with mandates established by an elected Governing Council accountable to ECOSOC.[11] This structure has been increasingly troubled by funding problems. The system of multilateral voluntary funding has been susceptible to free-rider problems as countries fail to provide their appropriate share in expectation that other more generous donors will pick up the tab.

In the absence of effective incentives or sanctions to correct such behaviour, the burden has shifted to a smaller group of donors and become increasingly vulnerable to shifting political sentiments. On the other hand, donor countries have argued that the existing organization of these programmes represents a cumbersome and unresponsive mechanism through which their contributions are channelled to perceived development problems. Addressing this problem has raised the question of effective governance as central to the strengthening of the development programmes. In part following from these two problems, a growing 'ad hocism' has characterized the funding programmes as the agencies have been forced back on their own independent endeavours to maintain adequate funding levels. As a result, coordination problems between agencies have shortened the horizon appropriate for organizing development programmes, increased transaction costs and duplicated activities, thereby undermining the collective performance of these programmes. Such developments raise the possibility of a vicious cycle of underfunding and 'ad hocism'; lack of funding makes for lack of coordination which reduces efficiency, justifying further reductions in funding. The signs of this process are clearly visible in the declining ODA share of the UN multilateral agencies in comparison with similar agencies, such as the development banks.

Any new funding strategy must address itself to these issues if it is to gain wider credibility with both donor and recipient countries, as well as the agencies themselves. The following tables offer some tentative figures consistent with the restructuring proposals currently being debated throughout the UN system. The focus will be the development programmes and funds, in particular UNDP, UNICEF, UNFPA and WFP.[12] Together these programmes absorbed US$3.1 billion in 1993. These funds have traditionally been provided through annually pledged voluntary contributions in national currencies and predominantly from the members of the OECD/DAC[13] (see *Table 1*).

As *Table 2* shows, while the OECD member-countries have increased their share of funding to the UNDP over the past two decades, there have also been significant regional shifts in funding patterns. The Nordic countries and the

TABLE 1. RESOURCES COMMITMENTS OF MULTILATERAL DEVELOPMENT INSTITUTIONS (US$10^6)

	1985	1990	1991	1992	1993
UNDP	567	1111	1159	960	834
UNFPA	141	211	212	164	206
UNICEF	452	545	947	917	655
WFP	872	956	1335	1575	1482
Operational activities of the United Nations	2032	2823	3653	3616	3177

Source: Annual Reports and information supplied by individual institutions

TABLE 2. CHANGING REGIONAL COMPOSITION OF UNDP CORE FUNDING, 1972–91 (%)

	1972	1977	1985	1991
Nordics + Netherlands	27.0	36.8	27.4	39.2
USA	32.0	19.1	24.0	10.3
Japan	3.0	4.2	9.3	8.7
Germany	5.6	7.5	6.0	7.5
Italy	1.5	0.8	4.7	7.0
France	2.2	1.9	3.7	5.0
UK	7.4	6.6	3.6	4.7
Remaining DAC	11.9	12.4	13.9	14.6
Others	9.4	10.7	7.4	3.0

Netherlands have increased their weight in funding—from an already high share—as has Japan, from a much lower starting point.

However, there are some noticeable national idiosyncrasies in the funding patterns of the different agencies, the USA showing greater generosity towards UNICEF and less to UNFPA, while the opposite holds for Japan, with WFP depending for a disproportionately large share of its funds on the USA and Canada.

Table 2 also reaffirms the generosity of a core group of small North European economies. The disproportionate commitment to the development programmes and funds by these countries is highlighted by comparing their voluntary contributions to the programmes with their assessed contribution to the UN system as a whole.[14] Although the main share of contributions originates in OECD countries, as *Table 3* shows, non-OECD countries also participate in the funding of the United Nations' activities in this area.

Undoubtedly, this divergence in funding lies behind the conclusion of the Nordic Project, that 'A stronger and more effective UN in the economic and social fields must be built on the basis of the joint responsibility of its members'.

The possible erosion of funding to the development programmes had led some donor countries to reconsider the financing of the agencies and to force recipient countries and the agencies themselves to reassess the present funding structures. By and large, most new funding proposals have suggested a more diversified funding structure than is currently found, involving assessed, negotiated/voluntary contributions. However, the precise funding modalities and structure remain open to negotiations and are being discussed in the 49th General Assembly in the context of the *Ad-hoc* Working Group established under the framework of 45/264 and 48/162.

TABLE 3. ASSESSED CONTRIBUTION OF NON-OECD/DAC COUNTRIES TO UN DEVELOPMENT PROGRAMMES

	Total contribution to programmes/$million	Contribution as % of non-DAC share
Brazil	35.00	6.70
Saudi Arabia	21.10	4.00
Mexico	19.40	3.70
China	16.90	3.20
Iran	16.90	3.20
Republic of Korea	15.20	2.90
Argentina	12.50	2.40
Venezuela	10.80	2.10
Poland	10.30	2.00
South Africa	9.00	1.70
India	7.90	1.50
Greece	7.70	1.50

Basic concepts underlying the sharing of expenses at the United Nations

Each member-state has, first and foremost, a direct responsibility for ensuring the timely availability of the funds necessary for the organization's well-being. Such responsibility is based on the obligations it individually assumed at the time of joining the United Nations.

The Secretary General reminded the member-states[15] that there are three basic criteria on which the sharing of expenses between the member-states is structured. The first criterion has been in existence since 1946. Under it, the expenses of the organization are apportioned broadly 'according to capacity to pay'.

Recommendations are normally made through the Committee on Contributions for periods of two or three years. Once the respective assessments are decided by the General Assembly, changes are normally introduced only under exceptional circumstances. They are normally gradual, since the 'capacity to pay' of countries does not, as a rule, change significantly from one year to another. The philosophy underlying this approach is to provide a high level of predictability and stability under the assessment mechanism, provided it can be assumed that all member-states do fulfil their obligations on time.

Under the second criterion, for the apportionment of the expenses related to peacekeeping operations, the Permanent Members of the Security Council must bear a special responsibility. It is expressed today through them having to pick up 'premiums' or 'surcharges'. Through them, they absorb the discounts granted to countries with a low capacity to pay. Those countries with greater resources should undertake to fund a greater share of the total burden.

Finally, to provide for the periodical realignment of the member-states' contributions to the organization, objective criteria are preferable.

In this regard, the Ford Foundation, in consultation with the Secretary General, requested from an independent and international advisory group a report on the financial problems of the organization and recommendations for solving them. This report, widely known as the 'Ogata-Volcker Report'—reflecting the names of the co-chairmen who led the advisory group—came out in April 1993[16]. Its main conclusions were:

- An examination of the United Nations' financial position is important because it is part of a broader issue, a debate on how to build a lawful and just world order, while we still have the chance to do so.
- All countries must pay their assessed dues on time and in full.
- While the United Nations' regular budget has remained stable in recent years, peacekeeping expenses have increased dramatically.
- The United Nations cannot be effective and will only invite criticism if it is forced to spread insufficient resources across its different missions, which are located all over the world.
- Proper financing is not enough. Funds and resources in general are to be at all times economically managed and efficiently spent.
- To carry out its duties under the Charter, the United Nations needs the timely availability of the necessary funds, in accordance with the obligations specifically laid down by the Charter.

It further, and more specifically, *inter alia*, recommended:

- Countries with past arrears should pay them as quickly as possible. This responsibility is particularly great for the large contributors.

- Annual dues should be paid in four quarterly instalments, instead of in a single lump, as is the practice today.
- Interest should be charged on late payments.
- The United Nations should not borrow funds from its peacekeeping operations accounts to cover deficits on regular expenditures.
- A US$200 million 'Working Capital Fund' should be put in place.
- The United Nations should not have the authority to borrow.
- The regular budget assessment scale should be based on a shorter three-year average of member-states' GDP, as opposed to the present 7.5-year average.
- For peacekeeping purposes, a special US$400 million 'revolving reserve' should be available, financed through three annual assessments.
- All member-states with above average per capita GDP should pay the same rate of assessment for peacekeeping as they pay for the regular budget.

The view from the member-states

In February 1994, the Secretary General invited 16 permanent representatives from a diversified group of countries to participate, in their personal capacities, in an informal dialogue on the possible ways and means of improving the financial situation of the United Nations.

After a frank and substantive exchange of views during a five-month period, they produced an informal document which included some concrete recommendations, reflecting the principal views of its members, and which can be summarized as follows:

- There was broad support, with some reservations, about the need for the United Nations to be given authority to charge interest on future arrears.
- The United Nations, at this stage, should not be given authority to borrow money.
- Prior to replenising the present 'reserve funds', for which action there was obvious support, large debtors should be current. Otherwise, contributions from member-states could be slow.
- Some proposed discounts or incentives for prompt payment. Others, however, were of the opinion that such mechanisms could only contribute to a further deterioration of the present difficult financial situation of the organization.
- A group of participants expressed the view that priority should be given to peacekeeping reimbursements, to those troop contributors who are current in their respective obligations. Others were of the view that developing countries contributing troops should be given some priority. This was to keep participation in peacekeeping operations always as wide as possible.
- Several participants supported the need to consider a unified peacekeeping budget to cover, as a minimum, costs which are common to all peacekeeping operations. In this manner, member-states could commit the corresponding resources in advance.
- Some member-states were of the view that contributions in kind, when specifically requested by the Secretariat, should be allowed for set-off purposes against such member-states' contributions. The above was to occur only provided that the specific criteria, terms of reference and costing were clearly defined as being on an *ex-ante* basis by the General Assembly.
- The need for rapid improvement in the present cash management procedures was also expressed by some member-states.

The problem of assessments

The assessment mechanism is the central component of the United Nations funding system. Provided member-states make timely and full payments, this method is probably the most effective, predictable and stable approach to fund raising for the organization.

The amount to be contributed by each member-state results from the operation of a formula which is determined in advance for a specific period. This formula is structured on the basis of various elements, the central one being per capita GNP, moderated by the size of the respective country's population and by the share of its trade in GNP.[17]

When member-states are slow or delinquent in their respective payments to the organization, this formula does not provide a stable resource base. This is clearly the case today, and has been the case prevailing for too many years.

The main component of the method is each country's 'capacity to pay'. Recommendations as to the specific scale to be used are made by the 'Committee on Contributions' to the General Assembly,[18] normally for periods ranging from one to three years. After the General Assembly makes its decision on this subject, amendments are not normally introduced, unless conditions have changed significantly. Although the Committee on Contributions has currently re-examined the ongoing methodology, no consensus has emerged on major reforms for its eventual restructuring.

In recent years, some member-states have expressed the view that there is a need for a long-term political reappraisal of the present assessment system. They would like to find a better structured and more equitable one. On May 1994, the US Congress, for example, unilaterally decided that the US contributions for peacekeeping should be reduced from its present level of approximately 31.4% to 25%. It may, or may not be possible. After the recent serious appeal to the member-states by the Secretary General[19] on all these matters, there is now a strong chance that such a long-term reappraisal will be made during the United Nations' 49th General Assembly period.

The very same definition of 'capacity to pay' is now under review. An *ad hoc* group is being organized for such a purpose and its mandate will be to revisit this notion. While there are changes in the levels of member-states' contributions over time, the fact that 'base periods' used for the purpose of calculating the 'capacity to pay' are pluri-annual, determines that such changes be somehow smooth and gradual. This makes sense as the 'capacity to pay' itself does not, as a rule, vary significantly from one year to another.

But there are also other aspects of the current methodology that may need some discussion, like the following recently suggested by the Secretary General himself:[20]

- Could the present system[21] be simplified?
- Could the system operate on a sliding scale?
- Could the 'base period' be shortened to try to diminish distortions in a world which is economically changing faster than ever before?
- Could the mechanism used to moderate the degree or speed of the adjustments be other than the 'base period' itself?
- Could the 'surcharge' on Permanent Members of the Security Council be made fixed, as opposed to the present fluctuating system? Should those members have a 'floor' or minimum contribution?

On the other hand, the concept of international peace and security can no longer be defined exclusively in military terms.[22] Notwithstanding that, during 1993, there was a major downturn in the flow of resources to the United Nations development funds and related programmes.[23]

The increase in having to finance not only emergency assistance but also various urgent humanitarian interventions seems to have led to a reduction of funding available for traditional development programmes. Member-states, however, through Resolution 48/162 of the General Assembly expressed the view that, as part of the overall United Nations reform process, there is a need for a substantial increase in resources for development activities. These types of activities are mainly financed through voluntary pledges. This mechanism obviously grants flexibility to donors when trying to respond to a wide range of needs and purposes. But it is also volatile from the recipients' standpoint. This is a drawback.

A mixed funding mechanism is probably the answer, combining both multiyear voluntary pledges and assessed contributions, thus highlighting the important principle of shared responsibilities among all members.

All these issues are, no doubt, for the member-states to decide. But they are of a political nature, and, therefore, need a political discussion leading to a political agreement to be technically implemented, at a later stage. The election of the forum for this long-term dialogue is crucial for member-states, to enable discussion of all presently available alternatives.

Member-states must avoid falling into the trap of resorting to specific fora which may already exist inside the organization, but which are not well suited for this limited, but important, political debate.

Other possible sources of income

The question as to whether the United Nations should—or should not—be granted authority to levy or collect taxes within its member-states for the support of the organization is also an old one.[24]

Some will argue that only through innovative approaches generating independent sources of income for the United Nations will its financial ills be cured. There are all kinds of proposals, some general in character, while others are highly specific. Again and again, levies on international sectors of airline tickets are suggested or even duties on forex transactions proposed. Irrespective of how realistic it is, for example, to dream about taxing forex transactions in a world which in fact wants to be as open and deregulated as possible, the present mood of member-states, as suggested by the day-to-day statements by their representatives at the United Nations, does not indicate that there is yet a will or an inclination even to start considering these types of proposals.

No matter how vigorously the proponents of independent sources of income for the United Nations make their case, the member-states simply do not seem to be willing to pursue these discussions related to an area which has traditionally been reserved within the exclusive jurisdiction of the member-states.

Far reaching proposals may require amending some member-states' constitutions. On the other hand, it is a fact that losing control of the United Nations' purse may have consequences which could be tantamount to eventually losing also, to a great degree, control of its programmes. This is, thus, not a simple political matter.

Back in 1954 it was said: 'given the present state of world affairs', the 'adoption of any UN tax system in the near future' is 'unlikely'. Correct then, but probably still correct today.

We agree with the Ogata-Volcker Report's conclusions on this issue, when it states: 'Current proposals for additional, non governmental sources of financing are neither practical nor desirable. For now, the system of assessed and voluntary contributions provides the most logical and appropriate means of financing the UN, as it permits and encourages member governments to maintain proper control over the UN's budget and it agenda'.[25] Clear enough.

Conclusions

The Secretary General has been courageous in calling on member-states to confront the gravity of the United Nations' financial situation.

The organization is being forced by some of its member-states to live in a sort of permanent financial emergency, with a cash-flow full of unpredictability and irregularities that, notwithstanding the substantial improvement in management resources made by the organization, do not allow its effective operation and, last but not least, without 'reserves' which, by definition, should be in place to be used and replenished as required.

We will soon commemorate the 50th anniversary of the birth of the United Nations. It is time to show with deeds the member-states' real commitment to it. Unless full compliance with financial responsibilities by member-states becomes a reality, the potential of the organization will always be restricted.

At the General Assembly it was recently stated: 'The United Nations works miracles with what we do not pay to it. But it cannot keep running on exhausted credit'.[26] True, but it is not only a matter of improving efficiency or effectiveness. Further, ensuring an adequate financial base for the organization has, in today's open world, become a question of commitment and self-respect. The United Nations can do no more than its members allow it to do.

Recently, Max Jakobson described the present situation vividly: 'Indeed, listening to what the experts have to say about the state of the United Nations, is a fairly melancholy experience. It brings to mind the sad fate of those fine old townhouses originally designed for a gracious living, which have been divided and redivided into poky little apartments and occupied by large families with badly behaved children and strange cooking habits. The more prosperous tenants have moved elsewhere, and the owners refuse to pay for necessary repairs leaving the poor janitor to take the blame for the failures of an antiquated plumbing system. The rational thing to do would be to tear the house down and build a new structure better suited for present-day conditions. But for sentimental reasons, or simply lack of energy, nothing is done and the place is left to decay. This must stop'.[27]

Just a few years ago, Dr Boutros Boutros-Ghali, stated 'A chasm has developed between the tasks entrusted to this organization and the financial means provided to it'. Time has now come to fill it.

Real internationalism, and, even more, supranationalism, can only exist if it is based on strong, coherent national support. With the United Nations, the world has the instrument and knows the techniques. It must still provide commitment.

There is too much at stake. Adlai Stevenson once observed: 'If the United Nations did not exist, it would have to be invented'. It does exist, and in its success lies nothing less than the hope of avoiding the end of the world. Let us all, in view of it, at least keep our promises.

Notes and references

1. Boutros Boutros-Ghali, statement to the General Assembly, 'Ensuring a viable financial basis for the Organization', 12 October 1994.
2. The Honorable Mr Gareth Evans, address to the General Assembly of the United Nations, 3 October 1994.
3. Boutros-Ghali, *op cit*, reference 1, page 1.
4. *Ibid*, page 1.
5. *Ibid*, page 3.
6. See Erskine Childers with Brian Urquhart, 'Renewing the United Nations system', Dag Hammarskjöld Foundation, Uppsala, Sweden, 1994, *Development Dialogue*, No 1, 1994. Also: Joachim W Müller, 'The reform of the United Nations', Vol 1, New York, Oceania, 1992, page 29, *et seq*.
7. See US Congress, Senate, 83rd Congress, 2nd Session, Budgetary and Financial Problems of the United Nations, Staff Study No 6, Subcommittee on the United Nations Charter, December 1954 (Washington, DC, US Government Printing Office, No 55432).
8. See Leland M Goodrich, Edvard Hambro and Anne Patricia Simons, *Charter of the United Nations, Commentary and Documents*, 3rd edition (New York, Columbia University Press, 1969), pages 177 and 178. Also Jean Pierre Cot and Alain Pellet, *La Charte des Nations Unies* (1985), page 399.
9. See United Nations A/48/935, 48th session, Agenda Item 91, Development and International Economic Cooperation, a report of the Secretary General, page 4.
10. United Nations Charter, Article 1 (3), United Nations DPI/511, September 1993.
11. WFP has a different organizational structure, jointly accountable to the UN and FAO.
12. In what follows the UNDP figures refer to the core programmes and the WFP figures to its regular programme activities.
13. The OECD member-states not part of DAC are Greece, Iceland, Luxembourg and Turkey.
14. Significantly each of these countries not only commits a greater percentage of its GDP to overseas aid but also channels a larger share of that aid through multilateral channels.
15. Boutros-Ghali, *op cit*, reference 1, page 3.
16. 'Financing an effective United Nations. A report of the independent advisory group on UN financing', New York, Ford Foundation, April 1993.
17. See United Nations A/48/940, 48th Session, Agenda item 56, 'Restructuring and revitalization of the United Nations in the economic, social and related fields', a report of the Secretary General, page 13 *et seq*.
18. For the latest one, see United Nations, Report of the Committee on Contributions, General Assembly, Official Records, 49th Session, Supplement No 11/A/49/11.
19. Boutros-Ghali, *op cit*, reference 1.
20. *Ibid*, page 3.
21. Here follows an overview of the present scale methodology and its application, as described by the Committee on Contributions itself. While preparing this document, the Committee recommended a 50% phase-out of the effects of the scheme of limits on the basis of a country-by-country approach spread over the 1995–97 period.

—The capacity to pay is the fundamental criterion for determining the scale of assessments. For ease of reference, the methodology currently used to approximate the 'capacity to pay' and its application are hereunder described.

The components of the methodology and criteria comprise the following:

(a) The national income data provided by all states for the statistical period;
(b) Debt relief reduces the annual national income of eligible countries with high level of external debt;
(c) The low per capita income allowance formula reduces the national income already adjusted for debt relief on the basis of its two parameters, namely the upper per capita income limit of the average world per capita income for the statistical base period and the relief gradient of 85%;
(d) The rates of assessment of member-states may not be lower than 0.01% (floor rate) or exceed 25% (ceiling rate);
(e) The assessment rate of least developed countries may not exceed 0.01%;
(f) The scheme of limits avoids excessive variations of individual rates of assessment between successive scales.

The national income data in United States dollars are prepared by the Statistical Division of the United Nations Secretariat for all member-states.

The part of the methodology described in paragraphs (a) to (c) above transforms national income in United States dollars into assessable income for the determination of individual assessment rates, which are then adjusted through the application of the various limits specified in paragraphs (d) to (f). The end result of calculations is referred to as 'machine scale' whose calculation is based upon the various adjustments steps defined above.

The adjustments for national income are:

(a) The national income of countries identified for debt relief, ie those with per capita incomes below $6000, is reduced by an amount based on a theoretical debt-service ratio. On the assumption that total external debt outstanding is repaid on the average in approximately 8 years, 12.5% of this debt is deducted from the national income of eligible countries. This adjustment increases not the absolute but the proportionate national income of the member-states that received no debt relief or whose relative debt relief reduction is lower than the amount of total debt relief, as a percentage of total national income.

(b) The national income figures resulting from step (a) are further adjusted for lower per capita national income. The national income of countries whose per capita national income is below the per capita income limit of $3198 for the period 1986–1992 is reduced by the percentage resulting from calculating 85% of the percentage difference between the country's per capita income and $3055 and $3198, respectively.

The total amount of relief granted increases the proportion of national incomes adjusted for debt relief of the countries not affected by the formula in proportion to their respective share (pro rata) of their collective national income. The national income figures thus adjusted constitute the assessable income.

Proportionate shares of national incomes are then adjusted as follows:

(a) The ceiling and floor rates are applied and the assessment rates of the least developed countries are reviewed to ensure that they do not increase. The points that make up the difference between the sum of the assessment rates thus adjusted and 100% are distributed, on a pro rata basis, among the countries with assessment rates below the ceiling and above the floor and that are not least developed countries.

(b) The scheme of limits is applied. It consists of eight rate brackets and two sets of constraints, ie, percentage and index points limits, which delimit the maximum possible individual rate increases or decreases between two scales. The level of maximum increase or decrease is defined by the limit with the lesser value. In applying the scheme of limits, the points that cannot be absorbed by countries whose rates of assessment have reached the level permissible under the scheme of limits are distributed, on a pro rata basis, among those countries whose assessment rate increases or decreases are within the constraints established by the scheme of limits.

After the application of the scheme of limits 50% of its effect is phased out. At this point the machine scales do not add up to 100% owing to the provision that, for developing countries benefiting from the application of the scheme of limits, the allocation of additional points resulting from the phasing out of the scheme of limits is to be limited to 15% of the effect of the phase out in accordance with paragraph 2 of resolution 48/223 B. The machine scales based on seven year and eight year base periods are then averaged. In the final adjustment of the machine scale to 100%, the unallocated points resulting from the 15% provision for certain developing countries are distributed, on a pro rata basis, among the countries which are not subject to the ceiling, are not least developed countries and are not developing countries benefiting from the 15% provision.

—The apportionment of the costs of peacekeeping operations is presently being made as follows:

(a) On December 11, 1973, the General Assembly adopted resolution 3101/XXVIII, on the financing of the United Nations Emergency Fund (UNEF II).

Under such resolution, the membership of the United Nations was divided into four groups: (1) The states that are Permanent Members of the Security Council; (2) Specifically named economically developed member-states, that are not Permanent Members of the Security Council; (3) Economically less developed member-states; and (4) Specified economically less developed member-states. The resolution also specified the amounts of the total appropriation to be distributed among each of the four groups.

Member-states in group (4) will pay 10% of the assessment rates established for the regular budget; those in group (3) would pay 20%; those in group (2) would pay 100% and those in group (1) would pay 100%, plus the amounts not otherwise apportioned.

Within each group, according to the terms of the resolution, the amount appropriated is to be distributed among the respective group members on the basis of the relative weight of each group member's regular rate of assessment in relation to the total rate for the group.

22. Max Jakobson, 'The United Nations in the 1990s. A second chance', UNITAR, 1993, page 8.
23. *Op cit*, reference 9, page 4 *et seq.*
24. US Congress, *op cit*, reference 7, pages 17 and 18. On international taxes, see also Harlan Cleveland, *Birth of a New World* (San Francisco, CA, Jossey-Bass Publishers, 1993), page 70 *et seq.*

25. *Op cit*, reference 19, page 24.
26. Speech by the Hon Douglas Hurd MP, to the 49th General Assembly of the United Nations, New York, 28 September 1994.
27. Jakobson, *op cit*, reference 22, page 15.

FINANCING THE UNITED NATIONS

Some possible solutions

Erskine Childers

This article suggests four basic propositions. First, financing is *not* an issue of UN policies or of UN management. Every member-state accepts an outright treaty obligation to pay its share of the organization's costs. The Charter gives no licence whatever to pay or not to pay one's dues according to whether one likes or dislikes some facet of UN work. Second, discussion of the financing of the UN should proceed from the Charter's principles of democratic revenue raising and governance, which plainly need reinforcement. Third, we should certainly explore additional sources, beyond the present triplicate framework of continuous dues assessment for regular budgets, *ad hoc* assessments for peacekeeping, and voluntary funding of development and humanitarian activities. But they should *be* additional sources—not devices to compensate for any state not paying its assessments. Fourth, UN financing is extremely vulnerable to disinformation and lack of information.

A picture has been painted for many years in some Northern countries of a UN budget that has massively increased. In 1946 the UN's regular budget—then raised from 51 states—was $21.5 million. In 1992 the budget was $1.2 billion. That looks like a 55-fold increase. But the budget has always been raised, and spent, in US dollars, and the dollar has lost about 85% of its value since 1946. In real terms the budget today is only eight times larger than it was 48 years ago for an organization

Erskine Childers (Ireland) retired in 1989 as Senior Adviser to the UN Director-General for Development and International Economic Cooperation. He may be contacted at 531 Main Street #1105, Roosevelt Island, New York, NY 10044, USA (Tel: +1 212 355 3174; fax: +1 212 980 0546). This article is an edited version of a paper presented to the Conference on Financing the United Nations, organized by the Society for International Development, New York, 30 March 1994.

starting virtually from scratch.

If we add the costs of peacekeeping and humanitarian relief, the UN's proper worldwide 1992 expenditures totalled a little over $5 billion. US citizens alone spend more than that on cut flowers and pot plants every year.[1]

The regular budgets of the specialized agencies are also financed by assessed membership dues, and they have also been the targets of demagogues. In 1992 the total worldwide expenditure of the whole UN system—the UN itself, all its development and humanitarian funds, and all its agencies except the World Bank and the International Monetary Fund, whose funds are raised in totally different ways—was $10.5 billion.[2] That, for example, would only sustain the alcoholic intake of UK citizens who so indulge for about 15 weeks.[3]

Table 1 shows all the expenditures including entirely voluntary contributions (for example to UNDP, UNFPA and UNICEF). Since the first pledging by governments of $20 million in 1950 this method has mobilized large additional sums for development and humanitarian assistance now aggregating to about $2.5 billion a year. But when high compound inflation over 40 years is factored in, that is nothing like the increase that is routinely claimed for this method.

Against record spending of about $*150* per human being alive in the world on military establishments and weapons every year, in 1992 governments spent through the UN system, in all fields, about $*1.90* per human being. Much of the budget goes on what we are constantly informed is 'a vast, sprawling, bloated bureaucracy'—a neat sound-bite and editorial phrase, powerfully conjuring up a picture of a huge and constantly multiplying staff, fecklessly frittering away the treasuries of the industrial countries.

First, as to the United Nations itself, its entire core, regular staff—general-service and professionals, worldwide, in New York, Geneva, Vienna, Addis Ababa,

TABLE 1. OVERALL WORLDWIDE EXPENDITURES OF THE UN SYSTEM IN 1992

Programme	UN and agencies (US$10^6)	Emergencies (US$10^6)	Per capita (US$)
Policy making	177.9		0.03
Political affairs	385.3		0.07
Peacekeeping operations		1400	0.25
Development	774.5		0.14
General statistics	145.9		0.03
Natural resources	403.5		0.07
Energy	81.5		0.01
Agriculture, forestry, fisheries	817.2		0.15
Industry	275.5		0.05
Transport	241.2		0.04
Communications	298.9		0.05
Trade and development	291.9		0.05
Population	268.8		0.05
Human settlements	127.9		0.02
Health	402.9		0.07
Education	418.5		0.07
Employment	284.4		0.05
Humanitarian assistance		2699.8	0.49
Social development	375.2		0.07
Culture	48.9		0.01
Science and technology	294.6		0.05
Environment	269.3		0.05
Totals	**$6383.8**	**$4099.8**	**$1.90**

Baghdad, Bangkok, Santiago and other offices—is now about 9000 (see *Table 2*).[4] That is less than the civil service of the City of Winnipeg in Canada.[5] It is some 14% less than the staff of the international advertising firm of Saatchi and Saatchi.[6]

The total regular and non-permanent staff of the whole UN *system*—the 9000 of the UN plus the staff of the agencies and the voluntarily financed development and relief funds, but not the Bank or IMF or, of course, contributed peacekeepers—is about 51 500. That is less than the total governmental staff in the state of Wyoming; it is less than the civil service of the city of Stockholm; it is less than the district health staff of the principality of Wales in the UK.[7]

We are not here discussing the inevitable improvements needed in the structure or the management of these civil services after 50 years. But let us be clear that we are talking about the financing of a world institution which has been kept perilously *small* and *under*-resourced because of all this disinformation.

When the UN was founded, only one method of financing it was envisaged. This was stated in Article 17 of the Charter: that 'the expenses of the Organization shall be borne by the Members as apportioned by the General Assembly'. This made payment of assessed dues obligatory in international treaty law. The method of apportioning these assessments is reviewed by the Assembly every three years. It allocates to each member a percentage of the total budget, calculated through a formula (currently) involving a 10-year average of its gross domestic product, with

TABLE 2. STAFF OF THE UNITED NATIONS SYSTEM[a]

Organization	Financed from regular budgets			Extra-budgetary (voluntary funds)			Total	
	Prof	*GS*	*Total*	*Prof*	*GS*	*Total*	*Prof*	*GS*
United Nations	3 265	5 829	9 094	1 604	3 198	4 802	4 869	9 027
UNHCR	106	179	285	643	1 198	1 841	749	1 377
UNITAR		1		10	8	18	10	9
UNRWA	51	2	53	67	7	74	118	9
ITC	1		1	181	192	373	182	192
ICSC	18	22	40				18	22
ICJ	19	28	47				19	28
UNU				36	65	101	36	65
UNDP				1 571	5 033	6 604	1 571	5 033
UNICEF				1 179	2 623	3 802	1 179	2 623
ILO	678	1 012	1 690	695	692	1 387	1 373	1 704
FAO	1 051	2 062	3 113	1 608	1 649	3 257	2 659	3 711
UNESCO	808	1 406	2 214	248	341	589	1 056	1 747
WHO	1 269	2 350	3 619	564	1 208	1 772	1 833	3 558
ICAO	248	350	598	231	223	454	479	573
UPU	62	84	146	25	1	26	87	85
ITU	240	395	635	135	99	234	375	494
WMO	104	124	228	78	72	150	182	196
IMO	88	146	234	34	47	81	122	193
WIPO	114	237	351	4	18	22	118	255
UNIDO	355	665	1 020	305	458	763	660	1 123
IAEA	684	958	1 642	15	108	123	699	1 066
Totals	9 161	15 850	25 011	9 233	17 240	26 473	18 394	33 090
Grand total UN system								51 484

[a] As of the end of 1990. There have been no major changes since then. Data derived from ACC document on 'The Budgetary and Financial situation of organizations of the UN system'. UN Doc A/47/593, 3 November 1992, and ACC/1991/Per/R 28, 5 July 1991.

downward adjustments for low per capita income and high foreign debt.

At the beginning, the US share of the regular budget was just on 50% and, of course, there were very few extremely poor members. Since then, in an agreed framework of special parameters, the US share has been adjusted downwards, and the contributions of the poorest countries cannot fall below 0.01% of the budget. To give a quick sketch of how the formula works, the USA is legally obliged to contribute 25% of the budget, currently $310 million; Japan half of that, 12.45%; Germany 8.93%; Russia 6.71%; France 6% and the UK 5%; Italy 4.29% and Canada 3.11% or $31 million; Brazil is assessed 1.59% of the budget; China 0.77%; India 0.36% which is $3.6 million, Nigeria 0.20% and Indonesia 0.16%; and so on down to 0.01%, or $102 000 for 87 member-countries at the bottom of the income scale.[8]

Late payment of these dues has been a chronic problem for decades, and there is to date no penalty interest charge. Late payments have steadily depleted the UN's Working Capital Fund (see *Figure 1*), and increased the running deficit, so that in October 1993, with 75% of the 1993 budget already spent, the equivalent of 72% of it had not yet been paid.[9] Governments have so far refused to allow the Secretary-General to borrow even for a week.

Every member-state has to pay its assessment in actual US dollars (we should actively campaign to establish a United Nations currency, a special drawing right (SDR) calculated on a representative basket of currencies). Protectionism in the North, and its refusal to discuss a fair trade strategy for the Charter's goal of the 'advancement of all peoples', have steadily reduced 75% of humankind to only having 18% of world trade, which drastically limits the ability of developing country members to earn hard currency. They have also suffered from unilaterally raised Northern interest on their loans. UNDP calculates that these North–South structural inequities are depriving developing countries of at least $500 billion a year in income that they could be earning.[10] Their indebtedness has multiplied 14-fold since 1970. Inevitably many have fallen behind in their payments, and we cannot hope for much improvement from that part of the assessment spectrum until industrial countries agree to discuss truly global all-win macroeconomic policies at the UN.

But the single most devastating impact on the assessments system came in 1985 when the US Congress decided to cut its legally obligated contribution by one-fifth

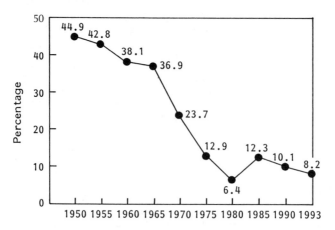

Figure 1.   Level of Working Capital Fund as % of regular budget appropriations.

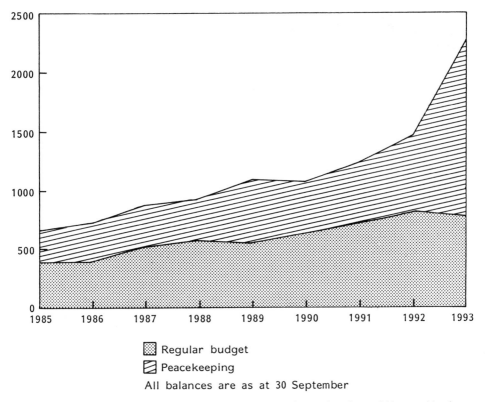

Figure 2. Unpaid assessed contributions—regular budget and peacekeeping activities combined (all balances at 30 September).

unless weighted voting was introduced in the UN, and then in 1986 when it applied an additional across-the-board reduction in US government spending.[11] *Figure 2* shows the impact.[12] Ever since the mid-1980s sheer cash-flow has been so uncertain that there have been times when the staff have not known if they would be paid the next month.

Peacekeeping costs are also assessed, but since 1973 the General Assembly has applied a slightly different scheme for these. Each of the five Permanent Members of the Security Council is supposed to pay 22% more than what its share would be under the regular budget formula; a second group of affluent countries pays the same percentages; a third group of the less well off pay one-fifth of their regular apportionment; and a fourth pay one-tenth. A major problem is that the Secretary-General only has a $150 million revolving fund, and each time the Security Council approves a peacekeeping operation he has to get a projected budget through the General Assembly before he can even send out a letter to members with their assessments for that new operation. That in itself results in delay in payments.[13]

The upper belt of unpaid assessments in the graph shows the consequences of this seriously inadequate method of raising peacekeeping funds. Here, the largest single delinquent is now Russia. Already crippled by Cold War armaments, its economy is now nearly wrecked by the hectoring priests of the new fundamentalist religion of the magic of the market. In October 1993 Russia owed nearly half the current $1 billion in peacekeeping arrears.

Finally, these arrears have a circular effect. Reimbursements to troop-contributing countries—more than half of which are developing countries—are delayed.[14] This in turn affects not only their ability to contribute more troops to more operations, but even their ability to pay their regular-budget assessments.

The history of official, intergovernmental efforts to reform the assessment system is pretty dismal.[15] Working Groups and intergovernmental Committees of Experts have been repeatedly convened over the UN's financing—in 1961, 1964, 1965, 1970, 1975, 1980, 1983 and 1986. But they have only tried to deal with its financial crises, and even then not to correct their causes but to reduce or freeze the budget, or UN salaries—or to liquidate arrears in peacekeeping costs when various members had refused to pay their assessed share.

By my reckoning, all these exercises have produced only five concrete actions:

- one issue of UN bonds—but only to liquidate already incurred costs of peace-keeping in the Sinai and the Congo;
- one increase in the level of the Working Capital Fund (now $100 million);
- under massive Northern pressure exploiting the US withholding of dues, the 1986 'Group of 18' exercise pressured the majority of members to accept that budgets are approved by consensus. This did *not* then improve the assessment process; indeed, even after this major concession by the South the USA did not resume full payment of its dues;
- a fourth action was to give the Secretary-General an inadequate $150 million fund for peacekeeping;
- and the fifth concrete action was the creation in 1991 of a $50 million revolving fund for start-up costs of humanitarian relief operations, which the regular budget could never have funded.

During the Reagan assault on the UN, however, there was one extremely important proposal. In 1985 the Prime Minister of Sweden, the late Olof Palme, proposed in the General Assembly that a ceiling of 10% should be put on the assessed contribution of any member-state, with redistribution of the difference among capable members. India endorsed this idea. It got only silence from Washington, but it was no secret that the US administration did not wish to have its share—and therefore its leverage—reduced at all. Other industrial countries might have supported Mr Palme's proposal but they refused to risk having such a reduction seem to reward the USA for defaulting on its legal obligations.

Mr Palme had diplomatically but sharply enough suggested that, 'a more even distribution of the assessed contributions would better reflect the fact that this Organization is the instrument of *all* nations'.[16] Once upon a time that was indeed the idea. If nothing else were to be done with regard to the financing of the UN for another decade, relieving the organization from its perpetual threat of either political dictation or bankrupting by one member-state—*any* one state—would be a marvellous achievement. In autumn 1993 President Clinton told the General Assembly that the USA does now want a reduction in its assessment share of peacekeeping costs. It is time to get the Palme proposal adopted first, for the regular budget apportionment.

In 1993 a 'first-ever' was, however, achieved in this rather gloomy history, when a blue-riband group of the world's financiers, co-chaired by Shijuro Ogata of Japan and Paul Volcker of the USA, met under the auspices and facilitation of the Ford Foundation, and sent their report to the Secretary-General.[17] The group's recommendations essentially addressed flaws in the present assessment system. The main recommendations were that:

- Dues should be paid in four quarterly amounts, with interest charged on late payments; and countries whose appropriations calendar is late in the year should re-phase it for UN dues.
- The Working Capital Fund should be doubled, to $200 million.
- The assessment formula should work from three- rather than ten-year averages of GDP.
- Governments should consider financing peacekeeping from their national defence budgets, and the revolving reserve for peacekeeping should be increased to $400 million.
- And along the lines of recent Nordic proposals the group also recommended that the administrative costs of the voluntary funds should be met by assessment.

We are now waiting to see what the action will be on these perfectly sound proposals. Governments should be nagged.

In the *Agenda for Peace* report Dr Boutros-Ghali had already suggested that alternative, additional means of financing should be considered, including a Peace Endowment Fund to which private sources could contribute. The Ogata-Volcker group, however, said that 'current proposals for additional, non-governmental sources of financing the UN are neither practical nor desirable, and that the present triplicate system is the most logical and appropriate means of financing the UN as 'it permits governments to maintain proper control over the UN's budget and its agenda'.

Financing possibilities

I briefly sketch here some possibilities for such additional and alternative financing, and then suggest some guiding principles.

Various sources have proposed a range of schemes in 'international taxation'.[18] This has a certain logic and equity to it: it would be automatic, fairly universal, with higher yields from those profiting more. Member-states could agree to levy a United Nations surcharge on any one or several of the following:

- all arms sales in the recently established UN Register (I do not much like that but I would acclaim an immediate and serious tax on every single land-mine produced from this day forward); or
- a tiny, fractional levy on all transnational movement of currencies (if governments came out of their current state of trance in market religion long enough to agree)—it has been estimated that a levy of 0.003% on the $900 billion being traded daily would produce some $8 billion[19]—or even on all international trade; or on the production of such specific (and polluting) materials as petroleum and hydrocarbons, or on all mineral raw commodities.
- There is, of course, the revenue from the Seabed Authority when that finally gets moving.
- One more often proposed is a United Nations levy on all international air and sea travel, on the grounds that the UN must maintain a peaceful environment for international travellers.

Common to all these propositions except the Seabed Authority is that each member-government would have to agree to levy the tax, collect it, and transfer it to agreed parts of the UN system. I mention this simply for us to be quite clear that international taxation revenue would essentially be raised through and stay under the control of governments. To what extent, also, would citizens of the United Nations—'We, the Peoples'—feel more involved as a result of such taxation, and how much importance would we attach to that as one purpose and product of additional financing?

That thought leads to another range of possibilities—still needing the initial assent of member-governments, but thereafter far more visible and tangible to citizens. For example, if someone has not already done so, the Universal Postal Union should be asked to calculate what revenues could accrue if the national post offices of every member-country agreed to contribute the proceeds of sales of stamps for one, publicly well announced, day in each year. To make it a real event for information about the UN system, a tiny surcharge might be arranged through the International Telecommunications Union on all telephone calls that day, with a free dialling number for a recorded explanation.

Of course, here again the revenues would still move through each government, to the UN. One possibility for income moving more directly to the UN—but still with initial governmental licensing and auditing legislation in each country—would be an annual United Nations lottery, administered by a special authority under the Secretary-General. This might be sensitive in one or more cultures, but it would be a form of very visible and citizen-involved 'voluntary automaticity'. Lotteries painlessly raise lovely pots of money.

Finally, we come to the various forms of endowment funds to which citizens, foundations or corporations could contribute. Here, however, I would suggest considerable caution, lest before we knew it some ebullient corporation CEO arrived with several billion very attractive-looking dollars, but perhaps with all sorts of conditionalities attached in extremely small print. Through voluntary financing the UN system is already in danger of drowning under waves of donor conditionalities that are flatly against the Charter.

I have only touched on some possibilities in three broad categories, but let me now offer some guiding principles.

First, any additional, alternative financing of the UN and its system should be *supplementary to* a properly worked, more healthily apportioned, and fully *honoured* assessment system.

Second, we should be clear what we mean in terms of who would *govern* any such additional contributions to the UN and the system.

Third, and closely connected, such additional financing, in one way or another a tax or donations from citizens, must be transparently accountable to citizens. Here I simply enter a plea for all-out support for a United Nations Parliamentary Assembly, one of whose functions could indeed be to watch over such supplements.

In conclusion, I make a plea for another 'first-ever' on this subject. The entire question of putting financing on a more stable and even modestly expanding basis has been plagued for many years by pressures and even outright demands from those who claim they are 'contributing the most'.

The assessment system is squarely founded on the principle of *relative capacity to pay*. It is a fundamental principle of democratic revenue raising and governance that it is as difficult for the poorer citizen to find his or her lower money amount of tax as it is for the wealthier citizen or corporation to find higher money amounts. Accordingly, the wealthier should have no special voice or voting strength in government; and they do *not* have it in any of the established democracies.

In the United Nations system, it is at least as difficult for Jamaica, Ireland, Tanzania, Australia or Nepal to find their smaller money amount of assessment dues as it is for Germany or Japan or the USA to find their larger money amount of dues. Yet it is from countries claiming to be models of democratic governance that there has for several decades come this insidious, totally *anti*-democratic talk of who 'pays most' for the UN's budgets, and of demands for special influence. If anyone tried now to revert their *own* system of governance to what they are demanding in the UN—the wealthier citizens and corporations to have special voting strength in their parliaments and hold key cabinet posts and civil-service jobs—there would be another round of the bitter and bloody revolutions it took to establish this principle in those same democracies.

It is often claimed that those contributing the larger money amounts are justified in demanding a special voice and voting strength, because the UN secretariats do not handle funds well. I find this difficult to accept from countries that are currently reeling from the exposure of massive corruption and ineptitude in their political and administrative systems. Citizens of one country whose officials constantly lecture the UN recently lost the equivalent in savings of 250 years of UN budgets through mismanagement and corruption in public organizations. The UN's management needs improvement, of course; but let us *improve* it, not surrender it to pre-democratic and semi-feudal control.

An all-time record would be set if no one again uttered those totally undemocratic words, 'who pays most'. The fundamental principle in our United Nations Charter, at the very roots of our one universal public-service institution, is that for all we want it to achieve, *everyone* 'pays most'.

Notes and references

1. *Surveys of Current Business* (Washington, DC, US Dept of Commerce).
2. UN Document A/48/1, Table 4 and paragraph 108.
3. *Social Trends* (London, Her Majesty's Stationery Office, 1991).
4. This and further staff statistics are assembled from UN Docs A/47/593 and ACC/1991/Per/R 28. Data are as of 1991; there have been no significant changes since then.
5. The City of Winnipeg was employing 9917 staff in mid-1993 (data from its Personnel Office).
6. *Financial Times*, 14 February 1994.
7. Comparative data respectively from *Public Employment 1991*, Table 6, Doc GE/91-1 (US Department of Commerce); *Kommunal Personal 1991* (Svenska Kommunforbundet); *Public Bodies 1991* (London, HMSO).
8. UN Doc A/48/503/Add 1, 11 November 1993.
9. UN Doc A/48/503, paragraph 31.
10. Data and graph from *UNDP Human Development Report 1992* (New York, Oxford University Press, 1992).
11. For useful summary accounts of this and other periods of UN financial crisis see Joachim W Muller, *The Reform of the United Nations* (New York, Oceana, 1992).
12. Graph on unpaid assessed contributions is from UN Doc A/48/503, in paragraph 14.
13. For much useful data on financing of peacekeeping, see, *inter alia*, Anthony McDermott, *United Nations Financing Problems and the New Generation of Peacekeeping and Peace Enforcement* (Providence, RI, Watson Institute/Brown University, 1994), Occasional Paper No 16.
14. See UN Doc A/48/503, paragraph 37.
15. For useful background to the whole history of the assessment system and its bargaining dynamics see, *inter alia*, John G Stoessinger, 'Financing of the United Nations', in *International Conciliation* (New York, Carnegie Endowment, 1961); Robert F Meagher, 'United States financing of the United Nations', in Trister Gati (editor), *The US, the UN, and the Management of Global Change* (New York, New York University Press, 1983).
16. Statement in the General Assembly, 21 October 1985.

17. *Financing an Effective United Nations: Report of the Independent Advisory Group on UN Financing* (New York, Ford Foundation, 1993).

18. For useful background see, *inter alia*, Eleanor B Steinberg and Joseph A Yager with G M Brannon, *New Means of Financing International Needs* (Washington, DC, Brookings, 1978); Paper on Automaticity in Electronic Transfers for the InterAction Council; United Nations Bibliography Series, Dag Hammarskjold Library. At the Conference at which the present paper was presented the author learned of a valuable paper, 'Financing mechanisms and their implementation' by the NGO UNCED Task Force, contact Dr Lisinka Ulatowska, World Citizens (Tel: 1-718-658-5872).

19. See, *inter alia*, Martin Walker, 'Global taxation', *World Policy Journal*, 1993.

A NEW SYSTEM TO FINANCE THE UNITED NATIONS

Hans d'Orville and Dragoljub Najman

The end of the Cold War has not delivered a peace dividend but, paradoxically, a peace penalty on the United Nations. This article argues that revision of the existing funding arrangements is inadequate and that a radical restructuring of the financial system is a prerequisite for successful multilateralism.

With the end of the Cold War, an almost religious hope had permeated the international community that the absence of ideological confrontation coupled with expanding disarmament agreements might yield a peace dividend—the proverbial manna—to provide the financial means for myriad multilateral programmes. Although global defence and military expenditures decreased, the truth is that any resultant savings have been absorbed and reallocated by individual countries to other domestic priorities and needs. Even more sobering, the decommissioning and elimination of weapons of mass destruction in the wake of the Cold War require previously unforeseen, substantial levels of national and international finance (eg the Ukraine alone was promised US$175 million by the USA to begin dismantling strategic warheads, and its Foreign Minister Zlenko suggested on 25 October 1993 that it would need a total of US$2.8 billion to dismantle and destroy all its nuclear warheads; or, the destruction of Russia's chemical weapons alone under the chemical weapons convention signed in January 1993 would require US$10 billion over ten years). On top of this, a dearth of international savings and the worldwide economic recession have reduced the inclination of industrialized countries to fund multilateral undertakings and have eroded the commitment of these countries to ever higher levels of development finance. A peace dividend will therefore elude the multilateral system in general, but more particular the field of development—the

Hans d'Orville was Assistant Secretary, UNDP Governing Council and Senior External Relations Officer (1982–88), and is now Executive Coordinator of the InterAction Council, 821 United Nations Plaza, 7th Floor, New York, NY 10017, USA (Tel: +1 212 687 2243; fax: +1 212 867 4810). Drago Najman was Assistant Secretary General, UNESCO (1975–86), and is now Executive Secretary of the InterAction Council. This article is adapted from Hans d'Orville (editor), *Perspectives of Global Responsibility: In Honor of Helmut Schmidt on the Occasion of his 75th Birthday* (New York, InterAction Council, 1994). The views expressed here are those of the author and do not necessarily represent those of the InterAction Council or any other organization.

peace dividend is nothing but a myth.

Instead, the United Nations and its agencies must paradoxically cope with an unforeseen 'peace penalty', ie more and exacting tasks are being thrust on the world body entailing exponentially growing costs, while it is already struggling with an endemic financing crisis. The scale and ambitions of UN efforts have rapidly expanded, as has the complexity of (often insoluble) issues—including new types of regional, national and ethnic conflicts, vast humanitarian assistance programmes, daunting ecological and developmental challenges—amidst a global economic recession, which also diminishes the willingness and ability of many countries to pay their share of the United Nations budget.

Radical structural change instead of piecemeal reform

Against this sobering background, revisions of and improvements to the existing funding modalities will no longer do the trick. Rather, what is called for is a radical, structural change in the financing system for the centrepiece of multilateralism. For this reason, we are convinced that recent international efforts, such as the recommendations of a panel headed by Paul Volcker and Shijuro Ogata, are bound to fall short of the challenge. The effect of their proposals will remain marginal at best as they merely tinker with the *status quo*, but do not address the fundamental underlying problems. Thus, even if fully implemented, they will be unable to prevent a recurrence of jittery periods and the spectre of bankruptcy.

The recurrent financial crisis of the United Nations and of many of its agencies is caused by the failure of a number of governments to pay their assessed—and obligatory—contributions in full and on time (by 31 January of each calendar year). It is absurd indeed that numerous member-states have not made any payments towards the end of a calendar year. By 30 September 1993, only 62 member-states had paid their dues in full, while 116 members still had to pay their outstanding contributions. It is equally intolerable that by the end of August 1993 the total outstanding contributions for the current year amounted to US$509 million, or roughly half the total assessed contributions (US$1070 million), and that at the same date, the total accumulated arrears of years prior to 1993 (US$330 million) was equivalent to a third of one year's budget. Hence, the organization has to operate with large arrears and unpaid contributions. Other intergovernmental organizations have never or rarely experienced comparable precarious and extreme situations, such as the EC or—from among the United Nations family—the Universal Postal Union (UPU), the International Telecommunications Union (ITU), and the World Intellectual Property Organisation (WIPO). While it is theoretically simple to solve the financial woes of the United Nations—namely that all governments in arrears pay their dues without delay—in reality the poor payment morale may continue or even worsen.

United Nations budget process

A brief analysis of the United Nations regular budget process might help in the search for alternatives of a more compulsory and automatic nature. Rightly or wrongly, the United Nations voting mechanism has been shaped along the precedent of individual countries, where rich and poor citizens have one vote each and assume equal civic obligations. The budget, however, is financed partly through taxes which differ from person to person according to their ability to pay.

A draft two-year programme budget is proposed by the Secretary-General to the

General Assembly. Prior to the Assembly's discussions, this draft budget is reviewed by an intergovernmental Committee for Programme and Coordination and a 16-member expert Advisory Committee on Administrative and Budgetary Questions. Apprised of the comments and recommendations of these two bodies, the General Assembly and its Fifth (Budgetary) Committee carry out an in-depth scrutiny of all sections of the budget, which goes through two readings in the budget committee and one final reading in the plenary of the Assembly. A few years ago, formal agreement was reached at the level of the General Assembly that the budget must be passed by consensus and cannot be adopted by a vote. This provision was supposed to prevent a recurrence of earlier votes when the industrialized countries, which contribute more than two-thirds of the budget, were outvoted by the numerical majority of other member-countries, most of whom contribute only a miniscule portion of the overall budget. Thus, this mechanism can be seen as a reflection of the time-tested principle of no taxation without representation.

At the same time it votes the budget, the General Assembly—on proposal by its expert Committee on Contributions—adopts a scale of assessments, which sets out the portion of the budget which each country must pay. This scale is essentially based on the *capacity-to-pay principle*, as it draws on GNP, population, membership and other factors.

The thus-determined amount of contribution for each country is mandatory (contrary to the voluntary contribution to the development and humanitarian organizations of the United Nations), as laid down in the Charter, to which all member-states have pledged to adhere on admission to the organization. Article 19 of the Charter stipulates that member-states with two years of arrears to the regular budget can lose their voting rights in the General Assembly. Would it not be time to tighten this provision to a voting forfeit after a one-year non-payment? Membership, after all, should have its privileges.

Hence, all incentives and safeguards would seem to be in place to enable a full implementation of the regular programme of the organization as voted. Nevertheless, a poor and worsening payment mentality abounds, catapulting the United Nations on an undignified roller-coaster. The lack of resources is now constricting the United Nations' ability to carry out its missions. Does this signal a low or even sagging commitment on the part of governments?

Setting global priorities collectively

One reason for the poor payment morale and record of many governments to the UN budget is evidently the fact that there is a divergence in the collective and individual will expressed by national governments. Often, a collective will is the expression of an unloved and unenthusiastic compromise. Yet, the maintenance of international peace and security and the promotion of sustainable human development are arguably the key areas among the many global priorities—as laid down in the Charter. The UN system is well placed and has a comparative advantage to act in these two areas. But if the United Nations system is not capable of dealing with them, other international organizations—already poised to get into the act—will increasingly seek to take the UN's place.

In the United Nations, governments collectively express and set global priorities, representing a reflection of the collective wisdom of humankind. In most cases, such general priorities do not allow a deduction of operable and accepted priorities at the national level. This must be accomplished individually by each government or parliament. More often than not, the sum total of the national priorities does not tally with the global priorities determined through the multilateral process.

This divergence is apparent in many areas. With respect to environmental issues, the alleviation and prevention of global warming is a stated global priority. But national perceptions and conclusions differ as to how this global goal should be translated into concrete national action-plans and targets. Or, take the tragic conflict in the former Yugoslavia: the Security Council members vote for safe havens in Bosnia, while knowing that they and other governments do not intend to supply the minimum necessary troops to protect them. Political grandstanding? On the other hand, a very specific global goal—smallpox eradication—was never presented by any government as a national priority for financing under the UNDP or WHO programmes. Consequently, it had to be subsumed under a facility and provisions for global programmes outside the scope of competition for scarce funds by national governments.

Or, the absence of peace in remote areas no longer triggers priority attention and commensurate action by a majority of member-states, especially if peace-making, peacekeeping and enforcement are likely to entail considerable additional financial and other obligations. Hence the emergence of a new debate that the UN should only get involved in situations constituting true threats to international peace and security. The verdict may be in the eyes of the beholder—to determine what constitutes such a true threat will be nearly as intractable as similar attempts in the past to define aggression, which lingered on unsuccessfully for more than ten years.

While concentrating on agreed global priorities, the United Nations may nevertheless involve itself in more limited and regional undertakings if certain conditions are met. In a reversal of chapter VIII of the Charter, which envisages regional arrangements for dealing with certain threats to peace and disputes, governments in a region, unable to tackle a particular problem or conflict situation effectively, may ask the United Nations to get involved and thereby take advantage of multilateral expertise. Such involvement should be subject to the condition that those governments concerned agree to finance fully all costs, either through direct payments or through funds plenished through mechanisms, such as

- governments of a particular region could contribute each 10% of their military budgets into a fund designed to finance UN operations in that region;
- governments of a region could contribute a certain percentage of their law enforcement budgets towards a fund for action to combat drug trafficking.

Financing global priorities

A key task facing the global community is to agree on ways and means to finance global priorities, once determined. One principle must be paramount in the decision-making process: whenever a decision is taken jointly to pursue programmes geared towards a realization of a global priority, full financing must be guaranteed and secured. If that cannot be ensured, decisions on the launching of such programmes are either delayed or alternative mechanisms must be agreed before-hand to ensure the financial viability of a global endeavour. To avoid a dilution of global priorities, we advocate that the numerous trust funds with extra-budgetary funds provided by some governments for the conduct of specific projects, should be merged into one single 'super' trust fund operating under the overall authority of the

UN Secretary-General.

The suggestion of integrating non-governmental and private sector organizations on a select basis into the activities of the United Nations might lead to a mobilization of supplementary resources from these quarters (ie an operationalization of the 'We, the peoples' concept derived from the Charter). Such an innovation would also mirror practices by two smaller UN organizations. Recognized private operating agencies and scientific or industrial organizations already contribute towards the expenses of certain activities of the ITU in which they have agreed to participate. WIPO receives its income almost equally from member-states and from fees coming mostly from private owners of industrial property rights using the services of the International Bureau of WIPO.

The Peace Endowment Fund—proposed by the Secretary-General in his 'Agenda for Peace'—might benefit from tapping such resources. In any case, it should be enlarged from its present level of US$1 billion to at least US$3 billion. The annual yields of such an enlarged endowment might well be sufficient to fund certain peacekeeping operations.

Confer national budget tools to the United Nations

While such a broader reach-out might bring some relief, it remains a palliative. One needs to go further. Given the analogy of the UN and the national budget processes, why can't the United Nations be authorized by its member-states to apply practices similar to those used by national governments, including measures adapted from collecting overdue taxes and other revenues? Consider the following:

- taxpayers are penalized if they are not paying their dues by a certain date;
- funds are regularly obtained from central banks and borrowed on international markets;
- in situations of current account imbalances, governments utilize their special drawing rights allocation and resort to other financing facilities made available by the international financing institutions.

But, unlike a national government, the international system has no comparable instruments at its disposal—unless specifically authorized by the governing bodies of the organizations concerned.

For example, the UNESCO General Conference authorized the organization's Director-General to borrow against the approved budget. This begs the question: why do the same governments act differently in the various governing bodies of the UN organizations, giving special financial tools to one organization only, which even has a controversial financial track record? Where is the coordination of the policies of one and the same government in different international fora? One wonders. This lack of uniformity can be taken to imply, however, that the financing approaches followed in the United Nations system are not sacred in any way and that different options can be pursued.

We submit that at the heart of a fundamental reorientation of United Nations financing must be a decision of principle to endow the United Nations with means and facilities comparable to those enjoyed by national governments. Why could intergovernmental organizations not be authorized by their member-governments to do what governments do, namely,

- to levy taxes;

- to borrow funds;
- to 'print' money?

What would that mean in practice for the financing of global priorities?

Financing the core budget

As a matter of principle, the core budget of the United Nations—its financial backbone—should be financed through some sort of international 'taxation' of the member-states, similar to the present system of assessments. The level of contributions should be directly linked to the current GNP data (and not based on the current practice of using data over a ten-year period)—despite all reservations as to the validity and reliability of GNP as an appropriate indicator. This approach would replace the present complicated—negotiated—formula of determining the UN's scale of assessment. Furthermore, we also suggest that the present ceiling for a maximum contribution by any single country should be lowered from the present 25% to, say, the 10–15% level. Permanent members of the Security Council, given their special privileges, responsibilities and possibilities for influencing the course of events, should each pay no less than 8%. Likewise, the present minimum 'floor' contribution of 0.01% for the poorest countries should be raised to 0.02%. Some smaller, technical United Nations organizations already operate under different provisions; at WIPO for example the highest contributions by any one member-state reaches less than 5% of the total contributions. This would reduce the excessive reliance on one single country and, in the process, would avoid sudden programme ruptures in the case of default or non-payment by a big contributor.

Commercial borrowing powers

As mentioned above, we call for a uniform decision by member-governments to allow the United Nations and all its agencies to borrow commercially under certain conditions, and initially up to an amount of 50% of the annual core budget.

Financing programme costs through international levies

In addition to the core budget, substantial funds could be raised for programme activities of the United Nations through levies and dues on various international activities, which are the glue of the growing global interdependence and which stand to benefit from collective security and stability, be it in the military or the economic and social field. International air travel (such as airport or departure taxes to be added automatically to ticket prices) and air freight; international telecommunications and postal services; certain transactions in globalized financial markets (to highlight the potential, eg in April 1993 foreign exchange trading was estimated as having a daily volume of US$1 trillion; or international bond issues exceeded US$300 billion in 1991); maritime shipping through international waters; conventional arms sales and transfers reported under the newly established United Nations arms register; and international trade might be the objects of such levies.

The revenues collected could be distributed among the United Nations and the specialized agencies, based on a yet-to-be-defined formula. In a similar vein, the US government plans, according to a recent report by the *New York Times* (9 October 1993), to raise US$500 million a year by imposing fees on travellers entering the country. These funds are intended to help pay for the North American Free Trade Agreement (NAFTA), which provides for the elimination of tariffs on imports and a corresponding reduction in federal revenue of US$2.4 billion. Yet, the immediately ensuing controversy in Congress points to formidable difficulties in implementing such ideas.

Financing peace-related activities through special drawing rights

In 1993, 11 peacekeeping operations were financed through separate budgets based on obligatory—assessed—contributions, utilizing a slightly different scale of assessment than that of the regular budget. The total peacekeeping budget has grown dramatically in the past two years from US$600 million in 1991 to US$2.8 billion in 1992. For 1993, operational costs may have totalled US$4.3 billion. This exceeds the regular budget substantially, but it suffers from the same late- and non-payment syndrome as the regular budget: as of 30 September 1993 overdue payments of obligatory operations amounted to US$1.5 billion—essentially preventing the reimbursement of costs incurred by troop-contributing countries (totalling US$605 million on 30 September 1993). This situation—which has more or less repeated itself in 1994—has scathingly been characterized as 'a financial bungee jump often undertaken in blind faith that timely appropriations will be forthcoming' (Richard Thornburgh). In December 1992, the General Assembly also established as a cash-flow mechanism a Peace-keeping Reserve Fund of US$150 million to enhance the organization's capability to respond rapidly to the needs of peacekeeping operations, especially if a crisis is at hand—of which only US$64 million could be paid in, due to financial needs elsewhere in the organization, and because even this amount had to be drawn on for other purposes. This is not auspicious.

In order to instil an element of automaticity into programmes fostering peace, an innovative procedure should be devised whereby the United Nations could be given access to monetary and currency-related instruments, especially special drawing rights (SDRs), for peace-related activities. This should be tapped when quick and assured action is critical—axiomatic for unexpected crisis situations. This would require a revision of the Articles of Agreement of the IMF—incidentally a member of the United Nations system of organizations—so as to permit the allocation of SDRs in some other way than currently envisaged, yet restricted to peace-related activities. As a trial preceding a formal revision, a group of like-minded countries might already agree to pledge some of their SDRs for the proposed purpose. The modalities would certainly have to be specified, ie that once the Security Council has taken a pertinent decision and authorized the scope and magnitude of a particular peace-related operation, the Secretary-General should automatically be empowered to draw on SDRs. To provide for a peace-driven SDR allocation would be the logical corollary to Chapter VII of the United Nations Charter on enforcement measures. The total budget for peacekeeping and peacemaking, if only kept at present levels, would be of the order of some US$5 billion annually—a trifle compared to US$1 trillion expenditures for global defence spending. Given the relatively modest amounts under consideration, such levels of SDRs are unlikely to trigger global inflationary effects. And let us not forget: making and preserving peace is infinitely cheaper than waging war!

The foregoing proposal is by and large in line with a suggestion made by the IMF Managing Director, Michel Camdessus, regarding the provision of funds for Russia and other post-communist states via new allocations of SDRs (*Financial Times*, 21

May 1993). According to Camdessus, the IMF's richer member-states should return their share of an SDR allocation—amounting to some US$5–6 billion—which would go towards a trust fund for support of the states concerned. If for Russia, why not for peace-related operations which are in the interest of the entire international community?

If and when the SDR articles will be amended, they should further be revised to stipulate that the UN Secretary-General be authorized to draw from a country's SDR allocation the amount of the annual contribution due to the regular UN budget if such funds have not been paid by the end of June of any given calendar year. This would take account of different budget years by member-states.

Financing sustainable human development—marshalling a critical mass of resources

Turning to the other key global priority, sustainable human development, most developmental and humanitarian work (operational activities) by the greater United Nations family (eg UNDP, UNICEF, UNFPA, WFP and relevant programmes by the specialized agencies) is financed from voluntary contributions by governments, pledged on an annual basis without legal obligations, but driven by the concept (and moral obligation) of burden sharing especially among the major donors. Efforts over several decades to bring about a system on a broader, more stable and more predictable basis have yet to be successful. The Nordic countries have suggested the adoption of a financing system combining assessed contributions (10% of total funding for the administrative budget), negotiated contributions (among donors, as in the case of the International Development Association, aiming at 60% of the programme resources) and voluntary contributions (about 30%).

The only true and significant developmental success story during this century, however, was the Marshall Plan, which involved the net transfer of 2.5% of US GNP over a period of four years. The failure of many international development efforts over the past 30 years might well be linked to mismanagement, corruption, lack of capacity and institutions—and lack of political will. But, most important, they failed for an absence of a critical mass of finance to underpin and jump-start development.

This problem—and its symptoms—cannot be resolved by organizing or reorganizing the United Nations and its economic and social sectors, as has been tried far too often with no palpable effect but an abundance of bureaucratic turf battles. Unfortunately, one long overdue, drastic reorganization has never been seriously discussed: the creation of a truly effective development organization—namely a *United Nations High Authority for Development.* The authority should combine the present multitude of often competing development and humanitarian programmes, agencies, offices and departments of the United Nations under one roof. This would minimize programme duplication, reduce redundant layers of staff and resources devoted to administration, finance, personnel, external relations and resource mobilization. Such a merger might not only increase the overall efficiency and delivery, but also generate annual savings in the amount of several million dollars which could instead be redirected to development purposes.

Would it be possible to marshal a critical mass of resources for a comprehensive effort to foster sustainable human development globally, spearheaded by the United Nations system? Global GNP is currently around US$22 trillion, with developing countries including China accounting for only some US$6 trillion. If a goal of 2% of global GNP were to be set (ie lower than that realized under the Marshall Plan) it would be equal to US$440 billion (and, by the way, had the 0.7% of GNP target agreed by industrialized countries for their development assistance been met across the board, it would by now have injected US$145 billion annually). We call therefore for a tripling of this—thus far unrealized—target. A substantial portion of these funds could already be raised through revenues from the abovementioned international levies and dues. The proposed infusion of financial resources into developing countries would be likely to lift the GNP of developing countries in excess of 13% per annum and might be capable of narrowing the present untenable development, prosperity and income gaps *vis-à-vis* industrialized countries, which defy the concept of 'one world'.

The United Nations should be mandated to prepare the blueprint for such a global economic recovery and development plan. A global programme on this scale would not only boost development, but would also give a significant boost to restart global economic growth. If the potential needs of three-quarters of the world's population are translated into effective demand, the resulting growth would resuscitate the world economy: hence, the North ought to have a considerable and enlightened self-interest in the realization of such a plan. This would mirror history: besides its benefits for the war-ravaged European economies, the Marshall Plan served precisely as a stimulus for the US economy in 1947, which was lingering on the threshold of a big recession in the wake of post-war military demobilization.

As a by-product, a global recovery plan initially aimed at the developing world would also revitalize the economies of the industrialized countries, reducing in the process their present high levels of unemployment—which for the OECD countries was estimated as reaching 8.5% of the total labour force by mid-1994, equivalent to 36 million people. Consider that according to the OECD, most member-countries of the EC spend at present annually between 1% and 3% of their GDP (for Germany even higher) on 'active' (various forms of training, youth employment measures, subsidized employment) and 'passive' labour market programmes (unemployment benefits, early retirement pay-outs). The case can be made that such expenditures could more productively be devoted to a global recovery and development plan.

Is the United Nations prepared for and capable of taking up this challenge? One should certainly resist the temptation to resort to SDRs for development purposes—as contrary to the peacekeeping area, the amounts required might indeed entail inflationary consequences for the entire world economy.

In conclusion, we want to re-emphasize that either a total, revolutionary approach will be adopted to financing the United Nations, and especially its peace-related operations and development activities, or one must be prepared to countenance other organizations filling the lacunae which might be left as a result of the financial difficulties of the world organization. Indications to that effect are already apparent. Whether the results would be better or worse, remains to be seen. But clearly, a courageous and major reorientation of the financing modalities for UN activities must be complemented by a host of operational, structural and managerial reforms, which are presently the principal focus of the public reform debate, virtually to the exclusion of the more fundamental issues.

BEYOND FINANCING

Giving the United Nations power of the purse

Inge Kaul

The present financial constraint on UN activities is primarily of a developmental—rather than strategic, geopolitical—nature. It stems from such factors as: the blurring of the dichotomy between North and South; caution about intergovernmental cooperation which might reduce national sovereignty; and hesitation to accept the need for a fundamentally new development paradigm. Yet, strengthening of the UN is at the same time one of the critical conditions required for the international community effectively to address the growing problems of global poverty, socioeconomic inequity and environmental degradation. It is, therefore, imperative urgently to find a way out of the present political stalemate surrounding the UN's role. The present article suggests two possible steps forward: (1) to shift the burden of financing the UN from national to global sources—by introducing charges for the use of global commons or levies on international activities such as trade and foreign currency transactions; and (2) to strengthen the UN's capacity to harmonize global policy priorities with global spending priorities—by creating under the UN's umbrella, an integrated international cooperation fund and an executive committee for ECOSOC.

The funding crisis of the United Nations (UN) dates back many years—even decades. Until the late 1980s the organization's financial problems were often linked to the then existing East–West conflict and accompanying superpower rivalries.

Inge Kaul is Director, Office of Developmental Studies, UNDP, 1 United Nations Plaza, New York, NY 10017, USA (Tel: +1 212 906 5064; fax: +1 212 906 5365; e-mail: inge.kaul@undp.org). Shareen Hertel kindly commented on the draft of this article and the author is grateful to her for giving her views and suggestions. The views expressed in this article are those of the author and do not necessarily reflect those of the organization with which she is affiliated.

Now, this conflict has ended, yet the UN's financial difficulties persist.

The reason cannot be cost. As Erskine Childers writes in this issue,[1] UN activities are relatively inexpensive. For example, the UN Secretariat manages the complex machinery of intergovernmental meetings, negotiations, research and studies on a budget of no more than approximately $1 billion a year—a figure equivalent to 0.004% of world income or $0.20 per world inhabitant. UN operational activities for development, which include those of the United Nations Development Programme (UNDP), the United Nations Children's Fund (UNICEF), the United Nations Population Fund (UNFPA), the International Fund for Agricultural Development (IFAD) and the World Food Programme (WFP), have a total annual expenditure of some $5 billion—roughly 10% of Official Development Assistance (ODA). Even UN peacekeeping operations, despite having rapidly expanded in recent times, will cost only about $5 billion in 1994—an amount equivalent to just 0.6% of world military spending.[2]

Nor can the reason be loss of public confidence in UN operations. Like any other organization of similar size and complexity, the UN has at times suffered from management problems. But, it has never been embroiled in any serious crises of accountability.

Thus, it would seem that the root of the present financial crisis of the UN stems from the far-reaching economic, social, political and environmental changes which development has brought about during the past decades. Three central elements of this changing global situation merit special consideration.

Blurring of the North–South divide

UN activities—whether economic, social or political—tend to have a strong focus primarily on developing countries; and therefore the UN has been affected by the gradual disappearance of a clear-cut dividing line between North and South and the ensuing 'aid fatigue' in some Northern countries.[3]

Developing countries are no longer just the 'poorer neighbours' of the richer, industrial countries. In fact, many of these countries have become strong and successful competitors of the North in a variety of international markets. Their products have caused whole industrial sectors in the North to collapse, forcing the developed countries into their own type of structural adjustment programmes. Just as with structural adjustment in the South, Northern adjustment programmes have often entailed high social costs—in particular, high unemployment and declining real wages. People in the North thus have a lot to worry about today in terms of their own well-being; and this might be one reason why there is less interest in and compassion for problems of people elsewhere. And because growing competition from the South has intensified in tandem with the lengthening of the North's own agenda of unmet social needs at a time of shrinking opportunities (ie when economic growth in the industrial countries is sluggish and budget deficits are running high), support for development cooperation abroad diminished considerably.

Questions are not only being raised concerning development assistance to better-off developing countries. Aid to least developed countries is also being watched with growing concern and mounting doubts about its effectiveness. The scepticism stems from the fact that after nearly five decades of development assistance to these countries, there are as yet no clear, reassuring signs that aid has succeeded in rendering itself superfluous. The opposite seems to be happening: the demand for aid is rising—in particular, aid for such basic purposes as humanitarian relief and rebuilding crisis-torn countries.

As a result, ODA allocations are stagnating, often even declining; and political support for multilateralism is waning.[4] Aid resources are thus being shifted towards bilateral programmes in an attempt to enhance the attractiveness of development assistance to Northern taxpayers and politicians by making aid work better for the domestic interests of the donor country. In the end, irrespective of the reason, the combination of fewer resources, on the one hand, and less support for multilateralism on the other, obviously places the UN in a doubly difficult situation.

Growing developmental interdependence of countries

Yet, multilateralism is not only being queried in the North, and not only for reasons of aid fatigue. It is also being re-examined in developing countries. In fact, governments worldwide are now realizing that they will have to confront the challenge of how to combine national political sovereignty—which remains an important political principle—with the increasing globalization of development, eg the growing internationalization of markets, the ever more dense global network of communication and transportation, and the accelerating rise in the number of developmental problems which assume border-transgressing consequences (such as environmental degradation, socioeconomic deprivation and poverty).

The globalization of developmental activities has increasingly eroded the decision-making capacity of nation-states, taking out of their realm of influence not only issues with an external policy dimension, such as trade, but also issues such as employment or social welfare, which have hitherto been at the heart of domestic policy making.[5] The current downward adjustment process of labour costs in industrial countries, aimed at improving the international competitiveness of Northern-based industries (a process which governments have largely watched as helpless by-standers), is but one trend which bears testimony to this dramatically changed context.

However, the public policy-making power 'lost' nationally has not yet been 'regained' globally. As a result, one could argue that there is currently an overall public policy deficit; and this could, in turn, explain why so many global social and environmental development issues at present remain to be tackled, and why so many global activities happen without any checks and balances. It should, therefore, also come as no surprise that relevant global development indicators are on the downturn. For example, global income disparities have dramatically widened since 1960, when the ratio between the income of the richest quintile of the world's population and that of the poorest was 30:1. By 1990 the ratio had doubled to 60:1. The global distribution of other economic opportunities is similarly skewed: the richest 20% of the world's population have more than 85% of virtually everything—be it trade, investment or commercial credit.[6]

Given the mounting evidence of growing international disparities and the continuing threats to global environmental conditions, it becomes increasingly difficult to deny the need for strengthened global governance. Such governance should be fully representative, ie involve all states, and truly concerned with restoring, maintaining and improving global developmental balances. Given its universal membership and its broad interdisciplinary mandate, the UN would probably be the international organization best poised eventually to assume such a global governance role.

Yet, the notion of global governance still meets with considerable reluctance, if not even resistance, on the part of both the developing and industrial countries. Indeed, the UN's very potential for playing an increasingly important role in the future would seem to constitute one of the strongest impediments to its current functioning—reason for governments to hold back full support to the UN, as long as there is lack of consensus on what precisely ought to be the organization's future course of action.

Developing countries voice two principal reasons for hesitancy concerning a stronger UN role. First, for many of these countries national political independence was achieved only a few decades ago; capacity building for sovereign national policy making is often still an ongoing process, and therefore still a major political preoccupation. Understandably, the notion of ceding powers, which are just being built up, to the UN (in the name of global governance) thus may look premature and untimely. The transition economies find themselves in a similar situation. Second, many developing countries—and transition economies—had hoped that the end of the Cold War would give them added, rather than reduced independence. Proposals for global governance are being perceived as running counter to this expectation.

Regarding the industrialized countries, their caution *vis-à-vis* global governance is no doubt related to the fact that the superpowers among them would have to let go of some of their present political decision-making privileges. Global development management—to the extent that it currently happens at all—is attempted either within the G-7 major industrial countries, or within the Bretton Woods institutions, where the weighted voting pattern places the richer, industrial countries in an influential position. Nevertheless, political support for global governance may grow as and if the industrial countries realize that high income alone is not the key to sustainable development and a comfortable standard of living in the long run. The attainment of these objectives also depends on other, non-financial factors, such as global peace, equity and social integration. Indeed, the industrial countries may well increasingly find that *not* opting for global governance, global meso-policies and global environmental policies is dysfunctional. After all, the world is coming close to being 'one'; and there cannot be durable prosperity in a sea of poverty, inequity and environmental degradation.

It may in fact be due to this realization of interdependence that countries worldwide—albeit for different reasons often still sceptical of global governance—are, nevertheless, inching towards it. For example, industrial countries have often insisted on international debates on such 'domestic' issues as poverty, the role of women, or human rights. Yet given the mistaken, but widely held, notion that development is something that has to happen only in the South (because the industrial countries are defined as 'developed' countries), debates on these issues have, in large measure, focused only on developing countries. The latter have tended to respond with great caution—just as the industrial countries have when the developing countries raised, within the UN context, issues of more equitable international economic relations and, related to that, such concerns as subsidies to Northern farmers. Nevertheless, pressures for global governance are building, both as the result of actual developmental crises and as a result of new political and developmental thinking. However, until such time that both developing and industrial countries fully realize that they basically want to see the same type of change in the UN's role, *viz* its moving away from being just a deliberating intergovernmental assembly towards assuming greater responsibility for democratic global management of development and peace, the present political stalemate on the issue of global governance, and as one of its consequences, the present funding crisis of the UN are likely to continue.

Change in the development paradigm

It is not only the *form* of developmental management and decision making which is currently under review and change. The *purpose* of development, too, is being re-examined.

There is growing recognition that past development strategies have in too single-minded a fashion pursued objectives of economic growth—to the detriment of the environment, and to the detriment of people. While world income has grown sevenfold over the past five decades (two-and-a-half times, taking population growth into account), poverty has nevertheless continued to persist, both in developing and industrial countries. The aforementioned continuing concentration of world income and other economic opportunities is, in fact, at the heart of persistent poverty. And this trend is likely to be exacerbated as economic growth continues to take the form of 'jobless growth' (wherein growth in output in many countries is nearly double the growth in employment). Given today's improved levels of education and information, most people know that their poverty and deprivation is not entirely a matter of fate or a developmental necessity; but rather, it is 'man'-made—the result of, for them unfortunate, *policy choices*, and hence a fact that can be changed. This experience has worldwide contributed to social and political tension, ethnic conflict as well as rising crime, violence and even terrorism. Thus, present development strategies not only clash increasingly with given environmental limits, but also with the limits of sociopolitical acceptability. As a result, there are growing political pressures, especially from the side of civil society, for a new development paradigm which would aim at greater consistency between the triple objective of economic growth, people's participation in development, and environmental regeneration.

A similar—and closely related—change in concepts is occurring in the security field. So far, security has largely been equated with defence or 'security through arms'. Yet, past developments, in particular the growing economic interdependence among countries, have helped significantly to reduce external threats to national security. At the same time, however, the failure of development to achieve more equity and social integration both within and among countries as well as the accumulated effects of environmental degradation are now posing new security risks. These risks do not 'violate' national borders in a classic sense, because they either emanate from within a country or cross borders in a virtually invisible way. Yet, they *do* violate people's security—the security in their jobs, income, health, communities, families and households. Thus there is a need for expanding the security concept to include (in addition to territorial security) human security, and in addition to military security also security through people-centred sustainable development.[7]

Many seeds for the emergence of these new development and security paradigms have been sown within the UN. For example, it is primarily within the framework of the UN Commission on Sustainable Development that the follow-up to the Earth Summit—the 1992 UN Conference on Environment and Development—is being negotiated. It has been from within the UN Commission on Social Development that the proposal emerged for holding in March 1995 the World Summit for Social Development in Copenhagen, Denmark. Furthermore, it has been from within the UN that a new understanding of peace has emanated, notably as a result of the Secretary-General's report on 'An Agenda For Peace'.[8] And it is in the Secretary-General's 'An Agenda for Development' that a new, more comprehensive approach to development has been suggested, which 'should not only generate economic growth [but] . . . make its benefits equitably available . . . enable people to participate in decisions affecting their lives . . . provide job-led growth . . . replenish the natural heritage . . . [and be] a necessary complement to preventive diplomacy'.[9]

Indeed, many of the new ideas, concepts and strategies of development and peace are 'UN concerns' rather than 'Bretton Woods concerns'. Yet, the Bretton Woods institutions are still the destination for the lion's share of development assistance provided by the major donors. The reason is not only that major donors enjoy a weighted voting share in these institutions. An additional factor is that the institutions still espouse a more traditional—economic growth-oriented, technocratic—approach to development with which the 'major powers' within the major contributor countries—especially finance ministers—tend to feel more comfortable. The same holds true for the 'major powers' from developing countries. Many Southern finance ministers also prefer to conduct developmental business with the Bretton Woods institutions rather than with the UN. This is another reason why the UN's lengthening development and peace agenda has not yet been matched by a corresponding increase in its financial resources.

Alternative sources of funding

In order for the international community to break out of the current political stalemate surrounding the issue of the UN's role and financing, it would be important to identify new, alternative sources of funding.

The main challenge would be to move away from national sources of spending for international cooperation towards global sources. The reason is that a reformed UN role of the type described above would involve a transfer of at least some policy-making power from the national to the international level. This would especially affect today's superpowers, many of whom are also major contributors to the UN. In addition, a strengthened UN—even if it were to work with the highest level of efficiency—would probably cost more than the present truncated UN. If one were to continue to rely on national sources (ie government budgets) for the UN's financing, all countries, in particular the superpowers, could end up in a paradoxical situation in which they would have to pay *more* for having *less* political influence.

Moreover, tapping global sources would in and by itself eliminate much of the present North–South divide. Indeed, it would mean that the UN would no longer have a 'class' system of 'major contributors', 'other donors' and 'recipients'. It would instead comprise uniform member-states. This would undoubtedly be a major step towards ensuring the type of democratic decision making on which effective global governance will depend.

The most obvious place to look for global funding sources are the use of global *commons* (eg oceanic seabeds or the air) and globalized *activities* (eg foreign currency movements and trade, especially trade in global 'bads' such as exports of arms and dumping of toxic wastes).

As discussed elsewhere in this issue, some of these global funding sources could generate considerable amounts of money. According to calculations presented in the *1994 Human Development Report*, a 0.05% levy on international currency transactions could yield annual revenues in the amount of $150 billion, some $900 billion cumulatively to the year 2000. A global tax on the consumption of non-renewable energy (eg $1 per barrel of oil and its equivalent in coal consumption) could generate $66 billion per year, totalling cumulatively up to the year 2000 some $395 billion. In addition, one could also tax (or, alternatively phrased, establish disincentives for) arms exports or any other activities which the international community deemed undesirable.

If there were the requisite political will among UN member-states 'to go global' in terms of the organization's financing, there would be no scarcity of funds. On the contrary, there would be much more money than the UN is likely to require for its own purposes in the foreseeable future.

Alternative patterns of decision making

In light of the foregoing, it should be remembered that the UN is not the only institution of international cooperation suffering from underfinancing. Most other concerned organizations—such as the World Bank, the regional banks, or non-governmental organizations—face similar, albeit sometimes less serious, problems. It would, therefore, only be logical—and pragmatic—to approach the search for better UN financing within the broader context of improved financing for international cooperation in general.

Indeed, the present system of international financing is marked by considerable inefficiency. To illustrate this point, each organization in the present system of international cooperation—and there is a multitide of them— has its own fund-raising process. Yet, the number of major donors or contributors is rather limited. The setting of global budgetary priorities therefore happens primarily at the level of the individual donor country—with little, if any, systematic coordination among the respective ministries and donor agencies. This may, in fact, explain why there has always been such a wide discrepancy between stated international policy priorities and actual international policy practice—for example, why the ten countries which have three-quarters of the world's poor receive only about one-quarter of all ODA, despite the fact that global poverty reduction has been a long-standing international policy priority.[10]

In order to ensure in the future greater efficiency in the utilization of resources available for international multilateral cooperation one could, therefore, envisage first depositing the monies generated through the new global sources into a general fund located under the roof of the UN. The various individual agencies within the system could, in turn, submit their funding requests in the form of budget proposals to the UN which would then be in a position to compare available resources with requirements and harmonize resource allocations with agreed political priorities. This would give the UN a global finance ministry role which it sorely lacks at present.

While the commonsense nature of such an arrangement may be attractive, it might not be acceptable without significant change in the UN's functioning—namely, without improved capacity for greater decisiveness in UN decision making. In the eyes of many observers, the UN's present decision-making process is too non-committal to entrust to it the sums of money in question here.

As suggested in the 1994 and earlier *Human Development Reports*,[11] this situation could be changed by creating a smaller but representative UN body, eg an executive committee (or extended Bureau) of the UN Economic and Social Council (ECOSOC). Like the Security Council, this committee could have permanent as well as rotating members and could function as a day-to-day 'management arm' of the General Assembly and the full ECOSOC. Among other things, it could assist in global budget management.

If such an arrangement were made, the UN would, for the first time in its 50-year history, have financial clout—financial backing for its broad developmental and political role, which, in theory, it has always had according to its Charter but which it is even more likely to carry out during the next 50 years; and if such an arrangement were made, the organization could set out to prove that indeed the Secretary-General was right when in his 'Agenda for Development' he emphasized the following three core principles as fundamental to successful UN operations, *viz* that 'more resources are needed; mandates and the resources provided for them must be in a sound relationship; and predictability in funding is essential so that operations are not undermined in the midst of performance'.[12]

Notes and references

1. Erskine Childers, 'Financing the UN: some possible solutions', *Futures*, in this issue.
2. The present article draws on the discussion in the *Human Development Report 1994* (New York, Oxford University Press, 1994). If not otherwise indicated, facts and figures mentioned here are taken from this Report.
3. See, in this connection also Inge Kaul, 'A new approach to aid', *Development and Cooperation*, No 3, 1993, pages 16–21; and *Human Development Report 1994, op cit*, reference 2, pages 61–81.
4. See Organization for Economic Cooperation and Development (OECD), *1993 Development Assistance Committee (DAC) Report* (Paris, OECD, 1994).
5. Keith Griffin and Azizur Rahman Khan, 'Globalization and the developing world: An essay on the international dimensions of development in the post-Cold War era', New York, Human Development Report Office (HDRO), UNDP, 1992, Occasional Paper No 2.
6. *Human Development Report 1992* (New York, Oxford University Press, 1992), pages 34–40.
7. See, in this connection, also Mahbub ul Haq, 'New imperatives of human security', Society for International Development (SID), 21st World Conference: Barbara Word Lecture 1994, Mexico City, Mexico, April 1994.
8. Boutros Boutros-Ghali, 'An Agenda for Peace', New York, United Nations, 1992, DPI/1247.
9. United Nations, 'An Agenda for Development; Recommendations Report of the Secretary-General', A/49/665; and United Nations, 'An Agenda for Development; Report of the Secretary-General', May 1994, A/48/935.
10. *Human Development Report 1992, op cit*, reference 6, page 42.
11. See, in this connection, also the paper by Hans W Singer and Stephany Griffin-Jones, 'New patterns of macro governance', New York, Human Development Report Office (HDRO), UNDP, 1994, Occasional Paper No 10.
12. United Nations, 'Recommendations . . .', *op cit*, reference 9, page 19.

RESTRUCTURING ECONOMIC AND FINANCIAL POWER

The potential role of a foreign exchange-transaction levy

John Langmore MP

National fiscal and monetary policies are dominated by financial markets, and the obsession of these markets with inflation is forcing governments to neglect other crucial economic and social goals such as growth of employment and reduction of poverty. Exchange rate volatility also adds to business costs and risk. Introduction of a small international levy on foreign exchange transactions would reduce short-term speculation and so the power of the markets to influence interest rates and to destabilize exchange rates. Revenue from the levy would be of benefit to both national governments and the UN for disaster relief, development and strengthened security programmes. Support for the levy is growing.

Before his inauguration Bill Clinton gathered his economic team at the Governor's Mansion in Little Rock to prepare the new administration's economic programme. Bob Woodward reports that Clinton was told by his new advisers that the highest priority had to be to reduce the budget deficit.[1] Deficit reduction was necessary not only because this would reduce the government's use of national savings, but also because it would encourage the financial markets to believe that interest rates would fall and enable the Federal Reserve (the US central bank) to keep interest rates down.

At the president-elect's end of the table, Clinton's face turned red with anger and disbelief. 'You mean to tell me that the success of the program and my reelection hinges on the Federal Reserve and a bunch of fucking bond traders?' he responded in a half whisper. Nods from his

John Langmore was Economic Adviser to the Australian Treasurer before being elected to the Australian parliament in 1984. He chairs the National Committee which is advising the Australian government on preparations for the World Summit for Social Development. He can be contacted at Parliament House, Canberra 2600, Australia (Tel: 61 6 2485222; fax: 61 6 2571781).

end of the table. Not a dissent . . . Their first audience would have to be the Fed and the bond market.[2]

Financial markets have been the most powerful constraint on President Clinton's capacity to stimulate economic activity and increase employment in the USA. He won the election having promised to increase employment by 8 million, yet was unable to introduce the infrastructure and training programmes he had planned because of the deficit reduction strategy.

Despite the introduction of the deficit reduction package, a year later the Federal Reserve made the first of a series of increases in short-term interest rates, in response to an increase they perceived in inflationary expectations. The increased rates were also said to be necessary to reduce long-term rates, for the Federal Reserve argued that the bond market would respond favourably to reduced risk of inflation. Yet long-term rates went on rising, for past experience suggests that once an interest rate hike begins it continues until well after the economic cycle turns down. This experience illustrates vividly that both fiscal and monetary policy in the USA are dominated by the financial markets.

In smaller countries this is even more readily apparent. For example, I remember an incident in Australia in 1987 when what many people considered to be an inhuman reduction in access to unemployment benefits for 16- and 17-year-olds was justified as a way of demonstrating fiscal probity to financial markets. A Wall Street dealer explicitly confirmed this view on national radio. Screen jockeys are quite happy to tell governments—of other countries as well as their own—not only what their economic policies should be, but also to prescribe their social policies.

One effect of this financial market dominance is to impose a deflationary bias on to the global economy. Since the self-interest of financial markets is entirely preoccupied with low inflation, they respond to any spirited signs of economic vitality by urging restraint. Argument for contraction of public outlays (though never increases in taxation) plus higher interest rates is their obsessive refrain.

A second aspect of the damage caused by anarchic financial markets is the growth of exchange rate volatility and unpredictability. Since the collapse of the Bretton Woods system the global financial system has gone through waves of instability during which the exchange rates of major—and minor—currencies have passed well beyond rates justified by economic conditions. Both this overshooting and the constant smaller movements in exchange rates impose greater costs and risks on trade in goods and services and on international investment. Even though hedging reduces risk, it is not costless.

The Volcker Commission on the international financial system argued that extreme swings on the foreign exchange markets have been a contributory cause of the low growth in industrial countries since the 1970s. It is certainly clear that floating exchange rates have not led automatically to external payments balance as the dogmatic advocates of floating asserted in the 1960s and 1970s would happen. And rather than liberating national monetary policy for use as a domestic policy instrument, as was also said to be a benefit of floating, monetary policy has become even more tightly constrained. Interest rates now commonly have to be set to placate the markets, not to maximize economic growth, let alone growth of employment.

In fact, floating exchange rates have had some quite perverse consequences for economic well-being. By abandoning most instruments for influencing the exchange rate, governments have been forced to use interest rates to achieve external balance. Current-account-deficit countries have had to maintain higher interest rates than would otherwise have been necessary in order to attract foreign capital. This kept their exchange rates high, discouraging exports and encouraging imports and so constraining the adjustments which were necessary to eliminate current account deficits. Average global interest rates have therefore been higher than would otherwise have been necessary, a tendency reinforced by the markets' preoccupation with inflation.

Financial transactions rather than trade now dominate most countries' balance of payments. According to the Bank for International Settlements (BIS), daily net turnover was close to $900 billion in April 1992, almost three times its value in 1986, and around 12 times the combined GDP of OECD countries on an annualized basis.[3] Only about 5% of this is related to trade and longer-term investment.[4] The BIS notes that even this 'pales' when compared with the growth in turnover in the securities markets, where the level of the total value of underlying transactions—all purchases and sales of securities by residents and non-residents—has multiplied several times in recent years.

The secretary of the committee which recommended the deregulation of the Australian financial system (the Campbell Committee) in the early 1980s said recently that 'financial markets have become a frankenstein monster which is devouring us'. Fortunately policies are available which would at least reduce the damage.

Among the proposals for greater control over foreign exchange markets are: strengthened requirements for the provision of information; tighter prudential controls over all financial institutions, not merely banks; compulsory non-interest-bearing deposits with central banks related to the size of foreign exchange purchases; capital charges on the net foreign exchange positions of financial institutions; and a transactions levy on all international financial flows.[5]

The Volcker Commission proposed the creation of 'flexible exchange rate bands', or target ranges for the three major international currencies, the US dollar, the D-Mark and the yen. The Commission considered that this would be feasible after a period of strengthened macroeconomic policies, by cutting budget deficits, and achievement of greater convergence of 'key' economic variables such as inflation.

The eminent New York investment banker Felix Rohatyn has proposed the establishment of 'a separate and comprehensive organization comparable to GATT for investment just as there was a GATT for trade, even though some aspects of investment are now covered under GATT'.[6] The central purpose of such an investment organization would be to set worldwide accounting, disclosure and other standards for the protection of investors. Without such standards Rohatyn considers that the big funds with fiduciary responsibilities will not be able to make investment available in the quantity required by developing countries.

Naturally there are technical and political difficulties with all these proposals. Most new interventionist policies involve issues of implementation and of opposition from entrenched interests. Yet the issues are quite pragmatic: does the proposed policy have greater potential net benefits for a nation or the globe than the net effect of leaving the problem unaddressed?

A combination of policies is certainly required which together would effectively reduce the influence of financial markets and the risks of instability or even of crisis. Among these, strengthened disclosure requirements, accounting standards and prudential controls are certain to be a part. Another which has much to commend it is a small multilateral foreign exchange-transactions levy (FEL).

This proposal, by the Nobel Laureate in economics Professor James Tobin, has two basic motivations. He writes that 'one is to increase the weight that market participants give to long-range fundamentals relative to immediate speculative opportunities. The second is to allow greater autonomy to national monetary policies, by making possible greater differences between short-term interest rates in different currencies'.[7]

Increasing the cost of short-term speculative transactions would reduce the extent of exchange rate fluctuations. The FEL could be set at a rate which would be too small to deter trade or movements of investment capital but which would penalize short-term speculation. By reducing the potential return to foreign exchange speculation the FEL would discourage the wasteful application of skilled personnel and scarce capital to such activity.

The principal criticism of the proposal relates to the difficulty of achieving agreement among all major countries involved in foreign exchange dealing. Yet in the late 1980s the BIS succeeded in achieving agreement between countries to set increased prudential reserve ratios for commercial banks. Since the FEL would be of benefit to everyone except foreign exchange dealers and the companies for which they work, such agreement could well be possible.

Governments would benefit from the greater capacity for discretionary monetary policy, and from the reduction in interference in national policy by financial dealers. Governments and the whole community would also benefit from the substantial revenue which the tax would generate, and which could be used for expansion of high-priority economic and social programmes or for budget deficit reduction. The FEL is also electorally popular: few people like speculators. An opinion survey in the USA found that about two-thirds of respondents supported introduction of such a levy. As Felix notes this is a tax on 'Wall Street' not on 'Main Street'.[8]

Part of the revenue could also be used for establishing a permanent, reliable source of funding for the United Nations system at last. The extent of this automatic funding would have to be settled at the time the administrative arrangements for the tax are negotiated and would no doubt depend in part on the tax rate. If the FEL were set at 0.1%, and the volume of transactions fell by a quarter as a result, and 10% of the revenue were allocated to the UN, receipts for multilateral purposes would total around $10 billion annually (after allowing for some exemptions and evasion).

Revenue received by the UN could be used for disaster relief, security and development. There would be widespread support for the establishment of a permanent disaster relief fund to ensure that substantial funds are readily and immediately available whenever crises occur, such as the civil wars in Rwanda or Somalia or natural disasters such as major floods or volcanic eruptions. Establishment of effective UN security procedures is being prevented by lack of finance. Automatically available, reliable revenue may well be a necessary condition for ensuring adequate peacemaking and peacekeeping activities. Substantially increased development assistance is essential too for improvement of living standards and reduction of poverty in many countries.

The question for business is whether the benefits for trade and investment from reduced exchange rate volatility, reduced investment risk and improved economic policy making would be sufficient to offset the cost of paying the FEL. This also depends in part on the rate at which the FEL is set and on the precise consequences of that, so the question should not be answered in principle only.

Tobin has suggested a rate of 0.5%. Others consider this too high and have suggested anywhere between 0.01% and 0.25%. It does seem likely that there would be some rate at which the benefits for business might well offset the cost.

Support for the Tobin levy is growing. Lawrence Summers (now US Under Secretary of the Treasury) and Victoria Summers published a case for it in 1989, based on empirical evidence that financial markets are less than fully efficient since they overshoot.[9] Another influential US economist who has supported an FEL is Professor Joseph Stiglitz (who is a member of the President's Council of Economic Advisers). *The Economist* has described the FEL as 'a nice idea'.[10]

Several multilateral agencies have recently put the issue of global levies on the international agenda. A recent report by the International Labour Office on global employment strategy included a brief discussion of the tax and concluded that '. . . proponents maintain that on balance the Tobin levy or a similar financial transactions tax would help to lengthen time-horizons and focus the minds of capital markets on enterprise and investment rather than on trading and short term speculation'.[11] The UNDP's *Human Development Report 1994* included the possibility of increasing development assistance funding by introducing the Tobin levy. The Commission on Global Governance, which is due to report just before the Social Summit, is including the Tobin levy among the possibilities it will discuss in its final report.

The Australian Foreign Minister has been canvassing this idea for some time, and a motion was passed by the National Conference of the governing Labor Party (and with the support of the Treasurer) in September 1994 that requires the government to advocate international study of the idea under the auspices of the UN. At the Second Preparatory Committee meeting the Australian delegation raised the possibility of the Social Summit deciding that a UN expert committee should be appointed to study the issue seriously. Some other countries also supported this idea.

The World Summit for Social Development offers an opportunity to take the idea further by authorizing the appointment of an authoritative committee to report on all aspects of an FEL which seems the best available option for reducing the power of financial markets, reducing exchange rate volatility and raising revenue for high-priority domestic and international economic, social and security programmes.

The objectives specified for the Summit . . . cannot possibly be attained if national and international economic and financial policies continue to be determined in the interests of financial and foreign exchange institutions and markets. Restoration of national government and international control over policies is a necessary condition for social integration, the reduction of poverty and full employment.[12]

Notes and references

1. Bob Woodward, *The Agenda: Inside The Clinton White House* (New York, Simon and Schuster, 1994), pages 82–85.
2. *Ibid*, page 84.
3. Bank for International Settlements, *64th Annual Report* (Basle, BIS, 13 June 1994), pages 174 and 175.
4. Wilfred Guth, 'The liberalization trap: how the free flow of capital is undermining multilateral trade', *The International Economy*, May/June 1993, page 57.
5. David Shirreff, 'Can anyone tame the currency market?', *Euromoney*, September 1993, pages 60–69.
6. Felix Rohatyn, 'World capital: the need and the risks', *The New York Review of Books*, 14 July 1994, page 53.
7. James Tobin, 'Tax the speculators', *Financial Times*, 22 December 1992.
8. David Felix, 'The Tobin tax proposal: background, issues and prospects', Policy Paper commissioned by UNDP for the World Summit for Social Development, page 13.

9. Lawrence H Summers and Victoria P Summers, 'When financial markets work too well: a case for a securities transactions tax', in Daniel R Siegel (editor), *Innovation and Technology in the Markets* (Chicago, IL, Probus, 1990).
10. *The Economist*, 25 June 1994, page 21.
11. International Labour Organization, *Towards Full Employment, Contribution of the ILO to the second session of the Preparatory committee for the World Summit for Social Development* (Geneva, ILO, 1994), page 7.
12. Russell Mathews, 'Financial and foreign exchange market constraints on economic growth and social development', Paper commissioned by the Australian National Consultative Committee for the World Summit for Social Development, August 1994, page 5.

THE TOBIN TAX PROPOSAL

Background, issues and prospects

David Felix

Less exchange rate volatility facilitates trade, investment and employment, for which, however, substantial international policy collaboration is needed. Tobin's proposal for a small uniform tax on foreign exchange transactions would be an important step, reducing fiscal deficits while discouraging exchange speculation. The fear of hostile reaction from the globalized financial markets makes putting the proposal on the table a more delicate matter for individual governments than for the UN. Doing so would strengthen the UN's claim for a slice of the prospective revenue.

Some 16 years ago, James Tobin, a prominent monetary economist and Nobel Laureate, proposed a tax on foreign exchange transactions with the following features:[1]

1. The tax would be applied at a uniform ad valorem rate by, at the least, all the key currency countries.
2. It would be administered and collected by each government on *all* payments by residents within its jurisdiction that involved a spot currency exchange, including, as in the case of Eurocurrency transactions, exchanges that do not involve the home currency.
3. The proceeds from the tax would be paid into a central fund controlled by the IMF or the World Bank.
4. Subject perhaps to prior IMF consent, countries could form currency areas within which the tax would not apply. That is, small countries that formally tied their currency to a key currency would not be required to levy the tax on intra-area currency exchanges.

The primary objective of the tax was to discourage speculative runs on the key world currencies. Such runs had contributed to the collapse of the Bretton Woods fixed exchange rate regime in the early 1970s and were intensifying under the flexible exchange rate regime that followed, contrary to the expectations of its advocates. To Tobin the runs were adversely impacting the real world economy. They heightened

David Felix is Emeritus Professor of Economics in the Department of Economics, Washington University in St Louis, Campus Box 1208, St Louis, MO 63130-4899, USA (Tel: +1 314 935 5670; fax: +1 314 935 4156).

exchange rate volatility between the key world currencies, which deterred international trade and shortened the investment horizon of foreign direct investment. And even more important for Tobin, monetary-fiscal authorities were deterred from adopting policies with socially desirable longer-term pay-offs out of fear of immediate hostile reactions of the financial markets.

The tax, in Tobin's words, would 'throw some sand in the well-greased wheels' of the global financial market mechanism, or would help, in Keynes's well known phrase, 'to mitigate the predominance of speculation over enterprise'. It would do this because a small transactions tax—Tobin tentatively suggested 1%—would cut deeply into the yield from currency speculation, since that involves 'short-term financial round-trip excursions into another currency', with the expected yield from each quick circuit usually a modest percentage of the mainly borrowed funds put in motion. It would, however, cut much less deeply into the yield from financial placements with higher expected returns and more delayed repatriation, such as in commodity trade and foreign direct investment. Moreover, while currency speculators, saddled with the tax bite and with less exchange volatility to exploit, would be clear losers, exporters, importers and long-term investors would get more stable exchange rates as a *quid pro quo* for their tax bite.

Governments in turn would gain more space for autonomous monetary-fiscal policies. For example, with a 1% tax, domestic interest rates could deviate an additional 2% from foreign rates without sparking capital flows to arbitrage the interest differences and set off exchange rate turbulence.

Tobin did not elaborate on his suggestion that the tax proceeds be transferred to the IMF or World Bank. Perhaps he had in mind compensation for the spreading foreign aid 'fatigue' of the 1970s. In any event, his proposal received little attention at first from either policy makers or academic economists. In 1978 policy makers were caught up in competitive pressures to deregulate financial and commodity markets, and most mainstream economists, conflating financial with trade liberalization, were egging them on by pointing up alleged efficiency gains from doing both.

More recently, however, worries over destabilizing financial dynamics and loss of monetary-fiscal policy autonomy that had motivated Tobin's proposal have been overtaking the earlier euphoria over the efficiency gains from the liberalization and globalization of financial markets. The greater rapidity and lower cost with which global markets can now exchange assets and hedge individual risks have been paralleled by efficiency losses as measured by more socially relevant welfare criteria. The performance of the world economy has worsened in each successive decade since the 1960s as regards global growth of output, trade, investment, and employment, and the domestic and international distribution of income. The October 1987 crash motivated prominent economists to propose taxes on transactions in domestic financial assets to dampen financial volatility and reverse the excessive absorption of human and physical resources in financial speculation.[2] The 'efficient market hypothesis', on which many economists had based their theoretical case for deregulating financial markets, is being widely rejected by mainstream economists on both empirical and theoretical grounds. Following the successful speculative runs in September 1992 which virtually demolished the EC's Exchange Rate Mechanism, the influential free-marketeering *The Economist* concluded an accolade to Tobin's 1978 article with the observation that 'lately, one imagines, a good many government economists have been dusting down their copies of that article'.[3] Even prominent international bankers, such as Wilfried Guth of the Deutsche Bank and Alexandre Lamfalussy, long-time General Manager of the Bank for International Settlements (BIS), are viewing free capital mobility as incompatible with free trade.[4]

These concerns have focused chiefly on the disruptive impact of free capital mobility on the advanced industrial economies. But the impact tends to be even more pronounced on the less developed countries (LDCs). Their less flexible productive structures adjust more slowly to 'real' shocks than do those of the industrialized countries, and their thinner financial sectors absorb financial shocks with more difficulty. As the governments of LDCs are even less able than those of the industrial countries individually to offset perverse capital movements with conventional monetary-fiscal policies, the contradictions between trade and financial liberalization are intensified for the LDCs.

Thus many Latin American countries are currently relying on inflows of hot money to stabilize their nominal exchange rate and slow inflation while they pursue trade liberalization. This has produced increasingly overvalued 'real' exchange rates that discourage exports and balloon imports. Financing the growing balance-of-payments deficits on current account has become dependent on a continual expansion of capital inflows, the likelihood of which diminishes as the deficits keep expanding. But alternatives more compatible with trade liberalization, such as devaluing the real exchange rate, and/or monetary-fiscal tightening to depress aggregate demand, evoke the fear that hot money outflows could reignite the explosive devaluation–inflation cycle which stabilizing the nominal exchange rate had damped. Even the East Asian countries, despite their booming exports, are registering discomfort. At the recent meeting of the 18 Asian-Pacific Economic Cooperation (APEC) countries, hot money was high on the agenda, Indonesia's finance minister complaining that 'our open capital account leaves us susceptible to potential disruptions by speculative flows of "hot money". Abrupt movements of such funds can disrupt local economies. Indonesia and others in the region are increasingly concerned'. The APEC finance ministers accordingly instructed their technicians to review jointly issues and policies regarding such flows.[5]

This convergence of advanced country and LDC concerns is creating a window of opportunity for proposals directed at curbing international financial volatility. A Tobin tax proposal entered formally into the international policy arena by, say, the United Nations, can no longer be peremptorily dismissed as addressing a non-problem. But while a Tobin tax, as argued in this article below, is probably superior on various counts, including technical feasibility, to alternative proposals that have been floated, getting it formally into the policy arena involves overcoming a 'bell the cat' obstacle. The financial sectors that have fattened on globalization have also grown sharper political claws. Academics run little risk in proposing measures directed at reducing some of the fat, but politicians do. So do career-minded economists and technicians of government agencies and international institutions like the IMF and the World Bank with financial sector links and a strong ideological commitment to full-scale market liberalization.

Thus recent IMF and World Bank studies, while highlighting various perverse aspects of financial globalization and their threat to global economic stability, nevertheless ignore or dance around proposals to tax financial transactions. They fall back, instead, on vague exhortations for broad-scale international coordination of tax, expenditure and monetary policies to tranquillize financial markets. In this they are evidently submitting to the IMF's party line as reiterated recently by its Managing Director, Michel Camdessus, in an address honouring the 50th anniversary of

Bretton Woods.[6] In it M Camdessus begins by acknowledging that 'exchange rate volatility hinders international trade and investment' and that the ability of official intervention to contain the volatility is very limited, but then goes on to urge that the Fund's Articles of Agreement be revised to require members to make their currency freely convertible for all capital as well as current account transactions, with the IMF to oversee compliance. The purpose of the revision would be to 'lock in the freedom of capital movements already achieved and encourage wider liberalization'. The United Nations, relatively untrammelled by such tight ideological inhibitions, thus seems best situated to 'bell the cat', ie to get the Tobin tax proposal into the policy arena.

The remainder of this article elaborates on the tax proposal by responding to questions and issues submitted by the UN. Many answers are necessarily tentative, but I hope they are of some value.

Responses to questions concerning the feasibility of a Tobin tax

How consistent is the Tobin tax proposal with free trade or free capital movement theory?

My short answer is that the proposal is quite compatible with free trade, but that free capital movement is not compatible with free trade. Since the latter was also the view shaping the Bretton Woods Articles of Agreement, and, as indicated above, is now once again on the rise, a comparison of the Bretton Woods monetary regime with the flexible exchange rate–free capital mobility regime that took over in the 1970s is a useful way of expanding on the answer and its theoretical and empirical basis. The focus is on the experience of the industrialized market economies, primarily because they hold the reins as regards prospects for the adoption and implementation of a Tobin tax. As indicated above, the incompatibility between free trade and free capital mobility is even deeper for the structurally weaker LDCs.

To the designers of the Bretton Woods regime, exchange rate volatility, hot money flows and international liquidity crises helped fuel the rise of protectionism and the collapse of multilateral trade during the interwar period.[7] They saw fulfilment of the basic goal of Bretton Woods—the restoration of a multilateral trading world moving towards free trade—as requiring an international monetary and exchange rate regime that would prevent a recurrence of the interwar turbulence.

Accordingly, participating nations were asked to peg the par value of their currency unit either to gold or the US dollar and to make their currency freely convertible at the par rate for current transactions. The newly created IMF was to be the central coordinating institution, overseeing member compliance and the orderly adjustment of par rates that had fallen into 'fundamental disequilibrium'. In fact, only the US pegged its currency to gold, the other members pegging to the dollar. But since the USA declared the dollar convertible to gold in official international transactions, the Bretton Woods exchange system was in effect a limited gold exchange system. The IMF was also to serve as the international lender of last resort, providing emergency finance to assuage liquidity crises.

The IMF's powers proved asymmetrical. It was able to pressurize small economies but not the large ones, and its resources were too meagre for it to function as the primary international lender of last resort. That task fell *de facto* to the USA. Possessed at the end of the war of about two-thirds of the world's monetary gold, over half the world's industrial capacity, and running enormous current account surpluses, the USA was able to perform the task easily in the first post-war decade.

However, the Cold War and decolonization in the 1950s made funding overseas military build-ups and foreign aid crucial instruments of its *Pax Americana* foreign policy, so that the aggregate of grants and capital outflows began outpacing the current account surpluses at an increasing rate. By the early 1960s *Pax Americana* outlays, the surge of US foreign direct investment sheltered by the *Pax Americana* umbrella, and diminished current account surpluses due to export competition from a revived Europe, were raising the stock of foreign-owned dollars to levels that dwarfed US gold reserves. Persuaded that the dollar was no longer as good as gold, speculators began driving up the price of gold in the private gold market to well above the official $35 per ounce. That tempted various central banks loaded with dollar reserves to begin exchanging them for official US gold, anticipating that the USA might be forced to raise its official gold price.

With the gold stock shrinking and the expanding Vietnam misadventure further augmenting foreign dollar surpluses, US policy makers in the late 1960s were seriously confronted for the first time in the post-war era with unpleasant policy trade-offs. Allaying balance-of-payments pressures and protecting the gold exchange commitment now required strengthening the current account balance, with monetary-fiscal tightening, retreating on capital and trade liberalization, or cutting back *Pax Americana* outlays.

After some dithering, the decision was taken instead to abandon the gold commitment. The dollar, and thus the Bretton Woods regime, was cut loose from its gold anchor in the early 1970s, and with that the official commitment of IMF members to defend their par exchange rates faded out. Superseding the fixed exchange rate regime was an informal regime of largely market-driven fluctuating exchange rates.

The theoretical case for such a regime had been put by Milton Friedman when Bretton Woods was still in its salad years. In a provocative 1953 paper, Friedman asserted that a flexible exchange rate regime with free capital mobility offered the following advantages over the Bretton Woods fixed rate regime:[8]

1. Allowed to adjust freely, exchange rate movements will act as shock absorbers, insulating each economy from disparate external monetary trends, thus strengthening the capacity of each economy to pursue independent monetary-fiscal policies.
2. This is because the nominal exchange rate and the price level will move in opposite directions, minimizing the short-term volatility of the real exchange and interest rates.
3. Speedy incremental exchange rate adjustments would discourage massive speculating on the exchange rate.
4. Long term capital flows will cause real interest rates to converge globally, optimizing the global allocation of physical capital.

By the end of the 1960s, the Friedman position had become dominant among mainstream US economists, who encouraged the shift among the industrialized countries and LDCs toward flexible exchange rates and the lifting of capital controls and regulatory barriers to free capital mobility that followed the demise of Bretton Woods. The consequences, however, have been generally unkind to that position. Virtually none of Friedman's predictions materialized, neither improved allocative efficiency, reduced macroeconomic instability, nor greater national autonomy over monetary-fiscal policies.

Empirical studies have identified only two clear-cut efficiency gains. The bid–ask spreads on deposits in different Eurocurrencies have narrowed and financial arbitraging has been eliminating with rapidity small differences in the exchange-rate adjusted price of short-term debt instruments of comparable maturity and risk. In the jargon of finance, covered interest parity has usually prevailed on short-maturity instruments of the G-7. However, the forward rates in the currency futures markets that sprang up with fluctuating exchange rates have proved to be very poor predictors of future spot rates. Rather, exchange rate volatility has been intensified by international speculation in financial assets with a penchant for self-reinforcing 'herd behaviour'. Real exchange rates and real interest rates have therefore oscillated, at times violently, with no sustained tendency for real interest rates to converge internationally.[9]

Volatility and financial market deregulation have encouraged the design of new financial instruments and other financial innovations at an accelerating pace to transfer the enhanced risks and exploit the profit opportunities. The contrast with the Bretton Woods years is striking, as is indicated by *Table 1*.

The pace has continued strong since 1986. Thus most of the boom in derivatives has occurred since 1986, their notional value reaching $1.6 trillion in 1987 and $8 trillion by the end of 1991.[10]

The innovations add to as well as defend against financial volatility. Walmsley writes:

A more controversial feature of the new shape of the financial system is that the bulk of its participants now have a vested interest in instability. This is because the advent of high-technology dealing rooms has raised the level of fixed costs. High fixed costs imply a high turnover is required for profitability to be achieved. High turnover tends to occur only when markets are volatile. The analysts at Salomon Brothers . . . put it clearly: 'Logically, the most destabilizing environment for an institutional house is a relatively stagnant rate environment'.[11]

Table 1, however, helps explain why Tobin's tax proposal initially had little impact. The pace of financial innovation was just picking up in the 1970s, as was the pace of foreign exchange transactions. By the mid-1980s the daily turnover on foreign exchange markets worldwide had reached about $150 billion, and by 1992 about $1 trillion, with only 5% related to trade and other 'real economic transactions'.[12] But in 1978 the daily turnover was as yet merely in double-digit billions, and it was still plausible to supporters of the Friedman case to rationalize the rising financial turbulence accompanying the shift from fixed to flexible exchange rates as a passing reaction to severe exogenous supply shocks, notably the OPEC oil shock.

In addition, the view then widespread among economists, that financial markets were inherently efficient, led many to reject Tobin's contention that, because 'goods and labor move in response to international price signals much more sluggishly than fluid funds, and prices in goods and labor markets move much more sluggishly than the prices of financial assets, including exchange rates', it was desirable to slow the reaction time of financial markets. Financial markets, they contended, were efficient

TABLE 1. DEREGULATORY MEASURES AND FINANCIAL INNOVATIONS IN THE G-7 COUNTRIES SINCE 1950

Interval	Number	Interval	Number
1950–59	2	1980–83	20
1960–69	5	1984–86	41
1970–79	9		

Source: Walmsley, *op cit*, reference 11, Table 1.1.

information processing institutions. When allowed to operate freely their continual revaluing of asset values provided the best available price signals on which to base long-term resource allocation. The 1970s' volatility merely reflected efficient financial markets at work, bidding up Texas real estate, transferring surplus OPEC revenues to capital-short LDCs, and in general moving asset prices and resource allocation to new equilibria as required by the OPEC oil shock.

The efficient market theory has a strong and a weak version. In the strong version market agents know the 'true model of the economy', ie its underlying structure and dynamic processes, and therefore where asset prices will ultimately settle when exogenous shocks hit the economy. These shocks, which include 'policy surprises', ie interventionist economic policies, initiate volatility, while speculators are merely socially useful abritrageurs who, by exploiting transitional differences between the current and the equilibrium asset prices, hasten the convergence towards equilibrium values.

However, the crucial premise of the strong version, that economic agents know the 'true model' and act primarily on that knowledge collapses under scrutiny. Decisions are unavoidably made on incomplete information, because neither the market nor any other social institution can provide the relevant information needed to make riskless choices, or to ensure against all possible future contingencies. Agents must form subjective judgments about the future, ie about equilibrium values, or 'fundamentals', to fill in the information gaps, in which the analysis of past and current behaviour necessarily plays a central role. A rational agent also knows that contrary judgments and degrees of confidence in those judgments by others can in the aggregate drive actual asset prices away from his particular vision of equilibrium values.

Two crucial corollaries follow. Volatile capital markets induce agents to try to reduce the risk of loss by taking shorter-term positions for which more hedging instruments are available. Since this increases turnover and makes financial innovating more profitable, the aggregate effect is to draw more human and physical resources into finance while deterring real capital formation.[13] Second, agents are induced to give more credence to their assessments of the thinking and behaviour patterns of other market players than to their own views on fundamentals. Chartism, which concentrates primarily or even solely on plotting past market behaviour as a guide, tends to become the preferred strategy. Thus recent surveys of London foreign exchange dealers show that over 90% rely on charting in taking short-term positions and that the chartists have consistently outperformed econometric models in forecasting the dollar–sterling exchange rate.[14] But such individually rational strategies can produce in the aggregate irrational results, such as increased volatility from 'rational bubbles' and abrupt deflation of asset prices, which then further encourage financial innovation and shortened investment horizons.

The weak version is a grin-without-the-cat version of efficient market theory. Agents don't know the 'true model' and are prone to speculative excesses, but government interference in markets to check the excesses will typically be so clumsy and ill timed as to backfire. Government failure dominates market failure. The weak version thus retains the *laissez-faire* policy stance of the strong version but from a lesser-of-two-evils perspective.

However, even central bankers and finance ministers who may exult in the Reagan dictum that 'the government is the problem not the solution', make an exception for financial markets, recognizing that they are vulnerable to system-wide liquidity crises originating in breaks in the complex chain of mutual payment obligations characterizing such markets. The panicky rush for liquidity in such crises can collapse asset values and block normal credit lines, converting the liquidity squeeze into an insolvency crisis with devastating consequences for output and employment. To allay such crises, monetary authorities must be ready to intervene as lenders of last resort, supplying liquidity, guaranteeing payments, and even closing asset markets as needed.

With financial liberalization and the globalization of financial markets has come an increasing incidence of global crises. The IMF has identified nine crises of global or near-global scope between 1970 and 1989, six occurring in the 1980s, all but one of which evoked central bank intervention, usually joint, to halt the spread of financial distress.[15]

Critics point out that such protective intervention has a negative feedback, that may account for the increasing incidence of such crises. It may have encouraged large financial institutions that have led the move towards globalization to pursue riskier strategies, confident that to the authorities they are 'too big to fail'. But since systemic financial blow-ups are not ruled out by the weak version of efficient market theory, the moral hazard spin-off from crisis intervention does not suffice to cement the case for non-intervention. Rather it can be viewed as requiring that protective intervention be balanced by strengthened controls against financial excesses. This has become the view of the central banks affiliated with the BIS, who have been engaged in a competitive regulation–innovation game with their private banks. Since the Herrstat crisis of 1974, a succession of Basle Accords between the central banks has coordinated tighter prudential banking regulation in the major industrial countries, while private banks have worked to weaken the impact through evasive financial innovating. Thus a recent IMF report urges further regulatory tightening, warning that the aggressive pursuit by US, British and Japanese banks of loan securitizing and other off-balance-sheet transactions that by-pass recently augmented capital adequacy requirements are causing 'a growing opaqueness of the financial system', making it increasingly difficult for supervisory authorities 'to assess fully the risk exposure of the entire consolidated balance sheet of financial institutions . . . Indeed, it is widely recognized that without reforms in financial policy and close attention by central banks, the new financial system could resemble a new high-speed train attempting to run on old, ill-maintained tracks'.[16]

Thus on both theoretical and empirical grounds the Tobin tax proposal may be an idea whose time has come.

Will it have any adverse effects on international trade as well as national and international capital markets?

The preceding discussion shows that international trade and long-term international investment would benefit from less exchange rate volatility and perverse trends of the real exchange rate, and that this view is now widely held. An obvious qualification is that stabilizing mechanisms must work, and the costs and other negative side-effects of operating them should not exceed the gains from stabilization.

There are broadly three approaches to such stabilization, of which the imposition of licensing and quantitative restrictions on Forex transactions can be ruled out as destructive of multilateral trade. Of the remaining two approaches now being suggested, one is for the industrial market economies to agree on a specific structure of exchange rates and to commit to keeping them at their assigned values, or within narrow bands around those values, adjusting their domestic monetary, fiscal, labour and social policies as needed to fulfil the commitment. The other approach is to tax financial transactions unilaterally or in concert so as to raise the cost of moving funds for short-term speculation. The Tobin tax proposal is a variant of this.

Stabilizing exchange rates by agreement is the Bretton Woods grin without the cat. Under Bretton Woods, stability depended on the USA performing as global economic hegemon, anchoring the exchange rate structure by its fixed price gold exchange commitment and supplying emergency liquidity to weaker economies in the throes of foreign exchange crises. As the world's leading international debtor, the USA appears no longer willing or able to assume that hegemonic role today. Replicating Bretton Woods would thus require hegemony by committee: the close coordination of domestic policies and international actions by at least the Big Three—the USA, Japan and Germany—an unlikely prospect for the foreseeable future. Even M Camdessus, who is now urging a return to pegged rates, admits that the major industrial powers are 'lukewarm' towards subordinating other national objectives shaping their economic policies to the needs of exchange rate pegging.[17] Nor is it clear how he reconciles his advocacy of further capital market liberalization with his support for pegged exchange rates. To defend fixed exchange rates against the enormous global volume of funds now available for speculative attacks could require coordinated monetary-fiscal tightening on a scale that would vitiate the stimulus to foreign trade and investment from stable exchange rates.

Taxing financial asset transactions is a more modest approach, with the more modest objective of merely reducing volatility. Two different versions have been floated, each based on the assumption that a small *ad valorem* tax on the sale or exchange of a financial asset will reduce the rate of turnover of the asset, which will reduce price volatility. Recent proponents of a security transfer excise tax (STET) focus primarily on excessive turbulence in the US markets for equities and debt instruments; they would apply the STET to the sale of equity shares, bonds, options, etc. Foreign exchange transactions are not singled out as such, but since the STET would also apply to domestic asset transactions by foreigners, it would presumably slow their turnover rate as well, thereby reducing the volume of foreign exchange transactions. Conversely, the Tobin tax, though directly applied only to foreign exchange transactions, would have indirect spillover effects on domestic assets markets.

However, the Tobin tax proposal has greater revenue and exchange stabilization potential than the STET proposals. In the STET proposals the tax is set unilaterally by each country, whereas Tobin's proposal calls for a uniform tax by at least the key currency countries. The Tobin proposal is thus largely free of the criticism levelled against the STET, that it would tend to shift speculative transactions to tax-free markets elsewhere, reducing the tax yield and the decline of volatility.[18]

The Tobin tax has a third important advantage; it would not merely lower exchange rate volatility by making speculation more costly, but would also reinvigorate the flagging capacity of central banks to alter exchange rate trends by buying or selling foreign exchange. In 1985, when the G-5 central banks successfully reversed the prolonged rise of the dollar with concerted dollar sales, the daily volume of Forex transactions globally was around $150 billion. In 1992 it had risen to around $1 trillion and the conventional belief now is that the resources of central banks are no longer adequate for effective intervention. By reducing speculation in Forex, the tax would also cut down the overall volume of Forex transactions, which would revive the ability of central banks to intervene effectively.

Would the burden of the tax negate the stimulus to foreign trade and investment from less volatility? Proponents of STETs or a Tobin tax both urge that the tax rate be kept low enough merely to return direct unit transactions costs to around their late 1970s level. The argument is that the subsequent decline of transactions fees due to computerization and the competitive deregulation of financial markets has encouraged more financial 'churning' and diverted more resources to financial pursuits without improving on the earlier growth rates of international trade, real investment and global output. To quote Tobin:

We are throwing more and more of our resources, including the cream of our youth, into financial activities that generate high private rewards disproportionate to their social productivity. I suspect that the immense power of the computer is being harnessed to this 'paper economy', not to do the same transactions more economically but to balloon the quantity and variety of financial exchanges. For this reason perhaps, high technology has so far yielded disappointing results in economy-wide productivity.[19]

That is, much of the financial sector's profits from the churning comes from the increased spending by firms engaged in commodity production and trade, who had largely self-insured against the risks from unexpected price movements during the more tranquil Bretton Woods era, on costly financial hedging instruments to offset the higher risks from the heightened post-Bretton Woods volatility. Reducing that volatility would depress the activity and profits of the financial sector by reducing the hedging needs of the productive sector.

As regards the Tobin tax specifically, the prediction is that with a modest tax rate the following social benefits will ensue. Firms engaged in foreign trade and overseas investment long-term investors will incur lower costs on net because of the reduced need to hedge against exchange volatility; they will be encouraged by more stable exchange rates to do longer-term investing and lending, and the tax revenue plus the downsizing of the financial sector will make more resources available for socially productive use. Needless to say, there is as yet a meagre experience base on which to test the predictions, including the inference that downsizing the financial sector will not cause much transitional disruption of the real economy. We know that the demand for risk-hedging instruments was much smaller during Bretton Woods; eg organized currency futures markets first appeared in 1972. And, as indicated above, the declining unit cost of exchanging currencies since the 1970s has not led to higher real growth rates of international trade or of global investment and output. Also, as of the end of the 1980s, seven EU and four major Pacific rim countries had STETs, with tax receipts reaching 0.5% of GNP in Switzerland without calamitous effects on the Swiss financial sector.[20] However, the rates and coverage have varied, and impelled by global deregulatory competition and pressure from the financial sector, the tendency has been to ease up on the terms or abolish STETS rather than coordinate them internationally.

What are the practical aspects—legal, legislative, political—of introducing such a tax?

Like other taxes, the Tobin tax would presumably require approval by the legislature of each participating country. As an international agreement, it would probably be submitted as a tax treaty. But legal matters, including how to reconcile the tax with existing treaties on double taxation, are for international tax lawyers not economists to assess.

The political aspects have two facets—forging an agreement between at least the major industrial economies to implement a uniform tax, and reaching an accord on the distribution of the tax yield. I comment on each in turn.

There are two main forces that could overcome resistance from the financial sectors to being taxed and downsized. One, discussed above, is the convergence of interest on the part of both industrialized countries and LDCs in curbing hot money flows and exchange rate volatility. A Tobin tax complements the more ambitious proposals to return to a Bretton Woods mode of fixed exchange rates; it improves their feasibility by strengthening the effectiveness of central bank intervention, a prospect that might bring M Camdessus and the IMF on board. The other force is the quest by governments, deficit-ridden but intimidated by current anti-tax populism, for new taxes that are not politically suicidal. A tax on foreign exchange transactions may meet this specification, since in US political jargon, it's a tax on 'Wall Street' not 'Main Street'. The titles of two US Senate bills introduced after the October 1987 crash and the political pedigree of their initiators are illustrative. The *Excessive Churning and Speculation Act of 1989* (S 1654) was introduced by Republican Senators Dole and Kassebaum, while *The Long-term Investment, Competitiveness and Corporate Takeover Reform Act of 1990* (S 2190) was introduced by Republican Senator Ford and Democratic Senators Sanford and Sasser. In each case the objective was to apply penalty taxes on excessive speculation by pension funds. Although neither bill passed, initiating them was evidently safe enough.

On the distribution of the tax receipts, it seems unlikely that the current fiscal tribulations and foreign aid fatigue in the collecting countries would allow the tax receipts to be fully passed along by the collecting governments to either the IMF or World Bank, as Tobin proposed, or to the UN. Nevertheless, the huge volume of foreign exchange transactions today makes even a modest share of the tax receipts a sizeable addition to the financial resources of the international institutions. The following 'back of the envelope' calculations, are illustrative of the astonishingly high revenue potential of a globalized Tobin tax. The calculations annualize the $1 trillion daily volume of global exchange transactions cited above, assume that 20% would be by governments, central banks and official international organizations and hence tax-exempt, that another 20% would be private transactions that elude the tax, and that the tax reduces the remaining exchange transactions by half (*Table 2*).

Research is, of course, needed to refine these very crude 'ball park' estimates. The $1 trillion trading volume figure needs more verification. The actual average ratio of official to total exchange transactions needs to be ascertained, as well as the percentage in the global volume of foreign exchange transactions that would ensue, were the EU countries to move to a single EU currency as called for by the Maastricht

TABLE 2.

Taxable foreign exchange	Annual tax receipts (10^9)	
	1.0% tax	0.5% tax
$1 trillion × 240 trading days less 20% tax exempts = $192 trillion less 20% evasion = $144 trillion less 50% reduction of trading volume = $72 trillion effective tax base	720	360
50% kept by collecting governments	360	180
Distributed to the UN, IMF and World Bank	360	180

Treaty. The reduction of exchange volume from the Tobin tax in the above calculations is a pure guess. It seems unlikely that a 0.5% tax would depress the volume as much as a 1.0% tax. A research group with an appropriate database and econometric skills should be able to simulate a reasonably plausible range of alternative estimates of the responsiveness of the exchange volume to different Tobin tax rates.

What institutional arrangements can one have to mobilize the resources through the Tobin tax and manage it? Can the UN be that institution?

Their crudeness notwithstanding, my 'back of the envelope' estimates suffice to illustrate two main points about the Tobin tax. It could be such a large revenue producer that getting even a modest slice of the revenue earmarked for United Nations operations is a goal well worth pursuing. And this could be true even if the World Bank and IMF were also assigned slices, provided that the collecting governments were willing to allocate a quarter or more of the tax revenue to international organizations. That likelihood would increase were the three international institutions jointly to mobilize their respective constituencies and lobbying efforts to that end. In initiating a Tobin tax proposal, the UN might consider including in it a tentative distribution of shares between the three institutions so as to help bring the IMF and World Bank on board.

Collecting the tax would be the responsibility of the individual governments, notably the industrialized countries, since most of the taxable Forex transactions are by their citizens and enterprises. An international board, however, ought to be empowered to oversee the sharing of the tax receipts, report periodically on results, and recommend changes as needed in the tax rate, coverage, enforcement, sharing and other relevant matters.

The board should have representation from the UN, IMF, and World Bank, as well as from the G-5. Whether or not the board is put nominally under the UN's jurisdiction, realistically the fundamental power will devolve, as has been the case with boards of the IMF and the World Bank, to the countries who most pay the piper—the USA, the EU and Japan. Moreover, since the 1950s the IMF and the World Bank have been the preferred international instruments of the USA, whereas the more ideologically heterodox UN has until recently been under a cloud and kept on short rations by the USA. With the end of the Cold War, the cloud appears to be lifting, and in the new international disorder that has followed, the UN has again become an international instrument of choice for the USA and the other industrial powers. Its bargaining power for a share of the Tobin tax receipts is thus considerably strengthened, although my hunch is that an equal share for each of the three institutions is perhaps the most that the UN could expect in the current political climate. However, were the climate to become more favourable in the future, the board would be a ready vehicle for initiating recommendations to enlarge the UN's share.

What are some of the practical problems in introducing as well as managing such a tax?

Assuming agreement among the major economies on applying a uniform tax and on the distribution of the tax receipts, the main practical problems seem to be the following:

Settling on a rate that offers an acceptable trade-off between deterring speculation and raising revenue. There is too little information now to compute reliable trade-offs, hence the sensible approach would be to agree on an *ad hoc* initial rate and provide for a corrective mechanism as results come in. A major function of the supervisory board, suggested above, should be to research the experience and suggest rate changes to the participating governments on the basis of that experience. Whatever uniform rate is adopted, however, should be only a floor rate. Countries should remain free to set higher national rates individually to allay severe bouts of turbulence. LDCs are especially subject to such bouts, and we do not yet know to what extent the globalized Tobin tax would reduce their incidence. Currently, for example, Chile and Colombia have imposed transactions taxes at rates that, I believe, are higher than Tobin's suggestion of 1.0%, in order to stave off disruptive hot money inflows.

Collection and evasion problems. Since large international banks do most of the handling of foreign exchange transactions, be it trade finance, interbank deposits, swap agreements between transnational companies, hedge fund speculation etc, tax collection should at least initially be quite manageable. The banks are few in number, and are required now to keep close records of their transactions for the bank regulators and tax authorities. Over time, evasive innovation could become more of a problem. Transnational companies could devise intrafirm accounting gimmicks to transfer funds, transactions could be shifted to offshore tax havens etc. Would the tax loom large enough for these institutions to incur the cost and risk of such evasive activity on a substantial scale? *Quien sabe?* Another function of the supervisory board ought to be, therefore, to assess whether evasion is becoming too prevalent, and if so, to suggest remedial action by the collecting authorities.

What recommendations can be made to the World Summit for Social Development for implementing the Tobin tax, generating the fund, managing it and using it for human development and human security?

Given foreign aid fatigue, there may be few alternative ways of funding the social objectives of the World Summit that are as promising as a global Tobin tax. A proposal for such a tax should therefore be put before the Summit for adoption. That would give the Tobin tax proposal a clearer moral dimension to reinforce its materialistic economic rationale, which should somewhat increase its prospects of adoption.

The proposal presented to the Summit should, however, provide more precise revenue estimates than I have been able to offer. This could easily be done in time for the Summit by a research group that has access to and has worked with international financial data. I suggest contracting with the UNCTAD economists for this research. They have been doing excellent analyses and reporting on international trade and finance, and, in contrast to IMF or World Bank economists, are sure to be appreciative of the proposal and its purpose. In addition, it would be advisable to get a legal expert to assess and perhaps help shape the international tax treaty aspects of the Tobin tax proposal.

On the remainder of this question, I have already said my piece in the preceding sections concerning implementation and management of the tax and distribution of the tax proceeds. And as for best applying the funds that might be made available to human development and security, you are much more knowledgeable about projects and programmes than I.

Notes and references

1. James Tobin, 'A proposal for international monetary reform', Presidential Address to the Eastern Economic Association, published in *Eastern Economic Journal, 4*, 1978.
2. Lawrence H Summers and Victoria P Summers, 'When financial markets work too well: a case for securities transactions tax', in Daniel R Siegel (editor), *Innovation and Technology in the Markets: A Reordering of the World's Capital Market Systems* (Chicago, IL, Probus Publishing Co, 1990), pages 151–181; Joseph E Stiglitz, 'Using tax policy to curb speculative short-term trading', *Journal of Financial Services Research, 3*, 1989, pages 101–115; Dean Baker, Robert Pollin and Marc Schaberg, 'Taxing the big casino', *The Nation*, 9 May 1994. Lawrence Summers is currently US Under-Secretary of the Treasury, and Stiglitz is a member of the President's Council of Economic Advisors.
3. *The Economist*, 3 October 1992, page 71.
4. Guth's position is evident from the title of his recent essay, 'The liberalization trap: how the free flow of capital is undermining multilateral trade', *The International Economy*, May/June 1993, pages 56–59. Lamfalussy, according to Guth, also contends that the free flow of capital and the free formation of exchange rates under financial globalization may be undermining free trade. This, Lamfalussy observes, 'would turn upside down the basic idea of Bretton Woods—to create the conditions for the greatest possible freedom of trade through orderly exchange rate relationships'.
5. William Murray, 'US and 17 countries meet to tackle finance issues of Asia's infrastructure', *The Wall Street Journal*, 21 March 1994.
6. Michel Camdessus, 'The way forward for the international monetary system, 50 years after Bretton Woods', an address delivered at Fundacion Ramon Areces, Madrid, 9 May 1994, and excerpted in *IMF Survey*, 30 May 1994.
7. Ragnar Nurkse, *International Currency Experience* (Geneva, The League of Nations, 1944) is a classic assessment along these lines, which Michael Bordo asserts largely reflected the views of Maynard Keynes and Harry Dexter White, the chief architects of Bretton Woods. Michael D Bordo, 'The Bretton Woods international monetary system: a historical overview', in Michael D Bordo and Barry Eichengreen (editors), *A Retrospective on the Bretton Woods System* (Chicago, IL, University of Chicago Press, 1993), page 30.
8. 'The case for flexible exchange rates', in Milton Friedman, *Essays in Positive Economics* (Chicago, IL, University of Chicago Press, 1953), pages 157–203.
9. These conclusions refer to G-3 and G-7 currency patterns as summarized in Ronald MacDonald and Mark P Taylor, 'Exchange rate economics: a survey', *IMF Staff Papers*, March 1992, pages 1–57; the International Monetary Fund, *Determinants and Systemic Consequences of International Capital Flows: Policy Issues in the Evolving International Monetary System*, IMF Occasional Paper No 96, Washington, DC, June 1992; and UNCTAD, *Trade and Development Report, 1990*, chapter 1, part 2.
10. 'Banks and derivative markets: a challenge for financial policy', *IMF Survey*, 21 February 1994.
11. Julian Walmsley, *The New Financial Instruments: An Investor's Guide* (New York, John Wiley and Sons, 1988), page 13.
12. Guth, *op cit*, reference 4, page 57.
13. Tobin emphasizes this in his essay, 'On the efficiency of the financial system', *Lloyds Bank Review*, July 1994. See also Stiglitz, *op cit*, reference 2, for a more extended theoretical treatment.
14. Helen Allen and Mark P Taylor, 'Charts, noise and fundamentals in the London foreign exchange market', *Economic Journal, 100* (Supplement), pages 49–59; Jeffery Frankel and Kenneth Froot, 'Chartists, fundamentalists and trading in the foreign exchange market', *American Economic Review, 80*, 1990, pages 181–185.
15. IMF, *Determinants and Systemic Consequences of International Capital Flows, op cit*, reference 9, Table 11.
16. IMF, *International Capital Markets: Developments, Prospects and Policy Issues* (Washington, DC, International Monetary Fund, September 1992), pages 7–8.
17. Kenneth Bacon, 'IMF chief urges changes to promote stability in currency-exchange rates', *The Wall Street Journal*, 8 June 1994.
18. See the discussion in *Tax Treatment of Short-term Trading*, prepared by the Staff of the US Congress, Joint Committee On Taxation for the US Senate Committee on Finance (Washington, DC, US Government Printing Office, 21 March 1990).
19. Tobin, *op cit*, reference 13, pages 14–15.
20. Summers and Summers, *op cit*, reference 2, Table 2.

0016-3287(94)00027−1

THE UNITED NATIONS SECURITY INSURANCE AGENCY (UNSIA) PROPOSAL

A preliminary assessment

Daniel M Smith

Success in peace operations requires solid financial support and confidence that the international community will respond to threats. These objectives could be achieved by creating a United Nations Security Insurance Agency (UNSIA) that links costs of peace operations to the probability that nations might be threatened. Using methodologies from the commercial insurance industry, UNSIA would conduct risk assessments and set 'premium' levels based on the risk level and the types of peace operations nations want. Even with such 'premiums', this arrangement would permit nations to reduce military spending and fund more human development programmes.

A recent issue of *Futures*[1] contains a document of the UNDP by Alan F Kay and Hazel Henderson that proposes a radical mechanism to finance future United Nations (UN) peace operations. To implement this mechanism, the authors propose a new entity called the United Nations Security Insurance Agency (UNSIA). Authorized by the UN as a public/private partnership corporation modelled after Intelsat, UNSIA would buttress and support the current and unreliable process of imposing regular and special assessments on UN member-states with a system of interlocking, prepaid guaranteed responses—insurance—against potential security risks.

As is so often the case with really innovative ideas, the fundamentals of this scheme are relatively straightforward. Nations with small or no armed forces and nations wishing to cut their military spending would contract with the UN for

Colonel Daniel M Smith (Ret), is Associate Director of the Center for Defense Information, 1500 Massachusetts Avenue, NW, Washington, DC 20005, USA (Tel: +1 202 862 0700; fax: +1 202 862 0708).

future national security guarantees ranging from simple border monitoring (as in Macedonia today) to peacekeeping (Sinai force) to peace enforcement (Bosnia).

In return for one or more of these security levels, a nation would pay the UN a predetermined sum of money—a 'premium'—which would be used to defray the costs of personnel, equipment and supplies needed by the UN should it be necessary to honour its guarantee to the insured nation. As with most private and commercial insurance, the expectation that most nations would never need to invoke their 'insurance policy' would work to keep 'premiums' down.

At the heart of such an international mutual insurance arrangement are the presumptions that most nations prefer peace and, when disputes arise, they prefer non-military resolutions. But occasionally this presumption fails and international action might be required to restore peaceful relations between countries.

Looking around the world today, one might almost conclude that the presumption for peace has not merely been breached but has completely collapsed. The end of the bipolar world seemingly has removed many restraints that dampened territorial, political, ethnic and religious divisiveness during the past 50 years. Our instant communications make us more aware of the resulting carnage, the suffering, the genocide. Our humanity is challenged, and with it our instinctive impulse is to stop the ongoing violence and to prevent future threats to peace.

In attempting to meet this challenge, we are placing significant burdens on our international institutions and resources. As more and more nations turn to or expect help from the UN, that institution, so long paralysed by the East–West Cold War confrontation, is in danger of being overwhelmed by the peacekeeping and peace enforcement burdens being heaped on it.

Rising expectations unfortunately produce rising costs, for peacekeepers and peace enforcers are expensive. Currently, UN member-states pay—often reluctantly when they do—millions if not billions of dollars for such operations. Citizens of many countries resent this expenditure. Seeing little benefit in comparison with spending money to alleviate significant domestic problems, they press their elected officials to reduce or skip payments. This leads to chronic underfunding and the debilitating unpredictability of the UN to respond to international crises. It also compels nations to maintain large standing military forces that consume scarce resources that could better be used for constructive economic and social development programmes.

Enter UNSIA, a small, well trained, professionally advised organization that would be the central clearing house for information and analyses associated with the development of an international security guarantee system.

UNSIA's fundamental responsibility would be to determine the extent of the risks of military action that each applicant country faces from its neighbours. This determination would drive the cost estimates of the UN guarantee for each level of potential intervention 'bought' by nation-states. By extension, UNSIA would be responsible for estimating the costs of having on-call UN forces able to respond to crises.

Before delving further into the problems of how to assess risks and develop costs—activities administered largely by UNSIA itself—it is important to note that UNSIA must integrate its activities with at least two other important UN bodies. Most notably, UNSIA would require guidance from the Security Council on the general conditions under which a UN intervention force would be authorized. Furthermore, since the Council authorizes UN peace operations, any 'insurance policy' written by UNSIA would also require Security Council assent to be an effective document.

UNSIA would also have to coordinate continuously with the UN Department of Peacekeeping Operations on the terms of each proposed and approved agreement as well as the probabilities and the effects of having to implement numerous 'policy guarantees' simultaneously.

This brings us back to the old sticking point of current UN peace operations—funding—and, by extension, risks. As with all kinds of insurance, the key for both the insurer and the insured lies in analysing the risks and establishing premiums that guarantee the 'company' has the resources to pay out in case an adverse event occurs. To achieve this risk–premium balance over the long haul, UNSIA would have to subcontract risk assessments to professionals in appropriate public and private organizations, including reinsurers, on fee-for-service bases.

Obviously, the premium amount depends on a realistic appraisal by UNSIA of the risks of military threats and military conflict. This evaluation must include a multitude of factors both within the country seeking 'insurance' and in countries with which it has borders. Because there are many potential and often unpredictable actors, the evaluation process is more complicated and interactive than might be the prediction of the location and probability of natural disasters such as hurricanes and earthquakes.

In support of the UNSIA concept, The Center for Defense Information has begun an initial canvass of existing risk assessment tools and models used by international agencies, government departments, multinational corporations, think tanks, insurance companies, and higher-level US military colleges.

Our investigation to date indicates that there is a wealth of data and a variety of methodologies that could be used as the bases for developing risk indices for nations. Data on the type of government, political stability, and the military's involvement in or influence over a nation's government are easily obtainable. So too are important economic indices such as gross national product (GNP), per capita income, the extent of natural resources, foreign trade figures (including arms imports or exports), and expenditures on armed forces and military production in absolute terms and as a proportion of GNP. Other widely available and novel risk assessment models look at global climate change.

Specialized economic and defence-oriented publications are vying to capture the public 'risk assessment' market. *Jane's Sentinel* has published regional assessments on three 'hot spots'—the Balkans, the Gulf states, and the South China Sea. The Economist Intelligence Unit (EIU) produces 'country reports' with fundamental information on markets and economic and political trends. The EIU has a specialized Country Risk Service that provides quarterly ratings for 82 economically burdened developing countries. Although oriented towards economics, these products include political risk analysis over a two-year horizon.

However, there are constraints on our investigative process associated particularly with multinational corporations which supplement their analysis of economic prospects with a hard look at political risks. As countries like Vietnam, China, the former Warsaw Pact nations, and potentially Cuba open their markets to Western investment, companies are increasingly guarding their risk evaluation methodologies jealously as high-priority proprietary information.

This reluctance to discuss risk methods looms as a significant missing link in any attempt to develop realistically weighted country profiles/risk models. One avenue, the most straightforward, is for UNSIA to contract for state-of-the-art risk assessments at market fees. However, this could add significantly to UNSIA's costs and reduce savings to participant countries.

An alternative approach that would at least partially compensate for the reluctance of corporations to share their methodologies is to determine what factors are used by public international financial organizations such as the World Bank, the IMF, and the Interamerican Development Bank. In making or guaranteeing loans, these organizations look at a nation's economic indicators and can require, as a condition of a loan or guarantee, that fiscal reforms be made. A nation's military expenditures are also factors that the World Bank and IMF consider in reviewing loan requests.

One interesting insurance experiment, one that focuses more on internal activities in a nation rather than interstate relations, is the Overseas Private Investment Corporation (OPIC). OPIC provides political risk insurance, direct loans and loan guarantees to qualified US private investors who are engaged in less developed countries. OPIC covers losses in business income and damage to tangible property resulting from currency inconvertibility, expropriation, and political violence—war, revolution, insurrection or politically motivated strife, terrorism or sabotage.

Our analysis has also highlighted another challenge, one at least as significant as obtaining information about methodologies currently in use. That challenge is the relative weight to give to quantitative and qualitative factors. In 1980, Ray S Cline, the CIA's Deputy Director for Intelligence from 1962 to 1966, published a detailed quantitative formula for what he saw were the 'elements of power' within a nation—economic strength and potential, political systems and historical stability, military capability and national will.

The Pentagon itself is a massive producer and consumer of quantitative and qualitative risk assessments, from the annual Joint Net Assessments to the 'Catalog of Wargaming and Military Simulation Models'. The latter lists various types of simulations for war games, risk methodologies, global games and demographic forecasts in general use by the US Department of Defense and the defence establishments of Australia, Canada, Germany and the UK. Factors examined by these simulations and their applicability to risk assessment for UNSIA include:

- the budget impact of executive decision making in the allocation of limited national resources—useful in evaluating a country's ability for increased social development by reducing military forces and 'buying' UN insurance;
- intent of high-interest hostile elements to pursue specific courses of action—attempts to develop 'pattern recognition' processes that can give early warning of belligerent intent;
- long-range (15–20 year) appraisal of demographic, political, economic, social and financial submodels that, in the aggregate, shape the future profile of a target nation—useful as a tool in predicting national capability for engaging in military adventures in the future;
- impact of policy alternatives on lesser developed nations—profiles trends in developing nations and then 'tests' various policy alternatives to project future courses of action in the target country.

In the end, all simulations, models and risk projections suffer from the same weakness—quantifying what are inherently non-quantitative influences on the evolution of a nation. This has been a particularly acute consideration as nations that have gained independence since World War II struggle to find their footing in a world no longer divided along East–West lines but now more on North–South ones. The old patterns and constraints are gone; new ones have yet to be determined, even for the powerful nations of the developed world.

In a sense, this fluidity in international relations provides a real window of opportunity for redefining and broadening the concept and content of intraregional security relationships under the UN umbrella. With a guarantee of an appropriate UN response, nations should be able to reduce their individual military expenditures significantly. The money saved through the UNSIA system could be channelled into programmes for food production, civilian infrastructure, job and income security, promoting human rights, and ensuring ethnic and religious tolerance.

In turn, with individual populations more secure in their personal lives, regional political and military stability and security would increase. Finally, by looking carefully at all these factors and employing a well designed, continuously updated quantitative/qualitative risk evaluation system, UNSIA would serve as the basis for effective, early conflict resolution regimes ranging from mediation of disputes to peacekeeping and, if necessary, peace enforcement activities.

The early stages of UNSIA will be ones of adjustment and learning. Undoubtedly, small nations seeking security without bankrupting themselves will be most interested in UNSIA. As more and more of these states opt for this plan and reduce or eliminate their military budgets, the web of individual UNSIA states will spread, eventually creating whole regions in which all countries are UNSIA participants. When such a critical mass is achieved, the costs of UNSIA would plummet even further, freeing more money for human development programmes.

Once medium and larger-sized nations become convinced that reducing their individual military expenditures provides greater security and more money for internal development, the world may finally make the psychological leap from reliance on war to reliance on peace. The remaining occasional breaches of peace, at whatever level, will then be easier to counter because the UNSIA system will stand as self-funding, self-sustaining protection from external aggression.

For such peace of mind and peace among nations, UNSIA is well worth pursuing.

Reference

1. Alan F Kay and Hazel Henderson, *Futures*, *27*(1), pages 3–10.

0016-3287(94)00013-1

FINANCING CIVIL SOCIETY FOR A GLOBAL RESPONSIBILITY

Robert Cassani

The global civil society is exercising an increasingly important role in supporting innovative, democratic people-centred policy changes in global affairs. For the majority of people, solutions for poverty alleviation, the security of productive employment and livelihoods and for the restoration of the integrity of the environment are rooted in private or community-based initiatives. The establishment of an independent global Civil Society Development Fund, with a web of regional and local affiliates, can create the basis for an independent civil society which is able to seek its own solutions to global problems.

At a certain point, the concept of citizenship began to take shape as individuals and their associations organized to contest and balance the authority of the state, of the nobility and of the clergy. This was the birth of civil society at the national level, of institutions in which individuals could pursue common interests without overdirection or interference from the government or other strong vested interests.

As the authority of the church or the state was challenged over time, the idea of government by consent ultimately derived from a mandate by the people. If those in whom power is vested for the administration of the public good misgovern, consent is withdrawn and authority vested on others. Only a viable and independent civil society can exercise this constant process of delegating power, monitoring its use to hold it accountable, withdrawing authority and bestowing it yet again. Civil society has made the transition from autocratic rule to democratic governance possible.

The transition to forms of democratic governance at the national level is still under way in many quarters of the globe. However, we have learned that civil society can only flourish if certain conditions prevail: the right to food, shelter, livelihood and security of family and person; the right to freedom of expression and association and the right to redress of grievances and due process. Transparency, access to public records, free press and media and public accountability of private initiatives which influence public well-being are critical needs in an open society.

The author is Executive Director of the Society for International Development, Palazzo Civilta del Lavoro, 00144 Rome, Italy (Tel: +39 6 592 5506; fax: +39 6 591 9836).

Necessary transition from national to global citizenship

It is easy for many to imagine how the above conditions ought to manifest themselves at the national level. It is less easy to imagine how the fundamentals for civil society can find expression at the global level; yet they must. Today we are at another pivotal point in history. The globalization of the economy, of information and communications systems, and of the impact of human activities on the environment, have created a world in which the nation-state is no longer the pre-eminent source of security. Individual rights and security must increasingly be found in satisfactory global relationships.

We may be global citizens at the level of rhetoric, but there is no equivalent to the state and its institutions globally; as the capacity of national governments to exercise control over global phenomena is steadily in decline creative ways must be found to respond to global challenges.

The institutions of global governance are patchy and unsystematically developed: international law is embodied in treaties and conventions, and redress for transborder violations is usually sought by governments or corporate bodies—seldom by individuals. There is political resistance by the major powers to create effective global judicial machinery to address the rights and obligations of individuals, for example for the creation of a world environment court or of a permanent war crimes tribunal.

The closest body we have which performs a legislative function at the global level is the UN General Assembly and periodic UN or intergovernmental conferences. The enforcement capacity is virtually non-existent, beyond moral suasion of governments, unless the five permanent members of the Security Council are prepared to apply economic or military pressure—again, on another state.

The institutions of global civil society are equally patchy and in need of undergirding if they are to exercise the necessary monitoring and political agenda-setting role which a civil society must perform.

Who is global civil society?

In the past it may have been easier to describe which organizations were *not* to be considered 'non-governmental' for purposes of formal relations with the United Nations—a government assembly in practice. According to a UN Economic and Social Council (ECOSOC) resolution of 23 May 1968, schools, universities, political parties, for-profit corporations, businesses or consulting firms, religious faiths, churches, orders or cults (as distinguished from religious councils or lay bodies) are not eligible to apply for consultative status with this organ as non-governmental organizations (NGOs). The resolution also specifies that an NGO's source of revenues should not derive only or primarily from governmental sources.[1]

Today, such a resolution would probably raise some eyebrows among the NGO community, at least concerning who is to be excluded. There would be little query as to the importance of financial independence from governments.

In 1994 over 1500 international NGOs retained some form of consultative status with the ECOSOC. And there is good reason to believe that this number would be much higher if the relevant criteria were not as confined and procedures for review of application and accreditation were not as time-consuming.

Although the implicit ECOSOC definition of NGOs is remarkably parallel to the 17th century French experience of viewing the political world as constituted by the state, the nobility, the church and the third estate, perhaps it is too restrictive to capture the true diversity of competing civil interests in today's context of globalization.

Today the NGO community is involved in virtually every aspect of development irrespective of a nation's income. NGOs work as relief and welfare agencies, they produce and implement technological innovations, they work as public service contractors for governments, they work as promoters of grassroots development, self-help and empowerment movements, and NGOs are active in information and advocacy work. Some are secular organizations and others are inspired by faith traditions.

We have seen that for every major UN conference since the 1992 Conference on Environment and Development in Rio (Vienna 1993, Cairo 1994, Copenhagen and Beijing 1995) *at least* 1500 people's organizations and citizens' groups mobilize in the preparatory processes in an effort to influence the official governmental negotiations. Indeed, it has become customary now that every official global conference is flanked by an 'NGO Forum'. This global networking by the civil society has stimulated the creation of new forms of association: from the creation of *ad hoc* 'coalitions', to 'constituencies' to 'caucuses' along thematic, national income or gender lines. The 'Women's caucus' for the World Summit for Social Development, for example, has proved to be one of the best organized and most influential networks, perhaps one of the few that manage to maintain a common identity and agenda from one UN conference to another.

The profile of NGOs that emerges from the engagement in the global conference process is that civil society tends to be increasingly organized in terms of almost seamless networks, rather than simply as a quantifiable group of territorial NGOs.

Networking for information, communication and advocacy

For many years associations of scientists, economists, environmental specialists, social activists and many other public-interest groups have been meeting, exchanging experiences and research and cooperating to identify and implement solutions to many specific and common problems. As problems and opportunities have globalized so have the communication and cooperation efforts. Advances in information and communications technologies have played a fundamental role in facilitating this interaction and emerging global identity.

Global lobbying, the coordination of campaigns and the exchange of information and real-time media relations via e-mail have become indispensable for the civil society. E-mail is faster and cheaper than the telephone, fax or courier service and is oblivious to time zones and to the limitations of postal services. This has permitted NGO representatives at UN conferences, for example, to inform their head offices about progress of meetings, receive guidance for lobbying positions and issue local press releases.

Internet, a collection of computer networks, has made this possible. The global network has nearly 1.5 million host systems serving an estimated 20 million people. Internet connections now reach into more than 50 countries. All are connected by computer and modem through telephone line. The access cost for users can be between $3–$20 per hour to be on the system, and an annual subscription can start at $100.

Less expensive alternative non-'phone and mixed systems for electronic communications are also available and spreading rapidly. There is a grassroots networking programme, for example, called FidoNet, which links computer bulletin board systems automatically through ordinary 'phone lines at night when 'phone rates are low. There is a growing market for joint private/public sector ventures to create digital communications utilities which combine packet radio, land lines and low-orbit satellites. The industry claims that one such utility can service 50,000 people for a per capita access cost of $12 per year. The utility approach frees the individual user of the obligation to purchase the hardware.

Balancing cooperation with independence

The non-governmental and voluntary associations have acquired a significant importance in development over the years. In 1992 official development assistance (ODA) to the developing world was $58.7 billion. In the same year, NGOs distributed $5.5 billion in grants—one-tenth of government aid and, as a group, the fifth largest aid donor after the USA, Japan, France and Germany.[2]

According to a recent study by the OECD Development Centre, increasingly large amounts of government money—as high as 25% of ODA in some OECD DAC countries—are passing through NGOs. The study confirms the risk which NGOs face when depending too much on government funds. As more and more funds are received from governments, through contracts as executing agencies for bilateral initiatives, they seem to form cluster organizations that differ only marginally from each other in terms of their product. This process of homogenization into, for example, development education, relief, volunteerism and operational groups, results from government pressure to conform to donor-designed norms and standards. Perhaps a greater risk, which is more difficult to demonstrate systemically, is the gradual loss of NGO independence in voice and action.[3]

The growing number of NGOs competing for stagnant or declining levels of government funds has pushed many to explore innovative and untraditional means to support themselves. In the North particularly, NGOs have increasingly set up commercial activities as a supplement to fund raising, with trading organizations for Southern goods, consulting activities, all designed to earn revenues that can be ploughed back into charity. As NGOs seek to raise funds directly from the public through media campaigns and direct mailing, however, their overhead expenses climb accordingly.

In some instances, governments (and the UN) have induced the creation of NGO coalitions to simplify representation or funding mechanisms, Some of these are short-lived or event-bound, while others are durable. Secular NGO groupings, such as EUROSTEP, InterAction in the USA and Canadian Council for International Cooperation, mostly engage in advocacy and information. National and international church networks have proved to be effective and lasting. As expected, genuine cooperation among NGOs tends to work best when it suits NGOs themselves.

A basis for an independent global civil society—seizing an opportunity

The World Summit for Social Development (WSSD) and the 50th anniversary of the Bretton Woods institutions this year offer a good opportunity to take some concrete steps towards the creation of more democratic institutions of global governance. It is also an opportunity to create the basis for greater financial independence of the civil society. The Summit themes of poverty, livelihoods and social integration, underscore the urgency of finding new solutions and means of cooperation for this venture.

In order to strengthen the capacity of civil society to contribute to finding its own solutions to the concerns raised by the summit, three conditions must be created and supported:

(1)   a continuous capacity for civil society to communicate, to associate and to obtain relevant information (eg about the state of the commons and of the world's communities);
(2)   reliable mechanisms which hold public bodies (governmental and intergovernmental) more accountable to civil society;
(3)   greater financial self-reliance of civil society.

These conditions are very much interrelated. The first, we have seen, is facilitated by information and communications technologies. The second requires the consistent institutionalization of procedures for consultation with and monitoring by civil society organizations in all global public institutions. To achieve the financial self-reliance of civil society institutions, new independent funding systems must be created. The following is a proposal in this direction.

A Civil Society Development Fund

The Preparatory Committee of the WSSD is currently considering a number of workable means for funding UN activities, particularly in the areas of health, education, productive employment and sustainable development activities. The need for a direct and reliable source of finance for the UN is evident, given the chronic delays in payment of member-government assessments and dues and increasing demands on national cooperation budgets. Efforts to create such an income stream for the UN, however, must not neglect the indispensable role that civil society plays in supporting the principles of the UN Charter.

A Global Commission to Fund the United Nations is being formed to explore alternative means to finance the UN. Several proposals are being elaborated which contribute to creating a coherent global fiscal regime. One such proposal is the 'Tobin tax' which could raise revenues through a uniform tax on international currency transactions.

The proposed beneficiaries of this revenue stream at present would be four categories of actors: (1) governments who apply the tax (50%); (2) the IMF; (3) the UN; and (4) the World Bank. Some estimates place the range of potential annual tax receipts from $360 billion to $720 billion, for a levy of 0.5% to 1%.[4]

Other international activities which are being considered for taxation include:

•   derivatives trading;
•   arms sales;
•   carbon combustion emissions;
•   international air and freight transport;
•   use of global commons generally.

All proposals would appear to be consistent with the generally agreed principle that a sustainable world economy should have a fiscal regime which discourages excessive consumption and the depletion of non-renewable resources and encourages economic stability and human security.

Parallel to these efforts to strengthen the UN's capacity, an independent global fund must be established to receive and administer a fair share of revenues generated by any new global fiscal regime. A Civil Society Development Fund would provide access, unmediated by governments, to development resources and provide the basis for the independent financing of needed civil society institutions.

Some basic principles

A number of critical issues need further thought in setting up such a global fund.

Governance. A Board of Governors should be created which reflects the diversity of civil society institutions and geographic balance. This will necessarily entail the articulation of a workable definition of civil society.

Structure. The Global Fund should support regional and local funds which adhere to common principles. Where possible, such local funds should be designed on a revolving basis and should encourage the reinvestment of local profits in the local community. Governments should be encouraged to provide fiscal incentives to individuals or corporations who make contributions to local civil society funds.

Transparency of activities. The Fund activities should be audited regularly by an eminent institution, such as the International Court of Justice, to ensure that resources are properly invested.

Beneficiaries. It is proposed that the information and communications 'infrastructure' needs of civil society in the broadest sense be the principle beneficiaries of the Fund. Individuals should not directly benefit, rather individual capacities to participate should be enhanced. The Fund should avoid supporting the purchase of hardware or capital assets, but invest in lowering the financial barriers to entry to those who cannot afford access.

Relations with intergovernmental agencies. A mechanism will need to be created to relate the proposed Fund and its governing body to the major institutions. The Consultative Status mechanism and supporting Conference of NGOs in Consultative Status with ECOSOC (CONGO) already in place, may provide a starting point for further strengthening, although similarly developed mechanisms do not exist for the Bretton Woods institutions and the regional development banks.

Some specific civil society needs

It will be important to identify the infrastructure requirements for civil society at the global level. Already it is possible to imagine that *subsidies for access fees* to electronic communications systems will be an important requirement. A July 1994 report of the ECOSOC on a working group concerned with reviewing consultative mechanisms clearly echoed a need repeatedly expressed by both governments and NGOs: means must be found to support the *travel and maintenance of NGO participants* in UN conferences and their preparatory meetings.

The information and communications needs of those who facilitate or engage in *fair trade* can be an obvious beneficiary. The NGO community in the UK and the Netherlands are particularly advanced on this front, with OXFAM- and NOVIB-supported initiatives among the most prominent.

There is a need for an *independent global non-commercial, non-governmental television network* to carry news and information from a plurality of perspectives, without the pressure of purely advertising-driven programming. Some efforts along these lines are planned, although the many partners in the venture have yet to achieve a critical mass.

Recently, the UNDP, UNICEF and UNFPA have agreed to push national governments to underwrite a '20/20' formula, whereby 20% of ODA would be matched by 20% of recipient-country earmarking of public expenditure for human development objectives. A portion of the national human development investment could be supported by a *'civil society 20/20 counterpart'* through the proposed Fund.

In low-income countries there is a general lack of computer-literate office workers, programmers and service technicians. Without affordable access to regional and global information and communications networks, the risk of further marginalization is even greater. Community projects which provide *access to digital communications on a utility or use basis* provide considerable scope if public/private sector partnerships are promoted and community control and access issues are carefully thought through. *Capacity building* to ensure effective use and maintenance of communications systems could also be supported by the Fund.

The use of debt-for-nature swaps for the purchase of local land preserves and community land trusts which aim to provide community or broad-based public equity control over natural resources can be an innovative approach to *regenerating the environment through land reform for sustainable agriculture practice.* A Fund could support this process.

Finally, the Fund could support the travel and communications expenses tied to civil society participation in *humanitarian or disaster relief* operations.

Conclusion

The moment has come to institutionalize the role and democratic participation of civil society in global responsibilities. Civil society is exercising an increasingly important role in supporting innovative people-centred policy changes in global affairs. For the majority of people, solutions for poverty alleviation, the security of productive employment and livelihoods and for the restoration of the integrity of the environment are rooted in private or community-based initiatives. These initiatives are assuming the characteristics of a movement. It is opportune to design an orderly means to finance and cooperate with these dynamic forces.

Notes and references

1. United Nations, Economic and Social Council, document E/C.2/1993/6, 1 December 1992.
2. *Report of the Development Assistance Committee* (Paris, OECD, 1994).
3. Ian Smillie and Henny Helmich (editors), *Non-governmental Organizations and Governments: Stakeholders for Development* (Paris, OECD, 1994).
4. David Felix, 'The Tobin tax proposal: background, issues and prospects', New York, UNDP, 1994.

Bibliography

John Clark, *Democratizing Development: The Role of Voluntary Organizations* (Kumarian Press, 1991).
Global Digital Utilities Corp. information sheets, 1994, 1600 Wilson Blvd, Arlington, VA 22209, USA.
Judith Randel and Tony German, 'The reality of aid: an independent review of international aid', ICVA, EUROSTEP and ACTIONAID, 1993.
John E Young, 'Using computers for the environment', in *State of the World, 1994* (Washington, DC, Worldwatch Institute, 1994).

0016-3287(94)00016−6

ALTERNATIVE FUNDING: LOOKING BEYOND THE NATION-STATE

Keith Bezanson and Ruben Mendez

The challenge for the UN and for all publicly funded institutions that distribute surpluses for international needs is nothing less than to devise new global mechanisms for the collection and distribution of the surplus generated in a global economy. A minimalist interpretation of when individual governments can and cannot provide public goods has exercised strong influences on perceptions as to what is appropriate at international levels and with regard to the financing of international institutions. There is a strong consensus on an important range of international social goods. Three kinds of financing alternatives should be accorded priority in policy research—charges for the use of the global commons, monetary measures, and international taxation.

Rather than trying to pump life back into the worn-out policy of year-to-year decisions by individual governments on how much to appropriate and to whom it should go, what is needed is a flow of funds for development which are generated *automatically* under *international control.* . . . The idea . . . should be treated as an idea whose time has come.[1]

The state has become too big for the small things, and too small for the big things. The small things call for delegation downwards to the local level. . . . The big things call for delegation upwards, for coordination between national policies, or transnational institutions.[2]

The future will be expensive:[3] a case for alternative funding

The nation-state everywhere faces a crisis of redefinition, a situation that will continue, at least for the foreseeable future. Capital and entire economies are

Dr Bezanson was Administrative Manager, Inter-American Development Bank (1988–91), and Canadian Ambassador to Peru and Bolivia (1985–88). He is currently President of the International Development Research Centre, PO Box 8500, Ottawa, Ontario, Canada, K1G 3H9 (Tel: +1 613 236 6163; fax: +1 613 235 6391). Ruben Mendez is a historian with UNDP, One United Nations Plaza, New York, NY 10017, USA (Tel: +1 212 906 5757; fax: +1 212 906 5190). The authors gratefully acknowledge the collaboration of Rohinton Medhora and Christopher Smart of the International Development Research Centre in the preparation of this article.

becoming increasingly borderless. Confronted with this economic globalization on the one hand, the nation-state also confronts 'globalization from below', to use Richard Falk's term. In order to meet basic economic needs, to preserve local traditions, religious and cultural life, to preserve the natural world and to struggle for human dignity, local citizens' movements and alternative institutions are springing up all over the world. Between these two tidal forces sits the nation-state, beset by demands for action, policy and finances, for the creation of public savings and the distribution of social goods.

Pity the government leaders caught in this vice. Much of the official truth that sustained and guided governments over the past half-century has collapsed and new political visions are in short supply. The most spectacular ideological shift of the past few years has been, of course, the repudiation of communism. In addition, however, the inexorable intrusions of a world economy over which national governments exercise diminishing control have drained other established political wisdoms of meaning and power. Both Keynesianism and Marxism were rooted in the idea that national economies were real and that, within the borders of a nation-state, governments could provide economic stability, development and social progress. No more.

The entire post-war international institutional system was constructed on those same fast fading wisdoms surrounding the nation-state. What this means for the United Nations system (in fact for *all* publicly funded institutions that distribute surpluses for international needs) is that new purposes must be defined and that, if those new purposes are to be met, alternative sources and mechanisms of financing must be established. This is much more than a supplementary requirement; at issue is the survival of internationalism as we have known it for much of this century.

For all the talk about rejuvenating the United Nations system on the occasion of its 50th birthday, the prospects are, in fact, not encouraging. Most attention is centred on administrative reform and modifications in the voting structure. The fact, however, is that current institutional arrangements are simply incapable of meeting the needs of a changed global order. The real challenge is nothing less than to devise new global[4] mechanisms for the collection and distribution of the surplus generated in a global economy. Failure to achieve this will, by default, cede authority to the market and the multinational corporations, many of which already manage large international economic systems. A very real prospect that must be contemplated is one where individual democratic franchise and state sovereignty become subservient to market-driven 'mercantile feudalism'.

The first quotation in this article is drawn from *The Planetary Bargain*, a publication by an eminent group of international scholars. We agree with their conclusion on the need for the funds to be generated *automatically under international control* and it is to this purpose that this short article is principally addressed. Such funds represent a necessary condition to the institutional arrangements that will be required if mercantile feudalism is to be avoided. We wish to emphasize in this regard that our concern is not with the financing of the United Nations system, *per se*. It is with the much broader issue of new financing mechanisms for new international purposes.

Indeed, in so far as the UN itself is concerned, it must be prepared to embrace far reaching reform in all aspects of its institutional arrangements as an integral part of its appeal for new sources of financing. This, broadly speaking, applies to all *status quo* international institutions seeking out new sources of revenue. New objectives (sustainable use of the environment), new definitions of leadership (local action for global results) and new forms of governance (popular participation, establishing links between communities with common interests, increased accountability of technology as a matter of public and social policy), are needed to clear the way to these new sources of financing.

The UN cannot expect enthusiastic support for its access to new sources of funding (nor of more from the conventional sources, for that matter) if it draws these into its central treasury. The UN must take note of the attempts of those progressive national governments which, in their efforts to empower their people by decentralizing decision making, or to renegotiate federal arrangements, are ready to limit their role to higher-order functions and devolve revenue collection and spending decisions to other levels and other actors. The UN can play a leadership role and will attract support if, when encouraging exploration of the new sources of funding, it makes it clear that it does not make an exclusive claim to such new revenues. On the contrary it must coordinate an arrangement designed to prevent mercantile feudalism, including the enabling of groups tasked with international mandates to gain access to new and adequate sources of finance. Peacekeeping and peacemaking, refugees and environmental protection are examples of the specialized areas that might be financed from new sources of money that are facilitated but not centralized within the UN's treasury.

The past is poor: national sources of finance are inadequate for global needs

The past half-century has led the citizens of many nation-states to expect to enjoy the consumption of public goods, typically financed by taxes and other public charges. At the national level, then, automaticism (as opposed to voluntarism) and other accepted principles of public finance became the guide to the finance and provision of many public goods.

The tendency of the past decade-and-a-half has been towards a minimalist interpretation of when individual governments can and cannot (and should and should not) provide public goods. That same minimalist interpretation has exercised strong influences on perceptions as to what is appropriate at international levels and most certainly with regard to the financing of international institutions.

Yet there is, generally speaking, a strong consensus on an important range of international social goods. Currency stability, for example, is widely seen to be an international social good. Concern is increasing over the globalization of monetary activity which has led to a situation where the volume of activity on the world currency markets exceeds the value of official foreign exchange reserves which are held to bring order to these markets. Clearly, policy coordination at the international level is the first best option to achieve currency stability. In reality, today's challenges in this regard are of a magnitude and complexity never before confronted, requiring especially strong international institutional arrangements.

The minimalist interpretation has served to increase the perception in the public's mind of large and unwieldy international bureaucracies. Whatever the defects of those bureaucracies (and they are both numerous and serious), the fact is that the size and resources of international organizations are hopelessly disproportionate to the issues with which they must deal. At a time when more peacekeeping is desired, and forays into peace*making* are being called for; at a time when stemming and reversing desertification, or in protection of the ozone layer, or a panoply of other green social goals, are thrust on the international governance system; at a time when the trends of globalization call for more international dialogue and harmonization of practices, not less; at such times, Erskine Childers reminds us, the total number of UN employees worldwide remains less than the number of civil servants employed by the city of Winnipeg, or the number of employees at Saatchi and Saatchi.

Even more spectacular tales may be told of the inadequacy of actual financial resources provided to address public good issues at the international level. This article, however, is not a plea to expand any particular international organization. Rather, the point being made in what follows is this: the finance and provision of international public goods require us to think beyond the capacity of individual national governments to deliver them, or manage their delivery. *New, innovative, stable and credible* sources of revenue and institutional arrangements are needed if the world is to come to view international public goods in the same manner that it views national public goods.

Treasure to share: international sources of finance are adequate for global needs

Future sources of financing must look beyond the nation-state to the world economy and to global resources. More than ever before, the world is replete with trans-national economic activities that depend on global resources. These activities generate increasingly vast streams of income and other benefits which do not accrue through rents or returns to the appropriate factors of production. By tapping a small part of these streams for international purposes, a more logical and efficient allocation of global income could result.

This notwithstanding, debates on this issue have tended to be characterized by high degrees of emotion, by advocacy without substance and by a lamentable absence of research and analysis. The net result is that the issue itself is becoming increasingly polarized between the 'reformers' (who argue that taxation and control on transnational economic activities are 'necessary' and 'moral') and the 'mini-malists', including an army of neoclassical economists (who argue that all intervention through tax or control would compromise economic efficiencies, distort markets and/or be simply unworkable). On both sides of the argument it is difficult to perceive anything that is not based on personal opinion, appeal to distant authority or undisguised emotion.

The task, we submit, is to move beyond the sterile debate which is occurring, to initiate serious, systematic and scholarly (the three S's) inquiry into possible alternatives. The results of such inquiry should be the subject of detailed public and international discussion.

Although there may be more, we would submit at this time that there are three kinds of financing alternatives that should be accorded priority in policy research. These are: charges for the use of the global commons, monetary measures, and international taxation. In all three cases it is imperative that the criteria for examination involve both the raising of financing for international social goods and the reduction of negative externalities (ie negative side-effects, such as pollution).

Costing the global commons

The global commons, defined as *res communis* or belonging to all humankind, may be said to include outer space including the geostationary and lower orbits, the electromagnetic spectrum, Antarctica (a disputed common) and the Southern Ocean, international air space and the other oceans (including their seabeds and subsoils). They are important international assets: for instance, the oceans are a source of living and non-living resources, a means of transport, a regulator of the weather and the world's main carbon sink. Outer space and its orbits provide the traffic lanes for geostationary and other satellites, and the lower orbits, which are being cluttered with dangerous space debris, are the gateway to our last frontier. The spectrum serves as a means of international telecommunications. Unfortunately, the commons are being misused or overused, partly because they are still perceived, erroneously, as 'free' and unlimited resources. There is a need to manage the global commons and to price and charge for their contributions to the various transnational activities that use them. A logical, efficient and socially responsible allocation of global income and resources should recognize and treat them as an important factor of production.

A system of user rights, regulations, rents and charges is one way of bringing governance to the commons and of using them to generate revenues. Preliminary studies carried out under the auspices of UNEP and the Brookings Institution and by Mendez (independently and as coordinator of UNEP teams),[5] indicate that this is a promising area to explore in the search for viable financing alternatives. Further work, however, is required, including research, the development of methodologies for global collective resources valuation, and legal policy analysis. These are necessary to assess whether any of these possibilities should be pursued and implemented over the near term and, if so, which ones.

Monetary reform

The globalization and growth of financial markets, starting in the 1970s, has led to a situation today where over US$1 trillion ($10^{12}$) worth of foreign currencies change hands each day—and to concern in several quarters, including central banks, over monetary volatility and even meltdown. This has stimulated a renewed interest in taxing foreign exchange transactions: the Tobin tax, which was first proposed in 1971 by Professor James Tobin of Yale, a Nobel memorial laureate in economics.

There are, unfortunately, formidable difficulties facing a Tobin tax. Among them are that: foreign exchange transactions are generally not registered or supervised and thus leave no paper trail; the creation of a tax regime would entail considerable administrative costs; since a universal and watertight system is improbable, money changers would easily evade the tax by moving 'offshore' to low- or zero-tax jurisdictions.

There may, however, be a viable alternative. It stems from the very fact that the present market is disorganized and consists, in actuality, of two markets: an inside interbank market where competition and the best prices prevail, and the publicly quoted market to which end-users—individuals, industrial corporations, importers and exporters—have access, but only at inflated prices and via intermediaries. The present pattern thus suffers from a market failure of incomplete information, which the banks are able to exploit with windfall profits.

The alternative, which would tap the same extensive base as the Tobin tax, would be the establishment of a foreign currency exchange. The exchange would serve the foreign currency markets as national bourses serve securities markets and, through an automated global computer network, would match buy and sell orders electronically. It would thus lower the cost to consumers of changing foreign currencies by giving them competitive prices and access to other buyers and sellers, which they now lack. It would also bring order and efficiency to the present chaotic market and, if properly designed, managed and sponsored, could generate considerable revenues from licensing and user fees from its member traders and customers. While preliminary analyses indicate that this is a viable variation on the Tobin tax, considerable research—in fact, an in-depth feasibility study—is needed to analyse the highly complex mechanics of foreign exchange transactions and technical requirements of a computerized system, to estimate costs, revenues and capital requirements, to assess the options for the organization, ownership and management of the system, and possibly to design a system, including the allocation of what could be vast revenues.

International taxation

International taxation, applied to transnational activities, is a third means of raising revenues. It is justifiable on the grounds that transnational activities use the global commons, often causing negative externalities such as environmental pollution. Such activities also benefit (without being charged) from global governance provided by the international public sector.

An obvious candidate for international taxation is world trade, in view of its large base—a volume of US$37 483 billion (as measured by imports) in 1992. There is a need, however, for careful policy research on various issues such as whether rates can be set at levels that would not inhibit trade, or what exemptions or allowances should be made for re-exports or trade-dependent countries like Singapore. Studies should be made of whether taxes should be limited to specific traded goods (and/or services) and, if so, which, or whether a tax on ocean freight would be preferable. Various legal and administrative questions should also be examined in detail.

There are other possibilities for international taxation—for correcting market failures as well as for revenues—that merit further exploration. These include: (1) activities with negative international externalities such as ocean dumping and other marine pollution, military expenditures and arms transfers; (2) the compensation of generators of positive externalities, such as the 'reverse brain drain', or the protection and enhancement by developing countries of 'global' environmental goods like tropical rain forests; and (3) other alternative measures, such as costly and marketable permits to pollute, charges for fishing rights in certain areas, surcharges on air tickets, and 'voluntary' taxes like lotteries. These are all items that should be on the agenda, but they call for careful policy research before any can be advanced to the advocacy stage.

The future can pay its way

While it is clear that there are a range of new, untapped and potentially rich sources of finance, it is equally clear that the critical factor delaying the uptake of these sources is the need for an acceptable answer to one of the key questions of economics: 'for whose benefit?'. Adam Smith's conception of self-interest has mobilized the development/exploitation of conventional sources of wealth: the unconventional sources that we have identified will be developed only when there is a strong, indeed overwhelming, conviction that they will be used in the common interest, that is, used to ensure the greatest benefit to the greatest number of people. We are only too conscious of past efforts in this direction and of the taint of any recommendation that invokes Marx. That said, we are reminded of the witticism that

'Communism, like Christianity, was a good idea that was never acted upon'. At the very least we would suggest that earlier attempts at systemic change to ensure economic justice and social harmony may be seen as false starts. Certainly, we cannot avoid the implication that only major institutional change at both the national and international levels will enable the exploitation of non-conventional sources of finance.

Although, *prima facie*, these are attractive, we repeat that research is needed if progress beyond the polemical is to be made on these matters. It is encouraging to learn that researchers and practitioners are engaging the problem from different perspectives. For example the Green Forum's 'People's Earth Fund', a major NGO approach to the issue of alternative financing; and the 'Environmental Finance Centre of the Coastal and Environmental Policy Program at the University of Maryland', which is researching creative approaches to funding environmental projects and treating finance as part of the strategic management process.

The search for alternative/innovative sources of finance must not be reduced to 'slogans' to stimulate UN reform. They should be approached as innovative ideas, fresh thinking—embryonic rational constructs that, in this time of uncertainty and crisis, deserve serious intellectual consideration, free of ideological bias and appropriation by self-interest.

We associate ourselves with those in the international community who recognize that current efforts to address critical areas of common concern are underfunded. Failure to resolve this in the next decade conjures the spectre of a disaster that will cause unprecedented dysfunction for the citizens of rich and poor states alike. For this reason, proposals for new sources of international finance to deal with global problems merit serious and urgent attention. And there is another reason: they offer hope for a renewal of spirit and optimism in the face of an increasing retreat into despair over the *status quo* in international affairs.

Notes and references

1. From *The Planetary Bargain*, cited in Harlan Cleveland, *Birth of a New World* (San Francisco, CA, Jossey-Bass, 1993).
2. Paul Streeten, quoted in Erskine Childers and Brian Urqhart, 'Renewing the United Nations', *Development Dialogue*, (1), 1994.
3. UNCED carries a price tag of $562 billion per year of which $142 billion are needed as concessional financing for developing countries. Peacekeeping has suffered from consistently late payments; 1994 budgets should be $3.3 billion and should grow steadily. One preliminary study (a personal communication to the authors) puts the cost of UN standing army at $50 billion per year.
4. *Global* rather than *international* is used here to suggest a future of options beyond the accepted interactions of nations. It invites participation from those who will make their contributions less because of allegiances based on citizenship and more because of their concern for and expert knowledge of the global problems that will only be resolved through cooperation across national frontiers.
5. For instance see UNEP, *Additional Measures and Means of Financing for the Implementation of the Plan of Action to Combat Desertification* (UNEP/GC. Add 1, 4 April 1978); and *Study on Financing the United Nations Plan of Action to Combat Desertification* (A/35/396, 17 September 1980); also R P Mendez, *International Public Finance: A New Perspective on Global Relations* (New York, Oxford University Press, 1992); and *The Provision and Financing of Universal Public Goods* (London, London School of Economics, 1993).

REPORTS

Innovative resource management for social development

In preparation for the World Summit for Social Development in March 1995, an International Round Table on Innovative Resource Management for Social Development was held in Berlin in June 1994. The findings and recommendations reported here were formulated by the participants as a contribution to the preparatory process for the Social Summit.

The post-Cold-War world is confronted with menacing challenges to peace and stability. The narrow concept of security in purely military terms is being replaced by the more comprehensive concept of human security in which social dimensions assume an important place. Poverty—a problem which has long blighted humankind—and social disintegration are now critical sources of conflict, instability and threats to peace. Recognizing this new constellation, the United Nations General Assembly is convening the World Summit for Social Development in March 1995 in Copenhagen, Denmark, in order to address possibilities for poverty reduction, the expansion of productive employment, and the enhancement of social integration.

The International Round Table was convened to review the scope for innovative resource management in the context of social development—rather than the social issues as such—in order to formulate suggestions for consideration by both the World Summit and its Preparatory Committee. It was attended by 37 participants, drawn from around the world and from a

The final report of the Round Table is published by the Development Policy Forum of the German Foundation for International Development.

broad range of government, international and bilateral agencies, non-governmental organizations (NGOs) and research institutions.

Under the chairman of the Development Policy Forum, Ingar Brüggemann, the Berlin meeting opened with addresses by the DSE Director-General, Heinz Bühler, the representative of the Federal Minister for Economic Cooperation and Development, Deputy Director-General Michael Bohnet, the representative of the Federal Foreign Minister, Minister Counsellor Wolfgang Gerz, and the representative of the Minister of Labour and Social Affairs, Rainer Pritzer. Introductory speeches were made by Cristián Maquieira, representing the Chilean Ambassador to the United Nations, Juan Somavia, Chairman of the Preparatory Committee for the Summit, and by Andrzej Krassowski, Assistant Director, UN Department for Policy Coordination and Social Development and Secretariat of the World Summit for Social Development.

All presentations emphasized the need to strive for a greater equilibrium between national as well as international measures geared towards enhancing economic and social development, in order to safeguard the needs and social security of all people, especially the poor.

The discussions which followed dealt with four key issues:

(1) mobilizing private initiative;
(2) improving efficiency and effectiveness of spending on social development;
(3) innovative sources of financing for social development;
(4) optimizing the use of national and external assistance resources.

The quest for social development

The quest for social development has emerged as one of the major tasks for governments in industrialized and developing countries alike. Persistent levels of high unemployment and underemployment worldwide, as well as deepening poverty in the developing world, graphically define the daunting dimensions of the problems at hand.

Social development is a complex process with many facets. It challenges all countries in different ways. The conventional dichotomy between social development and economic development is no longer useful in charting appropriate development strategies at national and international levels. Rather, both are integral parts of overall development that is sustainable. Furthermore, social development itself includes human resources and political emancipation which ensure fundamental human rights, such as food, health, housing, education, training, work and relevant information, as well as institutional development. In this broader sense, social and economic development must be pursued in tandem and in mutually supportive roles.

Although economic performance has long been regarded as the authentic indicator of a society's progress, it is now recognized that economic growth can no longer be the sole yardstick of its well-being. Rather, it must be balanced by and integrated with social development goals. Social stability is the bedrock for sustainable economic growth.

Towards a holistic approach

Effective action calls for a holistic approach with the principal responsibility for adopting and implementing appropriate and effective social policies resting with each country, and therein with the local communities, families and people. Yet, in an interdependent world, international cooperation has a crucial contribution to make in addressing and alleviating these complex problems. To be sure, all programmes must be in harmony with the culture and traditions of the people for whom they are designed.

The achievement of meaningful social development rests on a coordinated partnership between government, the private sector and civil society, involving:

- the optimum use and efficient management of existing resources by all involved;
- the contributions of central and other layers of government;
- the mobilization of private initiative in both the formal and informal sectors (domestic resource mobilization);
- the mobilization of citizens and community initiatives to address social problems of concern to them;
- the contribution by multilateral organizations; and
- innovative financing modalities to tap additional financial resources required to meet global needs.

Throughout the Round Table the consensus was that the most outstanding resource of any society is its people. Not only are they the beneficiaries of the process of social development, but they must also be the principal actors in achieving it. To unleash the creative potential and energy of the people, and especially the poor, there must be participatory development, empowerment, and a fostering of a sense of ownership in the social, economic and political development processes. To facilitate these ends several prerequisites were identified:

- political commitment to and unequivocal leadership at the highest levels and throughout the government structure towards agreed social development objectives;
- the systematic and organized devolution of decision making to and the implementation of policies and projects at the local and community levels; this will lead to social mobilization, foster participation, stimulate self-help and engender community cooperation and voluntary action; changes in the structure and mechanisms of governments as well as in

the approaches and training of bureaucrats must underpin these processes;

- revitalization of traditional values of community support and welfare;
- the encouragement of women's organizations, trade unions, farmers' associations and other interest groups through the provision of an appropriate legal framework and the taking of other steps to facilitate the interaction of civil society;
- the utilization and strengthening of self-employment, small businesses and local initiatives;
- the removal of obstacles to the creation of productive and remunerative jobs at the community and local levels and the provision of appropriate incentives; and
- an emphasis on catalytic strategies that stimulate greater societal awareness and involvement in social development processes.

Mobilizing private initiative

In the quest to alleviate the root problems of extreme poverty, the Round Table paid particular attention to unconventional approaches for income generation and asset building. It emphasized that low-income, self-employed and small-scale producers all need increased access to finance and credit, information and markets. Investment in activities of low-income women has proved to be particularly effective, as they have demonstrated to be excellent borrowers and sound credit risks. Thus, the Social Summit should also unambiguously acknowledge the role of women as key agents of economic and social development, and call for the removal of all legal and other barriers to their full economic participation and for their enhanced access to financial services.

The banking system has a responsibility to lend to low-income entrepreneurs and producers among the poor. This can be facilitated by creating links between the formal and the informal sectors. Such lending can be sustainable and profitable when lenders observe certain standards, including:

- providing quick and convenient access to small, short-term loans;
- being available in low-income areas;
- offering loans at unsubsidized rates;
- applying strict repayment criteria;

- minimizing the administrative costs of small loans;
- instilling confidence and mutual accountability;
- stimulating savings by facilitating small deposits, convenient collection, safety and ready access to funds for a significant number of customers.

A series of such financial intermediaries should be encouraged to enter the small and micro-enterprise financial market, including business, NGOs, cooperatives, credit unions and groups (including women's groups) at the local level, with a view to acting as direct lenders, savings mobilizers and providers of business development services. These financial intermediaries must strive to expand their own capacity quickly in order to meet the large numbers of low-income entrepreneurs. They should be supported through appropriate legislation and insurance, and by disseminating success stories. Private and public sector development banks should assume a supportive role by providing start-up money, refinance, innovative financial instruments and finance for capacity building.

In all countries, the creation of an enabling environment of appropriate laws; sound macroeconomic and fiscal policies; a regulatory framework for the functioning of a flexible and efficient labour market; appropriate administrative structures and workable institutions pursuing sustainable development; and the strengthening of civil society—all are indispensable for securing meaningful and enduring results. Governments should play a lead role in setting policies and funding activities. National independent and voluntary funding institutions and, in developing countries multilateral and bilateral funding organizations, enter the equation.

Human capital formation and investment in people are a key determinant in achieving socially sustainable economic growth. Investments in health, nutrition, education, training and family planning yield high social and economic returns. An efficient pattern of investment in people, especially when linked to the needs of the labour market, can lead to a virtuous circle of economic growth and increasing levels of human welfare, accompanied by major progress in poverty reduction and a narrowing of levels of income inequality.

Optimizing available resources—
a challenge to all actors

Given the scarcity of public and private funds, and taking into account the vast unmet basic needs, efficient and innovative resource management and resource use become imperative. In that regard, some approaches were discussed:

- a more rational allocation and management of resources with a view to realizing the highest possible sustainable social returns;
- the protection of development funding priorities, especially in the context of structural adjustment programmes;
- the defining of a suitable mix of the respective roles of the public, the private and the voluntary sectors;
- better coordination among government agencies, and also by and between the United Nations system, active in the social development field;
- private-sector involvement in training and retraining with a view to raising productivity and adjusting to changing economic conditions;
- the delivery by the private and non-governmental sectors of certain government-financed social services, as well as non-governmental financing of social services;
- improved information flows to maximize cross-fertilization of ideas and experience;
- the recovery of costs for services, especially where this would enhance equity;
- the reduction and containment of mismanaged projects and corruption;
- more effective coordination of all external assistance flows at the national level; and
- regular evaluation and identification of indicators of effectiveness and the impact of particular programmes.

In particular, there will be clear resource gains as a result of introducing national systems of accountability and transparency which succeed in lowering corruption at all government levels, and particularly in public procurement.

To ensure that public expenditures are focused to the maximum on social development policies and programmes, governments should review existing strategies and budgets and reorder priorities accordingly.

In that context, military expenditures should be reduced to the greatest extent possible—while making maximum use of the potential of the military in the national development process.

In the context of ensuring the flow of resources to social development, the suggestion was discussed that, on average, 20% of national budgets and of official international assistance flows should be devoted to priority programmes (the 20:20 compact[1]). While it was recognized that such a compact might assist in the mobilizing of resources, especially in countries allocating at present funds below that level, this approach has its limitations by focusing on expenditure levels and inputs rather than on outcomes, and on quantity rather than on quality. It was felt that this suggestion would require much deeper examination.

In order to inform national planning and to facilitate international comparison and action, agreement should be sought on all the elements included in the concept of 'social development'. Thereafter, countries should compile and publish relevant statistics regularly.

Tapping innovative sources of financing

Given the immense unmet needs and the scarcity of existing resources, innovative new sources of finance need to be identified and tapped. The tax on spot transactions in international currency markets proposed by Nobel Laureate Professor James Tobin,[2] which had the potential to raise very large sums, was discussed. The estimated amount that would accrue would be huge by developing country standards. Other ideas were also referred to, such as levies on international travel, arms sales, use of satellite time and tradeable pollution permits. The Round Table recommends that, in order to promote an informed debate, an independent group of internationally recognized financial experts be requested to prepare an authoritative analysis of the feasibility and implications of the various proposals presently under discussion and that their conclusions be made available in advance of the Copenhagen Summit.

Bilateral and multilateral donors are already committing an increasing proportion of their portfolios to social development. This trend should be reinforced by pursuing already agreed global targets such as health and education for all by the year 2000. Future replenishment negotiations for IDA and IFAD and the regional development banks should explicitly take into account the need for an increase in resources at concessional terms, especially for social development in low-income countries. Furthermore, expanded resources should be made available by industrialized countries in their bilateral assistance programmes and to multilateral development and financial organizations operating on a grant basis. Multilateral organizations act as catalysts and agents of implementation for social development programmes.

Debt relief is another means of creating financial breathing space for developing countries and freeing scarce resources for social development. The Round Table urges the full implementation of agreements already reached with respect to debt cancellation and debt relief, especially for the poorest countries.

However, the Round Table noted that liberalized and undistorted access of products from developing countries to international markets, especially to those of industrialized countries, might yield significantly higher financial benefits than existing flows of official development assistance, or the amounts likely to be realized as a result of all the measures discussed above. A progressive reduction in presently indefensible levels of subsidies by industrialized countries, especially in agriculture, would be a significant step in this direction.

Further arrangements for and follow-up to the World Summit for Social Development

With regard to NGOs, the Round Table also suggests to the Preparatory Committee for the Social Summit that it:

- urge countries to include representatives of NGOs in their delegations to the Summit;
- envisage an opportunity for NGO representatives to address the assembled leaders at a formal meeting of the Summit;
- recommend that, in any follow-up activity and mechanism established in the wake of the Summit, representatives of NGOs be included as an integral part;
- suggest that, as a follow-up to Copenhagen, hearings should be organized by the UN on a biennial or triennial basis whereby NGOs can present their views as to progress—or lack thereof—achieved.

As a follow-up to the Summit, the Preparatory Committee should include in the draft documents for the Summit the call for regular national progress reports about the state of social development, which should be complemented by assessments from non-state actors and reviewed by internationally appointed panels of experts.

Participants

Efried Adam (Friedrich Ebert-Stiftung, Germany); Nancy Barry (Women's World Banking, USA); Asoke Basak (Government of Maharashtra, India); Rattan Bhatia (IMF, USA); Michel Bohnet (Federal Ministry for Economic Cooperation and Development, Germany); Ingar Brüggemann (German Foundation for International Development (DSE), Germany); Barbara Bruns (World Bank, USA); Heinz Bühler (DSE, Germany); Dieter Danckwortt (German NGO Coordinating Committee for the Social Summit, Germany); Jeffrey W Dellimore (Caribbean Development Bank, Barbados); Lual Deng (African Development Bank, Côte d'Ivoire); Maymouna Diop (Senegalese Mission to the UN, USA); Peter Eigen (Transparency International, Germany); David Felix (Washington University, USA); Erich T Geis (Kreditanstalt für Wiederaufbau, Germany); Wolfgang Gerz (Federal Foreign Office, Germany); Hans Gsänger (German Development Institute, Germany); Robert van Harten (International Commission on Peace and Food, The Netherlands); Garry L Jacobs (International Commission on Peace and Food, USA); Inge Kaul (UNDP, USA); Pamidi Kotaiah (National Bank for Agriculture and Rural Development, India); Andrzej Krassowski (Division for Social Policy and Development, UN, USA); Dietrich Kurth (Federal Ministry of Economics, Germany); Götz Link (DSE, Germany); Johannes F Linn (World Bank, USA); Cristián Maquieira (Chilean Mission to the UN, USA); Ronald Meyer (Federal Ministry for Economic Cooperation and Development, Germany); Hans d'Orville (InterAction Council, USA); Krishnakumar Panday (National Planning Commission, Nepal); Jeremy Pope (Transparency International, Germany); Rainer Pritzer (Federal Ministry of

Labour and Social Affairs, Germany); Gonzalo Rivas (Chilean Mission to the UN, USA); Bruce Schearer (The Synergos Institute, USA); Bernd Schubert (Center for Advanced Training in Agricultural Development, Germany); Christoph Serries (Universität Göttingen, Germany); Andras Uthoff (Economic Commission for Latin America and the Caribbean, Chile); Kasba Venugopal (Prime Minister's Office, India).

Notes and references

1. *Human Development Report 1994* (New York, UNDP, 1994), pages 7 and 77–78.
2. *Ibid*, page 70.

Reforming the UN: the view of the American people

Alan F Kay

It may come as a surprise that surveys of the US people on the subject of the UN and global issues show that the US government policy of ignoring major UN reform is at odds with strong preferences by the American people for many major UN reforms. Illustrating both ignorance and some surprising discretion, it is also true that the US public opposes few of the many reforms tested. The Americans Talk Issues Foundation (ATI) has conducted six opinion surveys of US people on the UN and global issues in the past three years, the highlights of the latest of which are reported here.

The United Nations (UN) is not ready or able to handle many of the jobs the world wants to drop in its lap, either in peacekeeping (and making) or in support of global sustainable development, and member-states are not eager to reform the UN so that it can.[1] Handling these jobs successfully depends on resolving or sidestepping many thorny economic, social, political, military, financial, scientific, environmental, regional, ethnic, gender, health and educational issues. Whether the world will undertake any process that could restructure, reform, fund and empower the United Nations so that it *could* handle these issues well enough to do what the world

wants, depends critically on the support of world public opinion. Daunting as this task of UN reform is, the world has to undertake it, for after 50 years, with all of its weaknesses the UN has emerged for the foreseeable future as the only credible global authority under whose auspices these problems may be sensibly addressed.

The USA, as the world's leading economic and military power, could play a positive, lead role in envisioning, calling for, and initiating this necessary process of UN reform. The USA has endorsed and paid lip-service to 'multilateralism' and, starting with the Gulf War, the USA routinely seeks the UN umbrella and as much international support as possible for interventions that it supports. It is hard to imagine any engagement of its military (even one most logically suited for unilateralism, namely defending against an

The author may be contacted at 10 Carrera Street, St Augustine, FL 32084, USA (Tel: +1 904 826 0984; fax: +1 904 826 4194).

unlikely, direct attack on the USA itself) where UN endorsement and support would not be welcomed by the USA. Nevertheless the USA directs most of its 'external' funding into *unilateral* approaches and activities (for example, its entire huge military budget has no UN support item) and so far refuses to call for, or even envision, the necessary UN reform. Common to most governments and a vestige of an earlier era,[2] this attitude of the US government discourages much of the world which wants to move ahead to tackle the major global issues.

Accordingly, it may come as a surprise that six opinion surveys of national samples of the US *people* on the subject of the UN and global issues, conducted by the Americans Talk Issues Foundation in the past three years,[3] show that the US government policy of ignoring major UN reform is at odds with strong preferences by the US *people* for many major UN reforms. Illustrating both ignorance and some surprising discretion, it is also true that the US public opposes few of the many UN reforms tested.

We have space here for only some of the highlights from the most recent survey.[4] Approval ratings are shown here.

Even if UN restructuring or charter amendments were required, virtually all Americans favour US participation in a world conference to make the United Nations more effective in the area of

- global security—92% favour;
- global environmental issues—93% favour;
- helping to shift economies to sustainable development that uses resources less wastefully and does not foreclose continuing development for future generations—84% favour.

The US public does not approve of any increase in dues or assessments or permitting the UN to borrow against future earnings. However, Americans are ready to support some new funding approaches meeting these criteria: (a) be appropriate charges on international activities or services related to the UN's functions; (b) encourage desirable, or discourage undesirable, international activities (the 'sin tax' effect); and (c) be designed to be readily collectable (to minimize contention, litigation, or the need for a large bureaucracy for administration/enforcement). For the most part collection would be by member-states with strict authorization limits on any UN expenditures.

Promising approaches, with the percentage of Americans in favour shown, include:

- a tax of 1% on international arms sales and transfers (67%);
- a tax of 0.5% on international currency and currency derivative trades (Tobin tax, approved by 69%);
- pollution taxes, such as ocean dumping of toxic waste (82%) or carbon combustion emissions (79%).
- a novel insurance proposal, known as UNSIA, that contractually guarantees UN peacekeeping support to nations which agree to pay an annual premium for a defined degree of support with security risk assessment performed by insurance industry, military and financial professionals (62%).

A 77% majority favour the establishment of a Development Security Council with authority on social policy concerns and sustainable economic development, to coordinate all UN efforts and agencies dealing with health, education, human rights, employment, humanitarian aid and environment. A proposal to create a complementary organization, a new UN 'Parliament' with representatives elected directly by people rather than appointed by governments, is favoured by a plurality of 48% to 44%.

In regard to the creation of a new UN agency for advancing the education and status of women, 31% are in favour v 22% who feel that the additional bureaucracy makes this not worth doing and 43% who opt for the middle ground of strengthening UNIFEM, the UN's principal office dealing with women's issues and thus are in favour of both advancing the status of women and to some degree limiting the growth of bureaucracy.

How do the people of other nations see these questions? Although there is as yet no global survey research data directly comparable to the ATI US data, political surveys in many other countries over the years suggest that findings in other countries, at least the major industrial countries, might not be much different. As a consequence, dissemination of the results of the ATI US surveys should encourage complementary surveys of global public opinion on the readiness of other peoples of the world to undertake the tasks of major reform. Results of such surveys, carefully done, could be of enormous significance.

Notes and references

1. Harlan Cleveland, *Birth of a New World* (San Francisco, CA, Jossey-Bass Publishers, 1993).
2. The 'pre-1989' era of the Cold War.
3. ATI No 15, April 1991, *The New World Order—What the Peace Should Be*; ATI No 16, August 1991, *The Emerging World Order*; ATI No 17, March 1992, *Perceptions of Globalization, World Structures, and Security*; ATI No 21, May 1993, *Global Uncertainties*; ATI No 23, April 1993, *Structures for Global governance*; ATI No 25, July 1994, *The UN at Fifty—Mandate from the American People.*
4. *A word about methodology.* The Americans Talk Issues Foundation (ATI), does in-depth research on what the American people want for policy and legislation on major national issues. To design and conduct its surveys, ATI uses small balanced teams of issue and polling experts who make sure that both the questions and the analysis are fair and balanced and, within the limits of telephone interviewing, provide accurate contextual and factual information to overcome the public's lack of knowledge and attention to issues. The process allows the American people to exercise judgment on which policy choices they most prefer from among a wide menu of alternatives the expert teams cull from decision makers, policy analysts, academe, and grassroots sources. Such surveys are called educational or deliberative surveys and are quite different from the more familiar public or news media polls. The survey reported here (ATI No 25) was conducted of a random national sample of 1000+ adults by telephone 18–29 June 1994, with full sample probable sampling error of less than 3.2%. The survey and question design were supervised by Stanley B Greenberg of Greenberg Research Inc, of Washington, DC, and approved by Frederick T Steeper, of Market Strategies Inc, Southfield, MI. Input also came from Hazel Henderson, former Advisory Council Member of the US Office of Technology Assessment; Stephen Kull, University of Maryland; the Center for Defense Information; and from our three co-sponsors—the Society for International Development, the Earth Council, and Global Education Associates.

From Rio to Copenhagen

Maurice F Strong

The Earth Summit in Rio de Janeiro in 1992 made it clear that civilization has reached a crucial turning point. The economic model that has produced unprecedented wealth and power for the privileged minority of the world's people has given rise to risks and imbalances which threaten the future of the entire human community—rich and poor alike. It is no longer a model for progress; it is a recipe for disparity, division and disaster.

Agenda 21, the Earth Summit's action programme for implementing the principles agreed at the highest political level, provides the blueprint from which can be fashioned a new economic model. But much work remains to be done to build a new structure that will provide the world and its people with a more secure, more equitable and more sustainable future.

The United Nations World Conference

The author was Chairman of the Earth Summit, and is currently Chairman of Ontario Hydro, 700 University Avenue, Toronto, Ontario, Canada (Tel: +1 416 592 2130; fax: +1 416 971 3691).

for Social Development represents another important building stone in this new international structure. It is fitting that this 'Social Summit' should be held at this time, almost 50 years after the founders of the United Nations wrote the Charter in San Francisco. It is also worth recalling that the Charter aimed at the 'achievement of international cooperation in solving international problems of an economic, social, cultural or humanitarian character and in promoting and encouraging respect for human rights and for fundamental freedoms'.

It would be grossly unfair to blame the United Nations for the fact that these problems have most manifestly not been solved. But the fact remains that they have not been solved; indeed, economic and social disparities have deepened. And the UN founders' dreams of a more equitable distribution of the world's bounties and economic progress remain largely unrealized.

This is not the only early UN vision that disappointingly and dangerously remains unfulfilled. The Charter's most important objective—eliminating the 'scourge of war'—is also mocked by the past half-century of experience and the continuing regional conflicts which threaten global security.

Evidence prepared for the Earth Summit made it clear that there is an inextricable link among these issues—that a failure to address and reduce the dichotomy between the haves and the have-nots, coupled with a continued reliance on outmoded and wasteful economic theories of growth, is the surest way to perpetuate and exacerbate insecurity and strife.

The Earth Summit illuminated the inescapable fact that there can be no true social progress without economic development. But experience demonstrates that economic growth that deepens economic and social disparities, and undermines the natural capital on which future development depends, is not sustainable. It cannot be development in the traditional mode. If the newly industrializing countries follow that path, they will inevitably bring pressures on the Earth's resources and life-support systems to threshold levels beyond which all life will be imperilled. Yet their right to grow, and to meet the reasonable aspirations of their citizens cannot be denied. Nor should they be constrained by conditions and limitations imposed by those who were primarily responsible for creating the crisis.

The clearest message from the Earth Summit was that the only viable answer to the dilemma of economic and social inequity is to effect a global transition to a new development pathway that is sustainable in environmental and human, as well as economic, terms. This can only be brought about through a new global alliance embracing rich and poor, worker and employer, North, South, East and West, based on fundamental changes in economic behaviour and relationships.

The rich have a primary responsibility to lead the process of change that this demands. They must change their wasteful and environmentally destructive patterns of production and consumption, and move to an ecologically sound development model that will leave 'space' for developing countries to grow. And they must support the developing countries in their transition to their own models of sustainable development—through resource and technology transfers, through worker training, and through equitable trade policies.

There is a direct relationship between environment and the poverty issues which the 'Social Summit' will be addressing. Workers in a polluting factory in the developing world and farmers cutting down trees for firewood are innocent partners in the processes of environmental destruction which are undermining their own future and contributing to increased global risks. They are caught in a vicious circle in which today's needs for survival force them into actions that threaten the basis for tomorrow's existence.

For many of these people, the only resort is to move to the nearest town or city. They are currently doing this at the rate of about 60 million per year—a rate that is without precedent in the experience of the more industrialized countries. As Agenda 21 observed, 'This has put enormous pressure on urban infrastructures already under serious stress and unable to meet the needs of the existing inhabitants. Overcrowding, inadequate housing, inadequate access to clean water and sanitation, growing amounts of uncollected waste and deteriorating air quality are already serious problems in these cities'.

These problems cannot be resolved without financial resources. But financial resources continue to be difficult to come by and, in any event, will not in themselves be sufficient to enable the countries of the developing world to make the transition to sustainability. The answer surely lies in devising much more effective means of mobilizing the human resources of developing countries in the planning, development and management of their own economies. This will require new institutional mechanisms and programmes to enable people to acquire the skills needed at various levels to build sustainable communities and to give these people access to the information and the capabil-ities required to play an active role in the process of building a sustainable basis for their development.

I would submit that Agenda 21 provides the ideal framework for this. Leadership from the highest political levels is essential. And summit meetings such as Rio and the forthcoming World Conference for Social Development provide the fora for the required expressions of political endorsement. But broad participation of people is equally indispensable to achieve the vital consensus and grass-roots activities required for effective action on alleviating poverty, expanding productive employment and enhancing social integration.

Rethinking Bretton Woods

Jo Marie Griesgraber

Genuine development is now commonly viewed as a multidimensional, people-centred process wherein decision making is guided by the principles of participation, transparency, accountability and subsidiarity. By these criteria, the Bretton Woods institutions (BWIs), created 50 years ago, are in need of significant reform. Change must encompass the BWIs' own rules and policies as well as their relationships and responsibilities to the broader international community, from the immediate subjects of BWI projects to the United Nations and its specialized agencies. The practical segregation of the BWIs from the UN should be recognized as a hindrance to development, and governments and NGOs should promote their improved coordination.

The original premise for the Rethinking Bretton Woods project derived from the limitations of working on the debt problems

Dr Griesgraber is Project Director for 'Rethinking Bretton Woods' at the Center of Concern, where she has worked on issues related to Third World Debt and global economic justice since 1989. She may be contacted at the Center of Concern, 3700 13th Street, NW, Washington, DC 20017, USA (Tel: +1 202 635 2757; fax: +1 202 832 9494).

of countries in crisis, and from the vision offered especially in 'American economic policy in the antemillenial era', *World Policy Journal*, by Walter Russell Mead; *Human Development Report 1992*, by the UN Development Programme; and in *The Money Mandarins* by Howard Wachtel. The project proposed looking at the whole global economy, and all the significant actors, as they interact in a single, closed global system.

Project co-sponsors convened a conference in Washington, DC, 12–17 June 1994, to explore a broad range of proposals for achieving more equitable, sustainable and participatory development.[1] Participants came from 27 countries in Africa, Asia, Australasia, Europe, and North and South America, and included economists, historians, sociologists, lawyers, businesspersons, political scientists, theologians and representatives of the Bretton Woods institutions (BWIs).[2] The observations, judgments, and recommendations in the conference report reflect profound, joint consideration, and agreement shared in varying degrees by conference Working Groups and highlight many of their proposals.[3]

A core conclusion was the shared vision of development as a multidimensional, people-centred process. Decision making within this process must be guided by the principles of participation, transparency, accountability and subsidiarity. The principle of subsidiarity asserts that local problems should be resolved on the local level, national problems on the national level, and only international problems on the international level. Measured against this vision of development, current processes and policies were found wanting: in particular, structural adjustment programmes were criticized as being ineffective, inequitable, and adopted in an unfair manner.

The new vision of development served as the foundation for proposals to improve the performance of the BWIs—the World Bank, the International Monetary Fund (IMF), and the soon-to-be-established World Trade Organization (WTO)—now and in the longer term. The recommendations also challenge all actors, governments, NGOs, and intergovernmental organizations to assume their appropriate role in development.

Short-term recommendations would implement the principles of participation, transparency and accountability among all actors engaged in the development process. For example, national parliaments, acting singly and in interparliamentary fora, are encouraged to scrutinize the activities of the BWIs in implementing quality development, especially with and for the poorest people.

To begin to address the uneven distribution of power within the BWIs, the Report calls on the IMF to revert to the pattern of vote distribution that existed at the opening of the Fund when base votes (250 per country), distributed equally to each country, represented 12.5% of the total votes. Today, the base votes represent only 3% of the total.

Steps that governments can take immediately include implementing the UN's 20–20 proposal and establishing an IMF facility for fast-disbursing, low-conditionality loans to help countries counter speculative attacks against their currencies. The Report also recommends that the IMF re-create the Committee of 20 to review the state of the international economy in general and the international monetary system in particular. NGOs should establish a Shadow Committee of 20 to study the same issues and to monitor the official committee. If re-established in a timely manner, the Committee of 20 could provide global perspectives to the G-7's proposed review of the world's financial institutions at their July 1995 meeting in Halifax, Canada.

In its longer-term proposals, the Report affirms and builds on Agenda 21 endorsed at the 1992 UN Conference on the Environment and Development in Rio de Janeiro and calls for changes in Northern lifestyles. In this timeframe, the interests of the industrialized North and the developing South are very similar: productive growth that provides employment, distributes wealth and meets basic needs; fair rules of trade and a stable international monetary system; the protection of the environment with its biodiversity, reclaiming what is polluted, and reducing harmful contaminants; and respect for the rule of law.

Among the longer-term recommendations are calls for more equitable trade arrangements; more development funds from more diverse and secure funding sources; a more orderly international monetary system, effected through a global reference currency, regulation of speculative capital, and regulation of transnational corporations. Symmetry is called for in the execution of BWI policies (eg trade surplus countries should recycle surpluses to benefit the global economy). A comprehensive approach to the problems of severely indebted countries is proposed, including a complete overhaul of structural adjustment programmes. The recommendations are offered in the conviction that their implementation would promote the common good of people in the North and South alike.

The BWIs and the United Nations

The remainder of this report examines those recommendations that are particularly relevant to the relationship between the BWIs and the United Nations. To understand the particular power and poignancy of this relationship, and hence the context for these recommendations, it is useful to understand the evolution of relations between the BWIs and the UN—from dream, through legal fiction, to actual segregation and, most recently, to hope.

The dream

As World War II was drawing to a close, the allied leaders envisioned a system of global institutions capable of resolving underlying problems while maintaining open communication among nations to avoid another world war. The system envisaged had four pillars—the United Nations, the World Bank, the International Monetary Fund (IMF), and the International Trade Organization (ITO).[4] The United Nations Charter stipulated that all intergovernmental organizations would be affiliated with and incorporated into the UN system.

The division of labour intended in the UN Charter with regard to economic development was that the UN Economic and Social Committee (ECOSOC) would be the coordinating body; as UN agencies, the Fund would monitor exchange rates and would assist countries with short-term balance-of-payments problems, while the Bank would assist with reconstruction of Europe and, as an afterthought, with development in the poorer countries (the end of colonialism was not foreseen). The Bank would also leverage private capital for reconstruction and development.

Legal relations

Formally, the Bank and the Fund are UN agencies. However, within the UN system, they have unique relationships governed by recognition agreements, one each for the Bank and the Fund. These agreements recognize the 'independence' of the Bank

and the Fund, but require them to 'consider' UN decisions and recommendations.[5] The Bank and Fund are further required to give 'due consideration' to requests from the United Nations to place items on the agenda of the annual meeting of the Bank and Fund Board of Governors.[6] The parties to these agreements agree 'to the fullest extent practicable' to exchange information, special reports and publications,[7] while reserving the right to withhold—at each party's discretion—material that should remain confidential.[8] Each year the Bank and the Fund are to submit a Report on their activities to ECOSOC.

The practice: segregation

In practice, the Bank and the Fund have functioned as though unrelated to the UN system.[9] The annual report submitted to ECOSOC is a *pro forma* gesture. The Secretary General is no longer even invited to the World Bank/IMF annual meetings. The Bank and the Fund have acted totally independent of the UN and its specialized agencies. As the Bank's agenda has broadened to include issues such as the environment and women, the Bank has tended to develop in-house experts, rather than rely on the UN's specialized agencies. Occasionally, the Bank and Fund have recognized the expertise of certain specialized agencies: the World Bank consults with the World Health Organization (WHO) on health; and UNICEF's *Adjustment with a Human Face* influenced changes in the IMF's conditionality package.[10]

This divorce between the BWIs and the UN, despite their common membership of nation-states, relates to their different bases of representation. Within the UN the one-country-one-vote principle is enshrined, especially in the General Assembly (GA), making the GA a preferred locus for the weaker countries to raise their complaints with the powerful, and where the powerful (particularly the USA) are in the awkward position of currying votes from the weak, the needy, and often the unsavoury. In the political-military realm, the *status quo* powers have preferred the smaller forum of the UN Security Council; and in economic affairs, the *status quo* powers prefer the more secluded quarters of the Bank and the Fund—and even more so, those of the G-7. The *realpolitik* of power prefers a less public *modus operandi*—business can be done more expeditiously, messages conveyed more clearly. The Bank and the Fund have clearly been agents for accomplishing the foreign economic policies of their major shareholders.

The hope

The change in dynamics comes because many major powers also happen to be formal democracies, and some of their own people and legislators are insisting on greater transparency, accountability and participation on the part of the BWIs, aiming to transform those institutions into genuine instruments of development. It is in this current context of hope, as well as the history of visionaries and crass *realpolitik*, that the recommendations from 'Rethinking Bretton Woods' should be reviewed.

The BWIs and the UN

Three recommendations have direct bearing on the basic relationship between the BWIs and the United Nations. The first addresses the fact that the Bank and the Fund allegedly are bound only by their own articles of agreement, and they alone are authorized to interpret whether they are in compliance. This would seem to set them apart from international law. The Report therefore recommends that:

● Management of the Bank and Fund should explain publicly their interpretation of international law applicable to their programmes, as well as its operational significance. These explanations should include their interpretations of their recognition agreements with the United Nations, of their own articles of agreement, and of their responsibilities with regard to helping their member-states comply with their own treaty and UN Charter obligations. They should be willing to entertain well founded alternative interpretations of these matters.

The second recommendation addresses a country's need to balance its responsibilities to comply with financial agreements it has with the Bank and the Fund, and with other international legal obligations, including UN agreements, such as the Universal Declaration of Human Rights and UNCED's Agenda 21, as well as to meet the

basic needs of its citizens. Further, a government is obligated to handle its responsibilities in a manner that respects human rights and is environmentally sustainable. Therefore:

● The BWIs need to coordinate with the borrowing countries to ensure that implementation of these agreements is consistent with countries' other international legal obligations.

The third recommendation relevant to the fundamental relationships between the BWIs and the UN speaks to the BWI's responsibility to be accountable to ECOSOC. This reporting relationship could provide a forum for airing grievances and working towards common solutions to problems. Therefore:

● The Bank and the Fund, their Boards of Governors, the IMF's Interim Committee, and the joint Development Committee, should submit detailed public reports to ECOSOC and make spokespersons available for public questioning by representatives of ECOSOC and, when requested, by the UN General Assembly.

NGOs and the BWIs

The post-World-War-II institutional system recognized only nation-states. Since that time other major actors have appeared on the global stage, and the present system offers these new actors neither adequate voice nor adequate regulation. Two significant clusters of new actors are the NGOs and the transnational corporations (TNCs). The NGOs are significant because of two functions: first, their representational or interest articulation function; and second, their capacity to deliver services, particularly to the grassroots. Recommendations encourage giving NGOs an expanded voice, if not vote, at the various levels of meetings of the BWIs, including the WTO.

Regulating TNCs and speculative capital

The global economic role of TNCs, including financial institutions, deserves priority attention. They presently operate beyond the effective control of any single country, their size dwarfs many national economies, and efforts over the past decade to draw up a code of conduct for their activities have run into constant opposition from the industrialized countries, notably the USA. The 500 biggest TNCs account for 30% of gross global production, 70% of global merchandise trade, and 80% of international investment.

World Bank guidelines on foreign direct investment are insufficient because they discuss only the rights of investors, not their obligations. A code of conduct or a set of regulations is too urgent to wait for the longer-range judgment about what the role of TNCs in the global economy should be. The South needs investments which neither enrich investors at the expense of the poor nor create dependency and exploit natural resources. A first step with regard to TNCs is the recommendation calling for a TNC global code of conduct:

- Governments should collaborate to establish a regulatory mechanism to govern certain TNC activities. The mechanism should establish the rights and responsibilities of such companies and provide for enforcing them. First steps could include strengthening the UN Center on Transnational Corporations or the creation of a joint OECD–UNCTAD commission to look into the problem.

Closely related to the need to regulate TNCs is the need to regulate speculative capital. Foreign exchange transactions, of which capital movements represent some 95% of the total, now exceed $1 trillion per day. These capital flows have expanded rapidly in the unregulated Eurodollar market and have exposed the international monetary system to great instability, especially the less developed countries.

Therefore, member governments working with the IMF should develop mechanisms for limiting the destabilizing effects of capital flows and restoring the relative predictability and stability of exchange rates.

- Governments should jointly introduce a small tax on capital flows, as proposed by Nobel Economics laureate James Tobin, which would reduce financial instability. This tax would require global coverage and a global network to be effective.

Receipts from the 'Tobin tax' could be used to finance the UN system, provide environmental protection in less developed countries (LDCs), or selectively reduce LDC debt.

Symmetry

For an organization responsible for monitoring the global economy, the Fund has long had a myopic view, seeing only the problems of the poor indebted countries. The Fund regularly conducts its Article IV consultations with all member-states. However with the wealthy countries who can borrow on the private capital market and do not need to use IMF funds, the Fund's 'advice' can go unheeded. For countries borrowing from the Fund, however, their every economic policy will be shaped by the Fund conditionalities on the loans. Given this profound asymmetry of the Fund, the Conference recommended that trade surplus countries, as well as debtor countries, assume their responsibility to adjust. Taxes on these surpluses could become another source of revenue for the United Nations.

- The IMF should adopt a system of adjustment which applies to and is enforced equally to countries with trade surpluses and trade deficits, as well as on reserve and non-reserve currency countries. The adjustment process of surplus countries should take place through the expansion of domestic demand and through recycling their surpluses in a manner that ensures a more equitable process of global development.

Enhanced UN and BWI coordination

In general, there is profound need for much greater coordination among the UN specialized agencies and the BWIs. The conference report is lacking in that it does not call on all these actors to work affirmatively towards quality development. Rather, it seeks to restrict a further concentration of power in the World Bank as it incorporates issues other than economic growth into the understanding of 'development'. The recommendations nevertheless call for coordination among equals—the BWIs, the nation-states, and the UN specialized agencies.

- The BWIs and the specialized agencies of the UN and appropriate regional agencies need to coordinate programmes and policies, so that they are all promoting sustainable and equitable development in a manner that is mutually supportive. This coordination should include consultations, staff exchanges, and sharing of information and funding. Non-governmental actors should be included in these efforts. Specifically:

o The UN High Commissioner for Human Rights (UNHCHR) and the UN Human Rights Commission should determine when countries are in violation of human rights standards. These determinations should be communicated to the BWIs. Together, the UNHCHR, the country in question, and the BWIs should determine the appropriate response.

o The International Labour Organization (ILO) should identify labour rights and standards and report country compliance to the BWIs. When a country is not in compliance, the ILO, the country in question, and the BWIs should determine the appropriate response.

o The UN Environmental Programme (UNEP) should be authorized to set standards for environmental performance by countries and report country compliance to the BWIs. When a country is not in compliance, the UNEP, the country in question, and the BWIs should determine the appropriate response.

Finally, recognizing the UN's premier role in collecting statistics, the report affirms the greater awareness of gender and environmental dimensions of statistics. It then asks that attention go to the process of collecting data, as well as the need for greater disaggregation of the data.[11]

● The UN, the BWIs, governments, NGOs and local organizations should revise the indicators used to measure success in development. Traditional GNP-based measurements fail to capture the complexity of the development process. The new indicators should disaggregate information so that it more accurately reflects poverty gaps and the environmental, human rights, and welfare dimensions of people's lives. They should show the interrelationship of economic and social development and should be transparent, interdisciplinary,

and free of gender bias. The necessary data should be collected using participatory collection methods. Such indicators should be employed to measure each country's performance against its own previous achievements and against internationally agreed minimum standards.

Conclusion

Despite having been important instruments of economic policy for their major shareholders, the BWIs have spent most of their existence far from the spotlight of public attention in the economically powerful nations. But especially since the Cold War's end, the BWIs' relative anonymity in the North is beginning to give way to heightened concerns about international economic affairs in general, and to growing awareness of global economic interdependence in particular. Public attention to the role of the BWIs in development and their place within the UN system can be expected to increase, providing the opportunity to challenge current practices and institutional relationships, with the goal of more coordinated, complementary, and effective development efforts.

Notes and references

1. The project's 23 co-sponsors include persons from academic and non-governmental institutions in 18 countries; an advisory group has members from nine countries. The lead organization is the Center of Concern, a Washington, DC-based research centre founded in 1971 to provide ethical perspectives on global development. 'Rethinking Bretton Woods' has received generous support from the John D and Catherine T MacArthur Foundation, the Ford Foundation, the C S Mott Foundation, and the World Council of Churches. In addition, Catholic relief and development agencies in Ireland (Trocaire), the Netherlands (CEBEMO), and the UK (CAFOD) underwrote the expenses of their developing country partners who participated in the June conference.

2. Prior to the conference, some 25 papers were commissioned and disseminated over an electronic conference for broad readership and debate. They will be published by Pluto Press in London.

3. *Rethinking Bretton Woods: Conference Report and Recommendations*, is available from the Center of Concern. The Report

does not pretend to be a *consensus* document.

4. H K Singer, 'Rethinking Bretton Woods, from a historical perspective', prepared for 'Rethinking Bretton Woods' Conference, June 1994, The American University, Washington, DC.

5. Daniel D Bradlow and Claudio Grossman, 'A legal perspective on the principles for new international institutional arrangements' (Draft), prepared for 'Rethinking Bretton Woods' Conference, June 1994, The American University, Washington, DC, page 46, fn 69, Article IV(2), Agreement Between the United Nations and the International Monetary Fund. Article IV, Agreement between the United Nations and the World Bank.

6. *Ibid*, Article III.

7. *Ibid*, Article V.

8. *Ibid*, Article I(3).

9. The ITO's social agenda led to its still-birth. The commercial trade portion of the ITO agreement was salvaged and became the General Agreement on Tariffs and Trade which may yet result in a World Trade Organization (WTO). Like the Bretton Woods Twins, the WTO is envisioned to have quite an independent existence, apart from the United Nations.

10. Bradlow and Grossman, *op cit*, reference 5, page 48.

11. The political significance of statistics is evident in the South Centre's recollection that prior to the existence of UNCTAD, the poorer countries could not get access to basic information on shipping, invisibles, commodities trade or restrictive business practices. *The United Nations at a Critical Crossroad: Time for the South to Act* (Geneva, South Centre, 1993), pages 17–18.

Evolution of the market economy

The responsibility and contribution of business

Olivier Giscard d'Estaing

The scale and seriousness of contemporary social problems require a new form of cooperation among governments, companies and non-governmental organizations (NGOs). The Business Association for the World Social Summit (BUSCO) has undertaken a consultation exercise among heads of companies in various sectors (industry and services) and of different sizes in 30 countries. The business leaders who have been consulted are prepared to assume their civic responsibilities, and go beyond their traditional responsibilities towards their clients, employees, shareholders, suppliers and subcontractors. They accept the need to contribute to an unprecedented amplification of social progress, and to involve themselves in an action programme.

Aware of the gravity and extent of poverty and unemployment in the world and of the overwhelming necessity for solidarity without discrimination, the business leaders assembled within BUSCO and the personalities consulted have demonstrated their desire to contribute to world social progress and, more particularly and on a priority basis, to create productive jobs which are indispensable for conducting an effective

The author is Co-founder and Deputy-chairman of the European Institute for Business Administration (INSEAD), and Chair of the Business Association for the World Social Summit (BUSCO), Arche de la Défense, Paroi Sud, 92055 Paris La Défense, Cedex 04, France (Tel: +33 1 40 81 37 61; fax: +33 1 40 81 38 51).

fight against unemployment and poverty, by furthering everyone's participation in the collective effort. In the light of this, they thus propose an action programme aimed at involving the greatest number of corporations possible in a programme oriented towards renewed and accelerated social progress.

First, a few basic factors have been taken into consideration. Private companies are the most efficient ones for the production and distribution of wealth. Their activities have enabled the spectacular progress noted in these areas. Despite this, poverty, unemployment and exclusion are on the increase. If capitalism—or the market economy—is identified with unemployment in the opinion of the public, it will be rejected, and its creative and stimulating forces will disappear simultaneously.

The local and national parties responsible are not in a position to deal with the needs and expectations of populations. Under present circumstances, none of our governments is in a position alone to face up to the legitimate expectations of populations and even less to those unattainable ones promised by certain political demagogues.

Public and privately available finance and utilizable modes of credit probably represent one-tenth of what is required today to provide the world with modern infrastructures and to ensure its population satisfactory living standards. As an example, Germany is investing more than $100 billion per year to rehabilitate ex-communist Eastern Germany, and that involves a population of only 17 million inhabitants. This expenditure represents one hundred times the UNDP budget. The scale and seriousness of contemporary social problems require a new form of cooperation among governments, companies and NGOs.

The business leaders who have been consulted are prepared to assume their civic responsibilities and go beyond their traditional responsibilities towards their clients, employees, shareholders, suppliers and subcontractors. This is all very well, provided that they have the means and that their actions are incorporated into those of authorities and organizations responsible for social and humanitarian affairs. The objective is neither to work out a theoretical economic doctrine nor to propose a unique operating model for administrative bodies but—while taking account of the extreme diversity of situations, mentalities, needs, means and traditions—to open up priority attitudes and decisions likely to reorient collective efforts towards the needs of the most underprivileged.

The search for full employment and, more specifically, for job creation is at the heart of the problem. In an open economy the criterion is no longer to maintain as many existing jobs as possible, but to make sure that the private sector is able to create more new jobs than the number disappearing in the adjustment process.

The immense disappointment lies in the fact that employment does not 'follow' growth, especially in industrial sectors and in the EU. In the past 20 years this type of employment fell as a percentage of the total active population from 39% to 32% in Germany, from 37% to 22% in France and from 26% to 19% in the USA, while at the same time industrial capacity was increasing at a rate of more than 100%.

European firms, like the Japanese, used to have a tradition of maintaining jobs in spite of temporary recession. The present structural crisis questions its application. We hope that it is temporary. The same phenomenon exists in merchandising services, in banks and distribution, mainly due to computer technology. Airlines and hotel companies follow the same pattern, due to the important share of salaries in their costs and price reductions imposed by competition. On the day when staff redundancies are considered as open to criticism as a financial loss, we shall then have entered into a new era of capitalism, thereby enabling us to fight more effectively against unemployment.

From governments, business leaders expect clear, rigorous and sane policies, together with the efficient management of their activities. This is, in their opinion, much more important than financial assistance; this type of intervention should only take place exceptionally or temporarily.

(1) Policies for economic growth and new jobs

Five to ten years from now, the world production will—and should be—considerably increased to face up to demographic growth and to needs that must be satisfied.

It is expected that the growth of industrial production and production of services will reach yearly averages of 3% to 10%, with considerable disparities depending on sector and country. A recent estimate forecasts that from 1990 to 2000, production in rich countries (the G-7) will grow from $13 trillion to $24 trillion, ie 2% per year. During the same period, production in other countries will grow from $9 trillion to $34 trillion, ie more than 4.5% per year.

(2) An encouraging fiscal and monetary policy

To facilitate the development of companies, monetary and fiscal policies must be encouraging rather than uncontrolled or crushing. The stability of currency exchange as well as low interest rates are necessary conditions for company activities. Balanced policies should favour saving and consumption, both indispensable for economic growth.

International business leaders will carry out their investments on a priority basis in countries offering security and reassuring conditions of stability.

(3) An open social policy

Restrictive and compelling social legislation presents formidable obstacles to employment. The constraints regarding minimum remuneration, work duration and holidays, retirement age, hiring and firing etc, can reach a deterrent level. However, different national conditions make it impossible to achieve international harmonization of social legislation which, in any case, is not desirable at that stage.

(4) A clear and accepted definition of public functions and the role of the company

The oversimplified principle according to which corporations assume their traditional functions and lean on the state to manage their overall social problems, enabling them to utilize for this an increasing share of wealth they produce, must be superseded.

One of the main aspects of the proposed reform will consist of business leaders assuming civic responsibilities, and the state accepting the loss of its financial pressure on corporations, recognizing that it does not hold a monopoly on social action.

(5) To strengthen considerably the role of associations with a humanitarian purpose and non-governmental organizations

When public authorities are not in a position to assume their social responsibilities, a new type of cooperation should be established between private corporations and non-profit associations. Increased financial resources, through tax-free donations, should be made available to them.

(6) The promotion of small and medium-sized companies

Small and medium-sized companies are currently the most innovative ones, and those which create the maximum number of jobs. They experience, however, all kinds of obstacles to their creativity—administrative red-tape and discouraging regulations, risky financing, and often insufficient professional competence and connections. Their mortality rate is high.

The simplification of administrative procedures, attenuating social and fiscal charges, are necessary and must be achieved on a country-by-country basis. The creation of well equipped activity zones for the benefit of small and medium-sized craft companies and industrial and servicing companies is the best measure which the authorities could bring in to help the creation and development of companies and jobs.

(7) Second thoughts on training

We must re-examine training methods, both basic and professional, in the general development of training schemes, especially 'alternative' training. The struggle against exclusion is conducted through encouragement of greater equality of opportunities, including the career cycles of employees, workers and executives.

(8) Setting up necessary infrastructures

The smooth functioning of companies requires setting up efficient infrastructures in the areas of energy, transport, communications and harbour equipment. A great many achievements have been made in numerous countries since the 1950s, especially due to financing by the World Bank. The whole planet has equipped itself with roads, airports, railways and tele-communications networks, but these net-works have yet to be completed and their functioning and maintenance assured.

(9) An alleviation and better distribution of costs weighing on salaries and companies

The alleviation of costs will result in greater rigour in the administration of public funds. The living standard of the state must be better adapted to tolerable levels of levying by national economic authorities. Con-cerning social systems, minimum services should be ensured, eventually comple-mented by additional services determined by the professions and companies.

Fiscal alleviation on salaries and companies is only possible if savings on expenditure and in social benefits are possible and acceptable. Special measures should benefit small and medium-sized companies and companies which create jobs.

Heavy taxes and other social burdens on wages not only discourage job creation, but encourage illegal transactions and unfair competition.

(10) An active struggle against corruption

Corruption pollutes economic and social life. Its disastrous consequences on the functioning of companies and on the morale of populations are considerable. They cannot be calculated precisely but amounts to billions of dollars. This struggle should be a common effort on the part of the authorities and business leaders.

(11) A tourism and craft industry policy

Tourism, essential for certain countries, is a factor in creating jobs—not only for transport, the hotel business and catering, but also for local activities. Small and medium-sized companies—of the artisanal type—largely depend on it.

(12) Administrative simplification

The burden of accumulated regulations over the years and their local, national, regional and world imposition have become unbearable and discouraging. No one can deny the need for regulations and controls. These rules must protect citizens and the environment from all kinds of abuse and threats.

Their application, however, and their number are liable to cause great damage and to limit the creative power of business leaders. The choice of necessary regula-tions, their application and their control should systematically form part of a demo-cratic analysis.

(13) New civic and social responsibilities

The great change which should take place with regard to business leaders is based on an appeal to their conscience of imperative social and civic responsibilities. In this manner, a real citizenship of the company will develop.

In recent years, a large number of companies and international organizations have drawn up and applied codes of good conduct. From the traditional responsibi-lities of companies, we evolve towards individual and societal responsibilities which must also be assumed by citizens, workers and executives. Workers and unemployed people must be involved in a contribution to the good functioning of the social system.

Some large companies show, in their organization chart and at a high level of responsibility in the hierarchy, a depart-ment of external social actions, reflecting this preoccupation and regrouping their actions in this area. It would be desirable for this kind of initiative to become the norm in large companies. We particularly want to emphasize that this social responsi-bility has been remarkably felt and applied by great past and present industrialists. Some of them, like Henry Ford, have been the pioneers of salary increases; others, following the example of Michelin or Tata, were the driving force behind lodging, schools and hospitals. Most of them have applied effective policies of job creation and personnel training.

Social responsibility should be shared between the authorities and companies in applying the principle of subsidiarity, namely, that they act concertedly to solve problems which they cannot deal with separately.

The responsibilities of business leaders in relation to employment present conflicting aspects, making their task particularly complex. It is indispensable to admit a fundamental principle, namely that only 'the management of a company is qualified to determine the staff necessary to fulfil its function'. All constraints and rigidity dictating policy in this area for the company are, in fact, a cause of additional unemployment by leading to limitations on employment or to financial losses which put in jeopardy the survival of the company.

Controls are clearly necessary to avoid arbitrary and excessive firing. But by hindering a company from firing, one discourages it from hiring when the situation improves. What is more, responsible managers are well aware that well trained and experienced staff and their confidence and reliability are the most important company assets.

One way in which the business leaders' social preoccupation could be expressed is through the establishment of an annual social balance sheet. It is the opportunity to measure and make known the social realities of the year.

(14) Investment in low-salary countries

The salary gaps in industrialized countries and certain countries of Asia, Africa, Latin America and Eastern Europe result in considerable industrial displacements which have become an inherent strategy for all large industrial groups and now for service institutions. The beneficial effects for the world economy are clear—a lowering of costs and therefore of the price of products and job creation in developing countries. The immediate consequence is a loss of jobs in delocalized sectors of industrialized countries.

The world distribution of work is not immutable: low-salaried countries become perfectly able to produce for certain advanced technology services and industries because associated technology transfer and training are extremely rapid. On the other hand, advanced countries do not wish to renounce industries which require a large labour force.

The desirable political orientations are:

- to favour investments destined to serve local or regional markets;
- to increase remuneration and social protection quickly, but not too quickly, in countries in which they are weak, and thus where the labour force is relatively overexploited;
- to fight against work conditions inferior to those defined long ago by the ILO as representing the minimum acceptable standard, whether this concerns working hours, the hiring of women and children, the security of work conditions, or even the utilization of prisoners.

As long as these tendencies accelerate, we shall witness a double beneficial effect—a narrowing of the present excessive gaps and the creation of new purchasing power, which is the main driving force of economic growth and of raising the living standards of populations.

(15) Contributions to training

Companies are the best qualified bodies to conduct professional training—whether they carry this out on their own premises or whether they use external organizations. This professional training applies to all categories, ranging from the handicapped and illiterate to those with degrees and exceptional ability. It applies on a semi-continuous basis, namely to different ages and periods in careers in the framework of redeployment to different functions and in the updating of professional competence.

All training activities of the type described below are the safest investment which a society can make for its future, namely general professional and practical training relating to techniques and behaviour undertaken in a concrete and participative manner, based on practical cases using computer and audiovisual programmes:

- Professional organizations and chambers of commerce and industry are called on to make a contribution which can sometimes be decisive.
- Fiscal incentives, such as a tax reduction of up to 2% of total salaries, facilitate its application.
- If the authorities are to facilitate this practice, business leaders must take it on themselves to globalize it, that is to say, open it up to other companies and to other countries so as to involve younger generations in a new overall tendency in their collective effort of production and service.

The cost of this training must be spread between:

- the companies;
- the authorities, through fiscal allowance or subventions;
- the persons involved, either through unpaid work or through part-time work, with proportional remuneration.

(16) Products and activities for the handicapped

Among people who feel excluded from economic activities, the handicapped require special attention from companies; this has already yielded tangible results. It involves adapting working conditions and equipment to welcome employees who are affected by physical handicaps, such as the blind, the deaf and dumb, the amputated, partially paralysed people or people affected by various forms of illnesses and incapacities. Learning kits—more particularly destined for the mentally handicapped—have been perfected. Computer technology is at the service of the physically handicapped and speech therapists.

The cooperation between state, companies and NGOs will enable the amplification of the necessary actions.

Civic actions within the company framework

There are many companies which encourage the voluntary help of their employees for humanitarian purposes, and which have created foundations and associations for specific objectives. Generally, the reactions of employees are very positive and the social climate is improved as a result. One insurance company launched an information campaign for its employees to help children, sick people and the aged, and noticed that 30% of its staff made a contribution to its programmes outside working hours.

The cooperation state/companies/NGOs

One often has the impression of witnessing the existence of three different worlds which ignore or even sometimes fight each other—the world of civil servants, the world of business leaders and the world of volunteers or NGO employees.

The first duty of each is to assume their professional functions. But their second is to establish model cooperation in all possible ways to stimulate social progress. This presupposes a common will for concertation, a specific organization for sharing resources using the best means, and a new professionalism.

This cooperation can be stimulated by the agencies of the United Nations, by ECOSOC, involving directly the main actors of the economic and social life, and by the extension of 'Economic and Social Councils' already existing in 29 countries.

Unfortunately, the company alone can neither take charge of all unemployed people nor train them all. Even if some legislation imposes on the company a minimum number of handicapped employees as a percentage of staff, failing which a compensatory tax is levied, the problem is not resolved. In this area, the contribution of NGOs is mandatory.

Adults do not necessarily enter into the formal framework of public and civilian jobs. Society must be organized in a way which enables everyone to participate in social life in one form or another. The classic 'productive' salaried job must no longer be the only possible method of integration.

The contribution of companies to the action of NGOs for humanitarian purposes

The contribution of business leaders through donations varies according to country, fiscal system, tradition and attitude of top managers and employees.

In general, business leaders feel poorly informed on the actions of and results achieved by NGOs. They are pursued too frequently with innumerable requests, and they are often not competent to make the best choice. Sometimes, to avoid making many small contributions, they prefer to confine themselves to one or two major contributions which they choose by virtue of a special vocation or on the basis of the nature, the localization and culture of their company. All small associations will find their fragile financial equilibrium thrown out of balance.

Efforts should be directed towards:

- improving the defiscalization of gifts;
- promoting the donations of companies;
- organizing more efficiently the informa-

tion of business leaders and the collection of funds;

- obtaining the direct or indirect participation of business leaders in the management of the NGOs that they help;
- controlling the effectiveness of expenditures, such as, for example, placing a statutory limit on the accepted administrative expenses (15%).

Business leaders are essential contributors to NGO activities and it is desirable to involve them more completely. This should allow for a leap forward in those activities which offer the best contributions to the solution of numerous human problems.

It must be stated that these NGOs would not be able to depend solely on voluntary help but represent a considerable source of paid jobs likely to attract millions of people motivated by a spirit of enterprise and generosity.

Conclusion

Is it displaying excessive idealism to hope that we will witness a rapid and generalized evolution of the social attitudes of all persons and organizations concerned in order to unite further the efforts and means aimed at achieving clearly defined social objectives? Demographic facts remain at the heart of the problem and will evolve only slowly. Excessive demographic growth impoverishes populations, but an excessive reduction in the birthrate brings with it decadent societies.

The project of encouraging worldwide actions could be the object of the intergovernmental commitment of the Social Summit, supported by business leaders and NGOs, channelling their efforts and improving the functioning of existing organizations. Corporations must be considered as full citizens. This implies rights and duties.

We think that it is preferable to set up a system, through initiative and motivation, rather than to impose new behaviour by state intervention and the constraint of law. That is how a society will develop, where the human being becomes the focus of our preoccupations and the realization of our aims. After the ecology of the environment, the ecology of men and women will be promoted.

It is up to each one of us to contribute to this.

OTHER REFORM INITIATIVES FOR GLOBAL PEACE AND DEVELOPMENT

The articles included in this issue are but some of the most recent contributions of a continuously widening stream of activities aimed at examining the needs and possibilities for reform in international cooperation, peace and development. In order to place the discussion here into this broader context, the following pages present examples of relevant initiatives. While reference could have been made to major world events such as the UN Conference on Environment and Development —the Earth Summit—held in Rio de Janeiro in 1992, the World Summit for Social Development to be held in 1995 in Copenhagen, Denmark, the UN Secretary-General's most recent reports on 'A Development Agenda' (UN documents A/49/665 and A/48/935), and many other governmental, inter-governmental, civil society and private-sector endeavours—it was felt that those selected would probably best illustrate the spectrum of reform initiatives not directly undertaken by the UN system itself—but by independent commissions, national governments, civil society and the private sector. To focus on the latter type of reform activities is important to make the point that there is, among all global key actors today, growing interest in making the world during the next half century a more livable world—recognizing that we are one human race on one planet Earth.

The Commission on Global Governance

The Commission on Global Governance has been established at a time of profound, rapid and pervasive change in the international system—a time of uncertainty, challenge and opportunity.

Freed from East–West tensions, the world's nations have more favourable conditions for working together to build a better world for all. The need for cooperation among them has also increased. They have become more interdependent in many respects. New problems have appeared that call for collective action. Global society faces the forces of both integration and division.

These trends pose fresh challenges to the existing structures of international cooperation. It is therefore necessary to reassess their capacity and the values and concepts that underlie them. It is time to review the arrangements for the governance of our global society.

Five decades after World War II and in the aftermath of the Cold War, a new world is taking shape. It could give new meaning to the common rights and responsibilities of nations, peoples and individuals. It could bring greater peace, freedom and prosperity. The Commission has been established to contribute to the emergence of such a global order.

The elements of change

Wide-ranging changes have taken place in international relations. The number of nation-states has multiplied, and shifts have occurred in their relative importance. The

East—West division has come to an end. Several countries have formed closer relationships, ceding some sovereign power to collective entities. Other nations have fragmented, as ethnic, religious or other groups assert their separate identities.

Authoritarian rule is giving way to more democratic government, but the transition is not complete and human rights are still widely violated. Apartheid has begun to be dismantled but progress is halting and there has been a surge of racism elsewhere.

The two superpowers have started to disarm but the level and proliferation of arms, including nuclear weapons, continues to endanger peace. New sources of instability and conflict—economic, ecological, social, humanitarian—call for rapid collective responses and new approaches to security.

Economically, the past half century has seen unparalleled growth and transformation. They have been spurred by expanding world trade and investment and accelerating technological change. Widespread trade liberalization and financial deregulation have created an increasingly global market. But many protectionist barriers remain and weaker countries risk being marginalized. The gap between rich and poor, among nations and within them, has widened. Though economic progress has benefited billions, a fifth of the world's people live in abject poverty. Even rich countries are troubled by a deprived underclass. World disparities could deepen as the capacity to use knowledge through new communication and information technologies becomes the key to economic success. Growing disparities, made more visible by the media's wider reach, accentuate discontent and, among other things, produce pressure for migration, not just from rural to urban areas in developing countries, but now also from poorer to richer countries.

Migration has been a safety valve, easing pressure on and from desperate people. Today, while frontiers are breached by economic forces, they are being closed against people, even as poverty, famine, conflict and environmental deterioration drive more people from their homes. This narrowing of access could produce tension and potential for conflict.

The concept of the international system is also changing. People have begun to see it not just as a scene for states and their representatives but more as a global society with legitimate roles for many more actors. The new worldview values cultural diversity and sees equity and justice as essential underpinnings of institutions of governance.

Cultural variety and indigenous values suffer as homogenization is promoted by global exposure to Western communication and entertainment industries and other purveyors of Western lifestyle. This tends to create divisions between younger and older generations and to prompt countermovements that sometimes take extremist or obscurantist positions.

Despite greatly expanded international cooperation, global and regional institutions have not been able to keep pace with the challenges of increasing interdependence. At all levels, there is a gap between the demands of individuals, peoples and nations and the capacity of the system to meet their needs. In a world turning into a global village, the rights and responsibilities of its different actors must be redefined—and respected—as we move towards a new global democracy.

The task of the Commission

The Commission's basic aim is to contribute to the improvement of global governance. It will analyse the main forces of global change, examine the major issues facing the world community, assess the adequacy of global institutional arrangements and suggest how they should be reformed or strengthened.

The Commission will be able to draw on the work of the previous independent commissions chaired by Willy Brandt, Olof Palme, Sadruddin Aga Khan and Hassan bin Talal, Gro Harlem Brundtland, and Julius Nyerere. These contributed to a better understanding of policies and measures necessary to address key issues in important fields: North—South relations, security and disarmament, humanitarian questions, environment and development, and the progress of the developing countries.

The Commission does not have to go over the same ground, but will examine their proposals for continuing relevance and consider how their acceptability may be enhanced. It will explore what factors may have caused past efforts to improve global governance to fail—and what conditions helped them to succeed. The Commission will suggest how global, regional and national institutions should be developed to better support cooperation in today's world.

The principal challenge will be to mobilize political will for multilateral action. Attitudes must be fostered that enable enduring collaborative solutions to global problems to be put into effect. The political and economic arguments for action in the common good need to be well marshalled. It will be the Commission's task to articulate a vision of global cooperation that may inspire nations—leaders and people—to intensify their collective endeavours.

Some basic issues

The improvement of global society in its many aspects will be a prime concern of the Commission. The world has been spared a great war in recent decades, but conflict and violence have not diminished. In particular, there has been a rise in strife within states. Some conflicts have highlighted the vulnerability of minorities. Some have resulted in large-scale suffering, gross abuse of human rights and massive refugee problems; these have generated demands for external intervention. There is also cause for growing concern over the threats to stability that could arise from non-military factors. In considering security issues, the Commission will examine what approaches the world community should adopt to deal with threats to security in the broadest sense.

The Commission will study measures that could strengthen the system of collective security under the Charter of the United Nations to prevent or halt conflicts between states. An important linked issue is arms control and action by which the world community could prevent potentially destabilizing situations arising from arms proliferation and the trade in arms which assists it. A system of collective security that inspires confidence could reduce the urge of individual states to build up large arsenals, freeing valuable resources for socially useful purposes. The Commission will also pay attention to disarmament by the major powers and the prospects for securing a part of the savings for action to accelerate development.

The Commission's concern with security will extend to the considerations that should govern international action, whether preventive diplomacy or coercive intervention, to deal with conflicts within states that may trigger wider involvement or that cause outrage on humanitarian grounds. With increasing internal conflicts prompting calls for intervention, clear guidelines are desirable so that such action is both effective and consistent. The Commission will need to examine what the world community may set down as the limits of permissible behaviour in a range of areas, and consider mechanisms—in the context of a future regime of international law—to encourage and, if necessary, enforce compliance with these norms.

The values upheld by the international community must be reinforced by the regulatory framework of the global rule of law. As sovereign states remain the primary units of the international system, the changing nature of state sovereignty and the relationship between national autonomy and international responsibility will be germane to the work of the Commission.

Together with the worldwide movement towards participatory democracy, there has been greater attention to the rights of individuals and of minorities, and to the role of civil society and its voluntary organizations in advancing the people's interest. The Commission will be concerned with the protection of these rights. It will consider how individuals, peoples and nations can be empowered to exercise greater control over their fate and how democratic accountability can be fostered at all levels, from local to global.

The economic turbulence of recent times calls for renewed efforts to improve coordination in policy in the interests of achieving more stable conditions for investment and growth worldwide. There is also a need for nations to ensure that progress towards multilateral free trade is maintained. These issues will receive the Commission's attention.

A central concern will be the need to accelerate development in less developed countries, so that absolute poverty may be brought to an end and the living standards of billions of people raised to acceptable levels. The Commission will consider ways to foster an international environment that is more supportive of developing countries, and actions to reduce external obstacles to these countries' own efforts to earn their way out of poverty. Fairer conditions for selling to developed countries through the removal of import barriers, better terms for trade for primary commodities, and improved access to capital and technology remain key issues. The proliferation of trade blocks may adversely affect non-member countries, especially those in the developing world. The debt problem, which continues to burden many countries, draining resources that could be invested to raise output and living standards, also calls for further action.

Another important concern will be the environment, with its close links to development and population growth. Both affluence and poverty contribute to environmental stress, and so does population pressure which often accompanies poverty. Grave environmental problems beyond national remedy, such as greenhouse warming, ozone depletion and, in some cases, natural disasters, have linked the fate of nations more closely together. They call for cooperative strategies based on the principle of equitably shared responsibility. Such strategies must be responsive to a common danger and be guided by concern for the interests of future generations, in order to promote sustainable development on a global basis.

The Commission will consider how the limited progress made at the Earth Summit of June 1992 can be consolidated and extended, and how recognition of the interdependence of the human family, signalled by ecological dangers, can be widened so as to evoke greater international support for sustainable development.

Focus on international institutions

An extensive system of international cooperation has been built up over the past 50 years. With the United Nations at its centre, the system has an array of important organizations.

However, these institutions of global governance—mainly created for a much less complex world with far fewer nations— fall short of today's demands. In many cases, current arrangements inhibit the development of an improved system of global security and the advancement of the human condition. A key objective of the Commission will be to propose how an adequate international institutional framework can be achieved.

The Commission will identify the tasks that need to be performed as clearly as possible. It will study the requirements for carrying them out effectively and the adequacy of the existing institutional arrangements. It will then develop proposals for improving these facilities.

The United Nations, as well as its specialized agencies, the Bretton Woods institutions and the GATT, will be an important focus for the Commission's recommendations. The composition of the Security Council and the use of the veto will be matters for review. The Commission will also study how a number of functions can be performed at the regional level, frequently outside the UN framework.

A crucial factor in the effectiveness of organizations is their perceived legitimacy. This is linked to participation and transparency in their decision-making processes and to the representative nature of bodies that exercise authority. In considering how global institutions can be reconciled with these requirements, the Commission will examine how non-state actors—non-governmental organizations, business and labour, the academic community, cultural and religious movements, rights groups— can be usefully involved in the work of international institutions.

Effectiveness also depends on how well institutions are financed and staffed. A predictable and adequate resource base and a well-functioning international civil service are essential to the proper functioning of world organizations, which face rising demands. The Commission will suggest steps to improve the present position, which has manifest weaknesses.

In the spirit of San Francisco

The United Nations was founded and its Charter adopted at a conference in San Francisco in 1945. As 1995, its 50th anniversary, approaches, the adequacy of our institutions of global governance and the need to strengthen them will increasingly claim the attention of world leaders and citizens alike.

Recent improvements in international relations have created an exciting opportunity to construct a world system that is more fully responsive to the interests of all nations and people. It should be possible to move the world to a higher level of cooperation than has ever been attempted, taking advantage of the growing recognition of global interdependence.

In making its own contribution to this endeavour, the Commission will aim to invoke the spirit of multilateralism that animated those who worked together in San Francisco to form the United Nations. It plans to issue its report in 1994, so that its conclusions and recommendations may be discussed before the General Assembly of the United Nations holds its 50th anniversary session.

Members of the Commission on Global Governance

Co-Chairmen: Ingvar Carlsson (Sweden) and Shridath Ramphal (Guyana). *Members*: Ali Alatas (Indonesia); Abdlatif Al-Hamad (Kuwait); Oscar Arias (Costa Rica); Anna Balletbo (Spain); Kurt Biedenkopf (Germany); Allan Boesak (South Africa); Manuel Camacho Solis (Mexico); Bernard Chidzero (Zimbabwe); Barber Conable (USA); Jacques Delors (France); Jiri Dienstbier (The Czech Republic); Enrique Iglesias (Uruguay); Frank Judd (UK); Hongkoo Lee (Republic of Korea); Wangari Maathai (Kenya); Sadako Ogata (Japan); Olara A Otunnu (Uganda); I G Patel (India); Celina Peixoto (Brazil); Jan Pronk (The Netherlands); Qian Jiadong (China); Marie-Angélique Savané (Senegal); Adele Simmons (USA); Maurice Strong (Canada); Brian Urquhart (UK); Yuli Vorontsov (Russia).

Working Group on the Future of the United Nations System

In 1945 the nations of the world, emerging from World War II, envisioned a global institution that would promote peace, security, and cooperation among nations. After months of debate on the ways to achieve these historic goals of mankind, and determined to learn from the mistakes of the past, the Founding Members drafted and approved the United Nations Charter, signed in San Francisco in June 1945.

The great vision of San Francisco was partly frozen during the 40 years of the Cold War. The removal of Cold War constraints has both unleashed the potential of the United Nations and presented the world organization with new and tumultuous problems. The globalization and interrelatedness of problems of security, development, environment and population require new knowledge and fresh approaches. If the UN system, the only global forum with near-universal membership, is to maintain and increase its relevance, effectiveness and credibility, a great effort will be needed to analyse present and future challenges, to develop fresh ideas, and to rethink the role and functioning of the whole system.

Purpose of the Working Group

The need to improve and strengthen the present United Nations system is widely recognized. The UN system has remained essentially unaltered in structure since 1945. The enormous changes that have occurred in the world demand a reassessment, and possibly major reform of the present structure. While some parts may be overstaffed, in other respects it is clearly under-resourced to meet the fresh calls for help that are almost daily directed at it. There is little cohesion between the principal UN organs and many of the functional agencies, some of which existed prior to 1945. All this occurs at a time when regional dynamics and transnational forces have added new dimensions to the traditional state system. New concepts are also needed to encompass the various human needs that the present UN system means to address.

These challenges are not entirely dissimilar to those facing decision makers at Versailles in 1919, and at Bretton Woods, Dumbarton Oaks and San Francisco in 1944 and 1945.

The Report

The product of the Working Group's discussions ought, we think, to be a succinct document rather than an encyclopedic tome. Ideally, it would express a vision of an improved state of international security and 'human security', together with a set of practical proposals that would create a more coherent and efficient United Nations system.

Upon printing, *The Report of the Independent Working Group on the Future of the United Nations System* will be distributed to all of the member governments of the UN for consideration and debate. It will also have a wide distribution to non-governmental organizations, academic institutions, the media and interested individuals. We anticipate that the report will be a basis for discussion at the 50th anniversary session of the General Assembly meeting at the level of heads of state and government in New York in the fall of 1995.

Timing

In March 1994 the names of the Working Group members and the purpose of the project were officially announced. In early May 1994 the Working Group met for its first substantive conference. The second meeting took place in mid-September. Two more meetings will then occur, with the aim of producing the draft Final Report in the summer of 1995. A final report will be made available in time for the commemorative session of the General Assembly.

Organization

The Working Group consists of 12 members, including two co-chairs. They have been chosen from different regions of the globe, as well as different walks of life. While some may be familiar with the UN system, what all have in common is a long-standing interest in promoting international cooperation. A Secretariat co-directed by Professors Paul Kennedy and Bruce Russett has been set up at Yale University's UN Studies programme to prepare position papers, arrange the agenda, draft specific studies, and carry out whatever else Working Group members deem necessary to achieve their task. Consultants, practitioners and scholars outside Yale, from developing as well as developed countries, will be widely used.

Charter of the Global Commission to Fund the United Nations

An independent international organization, The Global Commission to Fund the United Nations ('the Commission'), is being organized by persons concerned with and knowledgeable about the United Nations and its needs for sources of funds to meet current and future daily operating requirements, beyond the current systems of dues and assessments of member-nations.

The United Nations is a unique global organization performing indispensable services for member-governments and the world's people. Its current funding from member countries' dues is inadequate and unpredictable. Dependable new income, even through new public/private partnerships, is needed if the United Nations is to take on additional assignments to solve global problems that individual nations cannot solve alone and which no other entity can be realistically expected to address effectively. The Commission will also take into account the importance of the growing global civil society of non-governmental scientific, social welfare, professional, environmental and business associations in a world now dominated by nation-states and international corporations. The 50th Anniversary of the United Nations in 1995 makes the work of the Commission particularly timely. Its initial efforts and findings will be presented at the UN World Summit on Social Development in Copenhagen, March 1995.

Advisers to the Commission are being sought who are experts or knowledgeable about, and can gain ready access to others expert in United Nations operations, budgets and practices; international monetary and fiscal policies and practices; global geopolitics and governance issues; international activities such as air travel, arms sales and transfers, currency and international securities trading, insurance, military issues; and global environmental pollution, resource protection, and sustainable development. The Commission will include high-level, internationally recognized persons and be balanced geographically and by expertise, viewpoint, gender etc with a broad range of practical financial, business, academic, government and non-governmental experience.

The Commission will study and develop workable plans for realizing one or more of various means that have been or may be proposed to fund the United Nations particularly its peacemaking, humanitarian, health, education, and sustainable development activities in a businesslike, fully accountable manner, including but not limited to:

- UN members required to pay interest on unpaid dues and assessments to buttress this bedrock financing system.

Taxation of international activities, including:

- international arms sales and transfers;
- international currency and derivatives trading (eg tax proposals by Professor James Tobin, recipient of the Nobel Prize

for Economics and Martin Walker, US Bureau Chief, *The Guardian*);
- dumping of toxic wastes in international waters;
- global carbon combustion emissions crossing national borders;
- international air travel and freight;
- use of global commons such as oceans, space, and electromagnetic spectrum.

Fees-for-service, barter, or service exchanges:

- facilities, equipment, supplies, weapons and training for peacekeeping/making forces;
- insurance for peacekeeping operations, such as those underwritten by a proposed public/private partnership—the United Nations Security Insurance Agency (UNSIA), which will contractually guarantee and underwrite UN peacekeeping support to nations which agree to pay an annual premium for a defined degree of support with security risk assessment performed by insurance industry, military, and financial professionals employed by or cooperating with UNSIA.
- other such innovative proposals that may be brought to the Commission which have been on the table for many years, for example, in such reports as Steinberg and Yager, *New Means of Financing International Needs*, Brookings Institution, 1978.

The Commission will develop and assess viable, alternative plans to fund the United Nations that will be as widely and deeply supported as possible. In the process, the Commission will obtain funds for its own work and will seek input and support from a broad range of constituencies. The Commission's plans will contain *pro forma* estimates of reasonable and acceptable levels and rates of taxation and/or fees; the methods and costs of collection and enforcement, including the roles of member-states and of UN staff; the expected revenues from and market acceptance of services offered and taxes assessed; the requirements of member-states and the United Nations as a whole for restricting and for empowering the use of received funds; the costs and compensation to member states, including those with deregulated financial markets who need to recoup tax losses, and to those in the private sector providing services that produce the UN revenues; and all start-up considerations relevant thereto.

The Commission will operate as a non-partisan, non-secretarian, non-profit organization and is applying for tax-exempt status for contributions. A committee structure will be developed for Commissioners interested in specific issue areas covered by the Charter. It is expected that consensus will be found among Commissioners co-authoring reports, while still reasonably representing diverse viewpoints within the Commission. Commission reports, while appropriately crediting all contributions, will make clear that individual Commissioners will bear no responsibility for report contents which they have not approved or authorized.

Information: write to Diane E Sherwood, Director, Global Commission to Fund the UN, 1511 K St, NW, #1130, Washington, DC 20005, USA (Tel: +1 202 639 9460; fax: +1 202 639 9459).

Commissioners of the Global Commission to fund the United Nations

Bella Abzug, Women's Environment and Development Organization (WEDO), New York; Christine Austin, Friends of the United Nations; Robert J Berg, International Development Conference, Washington; Keith A Bezanson, International Development Research Centre, Ottawa; Frank Bracho, former Ambassador of Venezuela to India, Caracas; Sam Brookfield, Business Council of the United Nations, New York; Ingar Bruggeman, Development Policy Forum, Berlin; Come Carpentier de Gourdon, WDB Group, British Virgin Islands; Ella Cisneros, Together Foundation for Global Unity, Caracas; Harlan Cleveland, World Academy for Arts and Sciences; Donald B Conroy, North American Coalition on Religion and Ecology, Washington, DC; J Elliott Corbett, Pax World Fund and Pax World Service, Washington; Jacques Yves Cousteau, The Cousteau Society, New York and Monaco; Sonia Gandhi, The Rajiv Gandhi Institute for Contemporary Studies, New Delhi; Olivier Giscard d'Estaing, Business Council for the Social Summit (BUSCO), Paris; Richard Y Hahnen, UN Support, Washington; Hazel Henderson, World Business Academy, St Augustine; J T Ross Jackson, Gaia Trust, Denmark; Nandini Joshi, Foundation for Constructive Development, Ahmedabad; Jagdish Chandra Kapur, Indfos Group of Industries, Delhi; Inge Kaul, Human Development Report Office, UNDP; Alan F Kay, Americans Talk Issues Foundation, St Augustine; Ashok Khosla, Development Alternatives, New Delhi; John Langmore, National Committee on the World Summit for Social Development, Canberra; Admiral Gene R La Rocque, Center for Defense Information, Washington, DC; Robert MacGregor, Minnesota Center for Corporate Responsibility; Alice Tepper Marlin, Council on Economic Priorities, New York; Honorable Cynthia McKinney, US House of Representatives, Washington; Morris Miller, University of Ottawa; Bradford Morse, former Administrator, UNDP, Florida; Robert Muller, Rector, University for Peace, Costa Rica; Claes Nobel, The Claes Nobel Institute for Environmental Technologies, New York; Nahed Ojjeh, Ambassador of Syria to UNESCO, Paris; Eva Quistorp, European Parliament, Berlin; Zhu Ronglin, International Technology and Economy Institute-Shanghai Branch, State Council, PRC; Sixto Roxas, former Finance Minister of the Philippines; Bruce Russett, United Nations in its Second Half-Century, Yale University; Marie Angelique Savane, Africa Division, United Nations Population Fund (UNFPA), Senegal; Roberto Savio, Society for International Development, Rome; Tessa Tennant, Social Investment Forum, London; David Trickett, World Business Academy, Washington, DC; Brian Urquhart, Ford Foundation, New York; Elizabeth A Ventura, Association of Professional Insurance Women, New York; Jakob von Uexkull, The Right Livelihood Award, London; Sir John Whitmore, Performance Consultants Ltd, London; Eckart Wintzen, BSO Origin, Utrecht; Diane E Sherwood (*ex officio*), New Paradigm International, Washington.

State of the United Nations: decline or regeneration in the next 50 years

The world has changed dramatically with far-reaching implications for the United Nations. As the economy becomes more globalized, as internal conflicts intensify, as modern communication systems expand the availability of information and the nature of political participation, and as the authority and legitimacy of the state erodes, the United Nations is called on to fill the void in a world state for which it was not designed. It is confronted with a paradox of escalating demands in the face of inadequate resources. Presented with these challenges, participants grappled with developing strategies for UN regeneration.

Future mandate of the UN system

Discussion focused on the principles around which a new UN mandate should be organized. Areas central to that mandate include:

- *Establishing universal norms.* This is one of the most important mandates of the United Nations. Standard setting gives the United Nations legitimacy to demand action and engage in strategies to alleviate the cause of conflicts.
- *Strengthening the UN role in collective security, peacekeeping, and cooperative security.* Most agreed that the United Nations must continue to play a key role in collective security, but were concerned about the role of the United Nations in contemporary crises and the risks to UN legitimacy. In peacekeeping, many were concerned that the United Nations' operations are blurring into peacemaking and peace enforcing. Participants also stressed cooperative and preventive measures to ensure security.
- *Developing a strategy for economic and social progress.* The United Nations could spearhead these efforts by bringing

---

This is a report of the Twenty-Ninth United Nations of the Next Decade Conference, sponsored by The Stanley Foundation, Santa Fe, NM, USA 19–24 June 1994.

states, community associations, and NGOs together to build a common notion of security—one which bridges the division between the political and military activities of the United Nations and its socioeconomic programmes.
- *Engaging in capacity building.* Capacity building is concerned with addressing root causes of conflict by strengthening local forces for development, the promotion of human rights, conflict resolution, and democratization. It is an integral part of alleviating the root causes of conflict, and also serves to enhance the degree of democratic participation at the local, national, and global levels.
- *Operating as a global forum.* Prodded by trends towards democratization and the proliferation of NGOs, such a UN forum would help to prioritize, disseminate information, integrate policy, and give voice to the historically voiceless.

Structural impediments

As an interstate system increasingly charged with global responsibilities, the United Nations is not ideally equipped to meet necessary global mandates in the future. The question is whether the United Nations can adapt to be both legitimate and effective in the midst of competing within civil society and states.

The lack of coordination among specialized agencies, between specialized agencies and the central United Nations, and between major UN bodies was also cited as an obstacle to policy making as are financial problems presented by recalcitrant contributors.

Proposals for regeneration

Proposals for change in the United Nations fell into three categories, fundamental reconfiguration, long-term reform, and near-term adjustments.

Fundamental reconfiguration:

- Establish a global directorate consisting

of major powers and regional representatives to act on matters of global security and to discuss issues.

- Create a representative parliament which might consist of national parliamentarians or representatives elected directly.
- Develop verification principles in the areas of human rights, democracy, minority protection, and arms reduction.

Long-term reform:

- Develop ways to compel contributors to pay their arrears and find additional forms of financing, including global taxation.
- Create an economic security council.
- Strengthen the international legal system.
- Institute an international professional civil service.
- Improve public perception of United Nations efficacy.

Near-term adjustments:

- Improve coordination of the UN system, including Bretton Woods institutions.
- Increase access by permitting greater NGO input and increasing the flow of information.
- Enhance UN military response capability.
- Build on existing human rights machinery.
- Strengthen arms transfer control measures.
- Solidify working relationships with regional organizations.

Prospects for change

Implementation of these proposals will require a profound shift in attitudes towards the role of the United Nations for the future. The momentum for change will not come primarily from within the United Nations or from national governments whose role and authority are called into question. A real source of hope rests in the transnational movements for change and progress. All agreed that with proper support from a broad range of these actors, the United Nations can develop the tools to meet the new challenges of the 21st century.

Participants

Richard H Stanley (Conference Chair); Ellen Dorsey and Bruno Pigott (rapporteurs); Diego Arria; Maurice Bertrand; Emilio J Cárdenas; Francis M Deng; David J Doerge; Louise Frechette; Ibrahim A Gambari; Chinmaya Rajaninath Gharekhan; Karl Frederick Inderfurth; Frank Judd; Abraham Katz; Li Zhaoxing; Ian Martin; Charles William Maynes; Jorge Montaño; Simbarashe Simbanenduku Mumbengegwi; Margaret C Snyder; Brian Urquhart; Joseph Van Arendonk.

CODES OF CONDUCT

Introduction

At least since the Industrial Revolution in the UK, 'social responsibility' has been gradually imposed on private, for-profit corporations by electorates, courts and legislators. From the passage in Parliament of the child labour laws in the middle of the 19th century until today, activities of entrepreneurs and industrialists have been circumscribed by laws and regulations to prevent them 'externalizing' their social costs from their balance sheets—on to unsuspecting taxpayers. 20th century capitalists now routinely embrace such social contracts.

As we approach the 21st century, many business leaders are updating their attitudes to traditional rearguard lobbying for 'voluntary compliance', 'self-regulation' and foot-dragging. Instead, companies of many kinds and sizes in many countries are proactively declaring their own principles and social codes of conduct. While the cynics will scoff, such written and published codes of conduct are often precursors to compliance, contract law and even international agreements, such as those on chlorofluorocarbons and other ozone-depleting substances, production of which has now ceased in all industrial countries. Since this edition of *Futures* addresses issues of taming global capital markets and how best to reduce the social and environmental costs they inflict, the following examples of corporate codes of conduct are relevant.

Calvert Group

Mission

Calvert Group's mission is to be a premier asset management company recognized both for the quality of our investment programmes and for our commitment to improving quality of life in society.

Vision/operating philosophy

Calvert Group is committed to constant improvement. We choose to make a difference in our world by working to improve the quality of life for our customers, employees and the communities in which we live and work. We strongly believe that the spirit of Calvert Group is embodied in our shared values. Our growth and long-term success will directly result from meeting the continually changing needs of our customers and employees with unflinching integrity. All decisions are made with consideration given to their effect on all of Calvert Group's constituents, balancing our growth and our responsibilities to society with fair profits.

Shared values

The following value statements are placed in categories which correspond to an adapted version of Maslow's hierarchy of needs model. We want to view the organization as a living organism, with needs that are very similar to those of a human being.

It is the responsibility of management to foster an environment which reflects the following shared values, beliefs, philosophies, norms, and principles:

Survival

(1) The organization must be profitable to survive. All business decisions should include a profitability analysis of what is proposed. If a decision is made, taking profitability into consideration, that will result in an unprofitable situation, then it was made consciously. Decision making without real knowledge or projection of profitability (cost/benefit) should be discouraged and eliminated. We are committed to returning a fair profit to our customers and parent. It is our belief that the ongoing evaluation of the progress we have achieved relative to our goals is of paramount importance.

Security

(2) Management recognizes the tangible and intangible benefits of good planning. Planning should be viewed as an ongoing responsibility. The process of planning, even at an informal rudimentary level, fosters good decisions, more efficient and effective implementation, and, in general, a proactive *v* a reactive approach to our business. We subscribe to the belief that the effective management of our time is a critical tool in better planning.

(3) There is value to stability and form. Keeping established procedures relatively constant over a certain period of time enables the efficient and effective handling of routine daily tasks. Solving the same problem more than once, regular firefighting, lack of accountability, and low productivity are symptoms of too loose a structure and a lack of well-established processes and systems. But Calvert's organizational structure, processes, and management systems should remain flexible to the demands of a changing world. We must not have such a rigid process and structure that we stifle creativity and innovation. This flexibility will be a competitive edge since we will have the ability to research, plan, and respond more quickly than our competitors. But this flexibility must also reflect an orderly disciplined approach to the normal work at hand.

Social

(4) Another critical component of every decision we make should be an assessment of the value to or impact on Calvert's stakeholders (customers, trustees, employees, vendors, parent etc). Our goal should always be to provide the most value we can while maintaining a fair profit for ourselves. Gimmicks or programmes which verge on the line of 'ripping people off' will have no place in our organization. Our attention to quality in all we do will guarantee high-value products, services and relationships.

(5) As members of the financial services' industry, Calvert's employees will conduct themselves at all times in a manner which reflects the highest ethical and professional standards. We are committed to conducting business internally and externally honestly. Everyone will be treated as an individual by respecting her/his dignity and recognizing her/his merit. We shall handle ourselves, as John Paul Jones stated in his Code of a Naval Officer, with a 'refined manner, punctilious courtesy and the nicest sense of personal honor . . . to be the soul of tact, patience, justice, firmness, and charity'. Developing effective listening and communication skills will be critical to working with each other in a professional courteous way. Compensation must be fair and competitive, working conditions safe, orderly and clean. We are committed to providing a climate that fosters a high degree of trust and openness in which employees can feel comfortable expressing their suggestions and concerns. There must be equal opportunity for employment, development, and advancement for those qualified.

(6) The organization is committed to being socially responsible in a proactive way. The intent behind this guiding principle is 'to make a difference in the world'. We will make a fair profit through being proactively responsible. This social responsibility is not only reflected in our investment strategies and products, but in the way we are responsible to the communities in which we live and work. Calvert actively promotes and supports civic improvements, charities, better health and education programmes, and recycling/conservation efforts. We maintain in good order the properties we are privileged to use, protecting the surrounding environment and natural resources.

(7) The people of Calvert are committed to working as a well integrated team. Teamwork enhances communication, eliminates invisible walls, enables fuller participation, provides all employees with a 'big picture' rather than a 'compartmentalized' orientation, and fosters better decision making and implementation. We believe that if all employees understand their roles and the significance of their individual contributions to the whole, then they will think and act with a responsibility derived from 'ownership'. The comradeship and commonality of goals and purpose which emanate from this environment provide the primary driving forces for our organization.

(8) We believe strongly that 'fun' is a critical element in our culture. Calvert's employees have always drawn a great deal of excitement and enjoyment from overcoming the challenges that their work presents. And we will continue to foster these attitudes through the development of meaningful and rewarding jobs and responsibilities. People are also encouraged to balance 'working hard' with 'playing hard' through contests, company-sponsored sporting and entertainment events, retreats, and celebrations. Our history is important to us and an integral part of our future so we will take the time to carry on meaningful traditions. Also, humour is cathartic and known to be one of the best diffusers of stress. Since stress cannot be avoided, we must encourage ways to channel it so that it does not damage any individual. Sharing stories, jokes, and taking time to see the lighter side of things are excellent 'preventive medicines' for the health of our company and its people.

Esteem

(9) The organization is committed to the growth and pursuit of excellence of each and every employee. We firmly believe that Calvert's growth and continual improvement are dependent on the growth and improvement of our people. If an individual's growth evolves into a new direction that cannot fit within the organization's framework, then we are committed to assisting the individual find

a more appropriate situation. By operating in this way, we are constantly striving for win—win solutions with all our people. We will continue to foster an environment which is receptive to all ideas no matter at what level of the organization they originate. We believe this approach will result in a high degree of organizational credibility within each of our markets, in the financial services industry, in the communities in which we operate, and within the business world in general.

Autonomy

(10) Calvert dares to be different, if being different makes good business sense. The organization prides itself on its individualistic, unconventional and non-traditional approach to the businesses in which it chooses to be. Independent thinking will be valued and encouraged as long as it benefits the organization and is not voiced just for the sake of being independent. We firmly believe that the more heterogeneous and diverse the organization is, the more creativity and entrepreneurial spirit it will possess. Therefore, we will hire and promote individuals based on potentials demonstrated, accomplishments, creativity, ambition, willingness to learn, and flexibility. We will constantly encourage risk taking and recognize creativity, hard work, and initiative even if the end result is not successful. In a more complex and sophisticated world, high levels of creativity and entrepreneurial spirit will be required to excel. Our experience has proven that freedom to be oneself actually promotes higher levels of personal commitment and responsibility than does the more conventional, highly structured organization.

Fulfilment

(11) We believe that all the previous statements of value are intertwined, and, taken together, result in a climate which fosters passion, pride in what we do, and high energy in employees about the organization they work for and their contribution to it. Calvert's commitment (a) to its vision of 'making a difference', (b) to a continual endeavour to be creative, innovative, and unconventional, and (c) to the growth and well-being of its employees and customers—are the main drivers of the organization. These drivers are appropriately summed up in the phrase 'a passion for excellence'. It is this 'passion' which can only be truly experienced in the excitement and enthusiasm you feel when you work for or do business with Calvert Group.

Contact: Calvert Group Inc, 4550 Montgomery Ave, Bethesda, MD 20814, USA (Tel: 1-800-368-2745).

The Caux Round Table: principles for business

In a world which is experiencing profound transformations, the Caux Round Table of business leaders from Europe, Japan and USA is committed to energizing the role of business and industry as a vital force for innovative global change.

The Round Table was founded in 1986 by Frederik Philips, former President of Philips Electronics, and Olivier Giscard d'Estaing, Vice-Chairman of INSEAD, as a means of reducing escalating trade tensions. It is concerned with the development of constructive economic and social relationships between the participants' countries, and with their urgent joint responsibilities towards the rest of the world.

At the urging of Ryuzaburo Kaku, Chairman of Canon Inc, the Round Table has focused attention on the importance of global corporate responsibility in reducing social and economic threats to world peace and stability. The Round Table recognizes that shared leadership is indispensable to a revitalized and more harmonious world. It emphasizes the development of continuing friendship, understanding and co-operation, based on a common respect for the highest moral values and on responsible action by individuals in their own spheres of influence.

Introduction

The Caux Round Table believes that the world business community should play an important role in improving economic and social conditions. As a statement of aspirations, this document aims to express a world standard against which business behaviour can be measured. We seek to begin a process that identifies shared values, reconciles differing values, and thereby develops a shared perspective on business behaviour acceptable to and honored by all.

These principles are rooted in two basic ethical ideals: *kyosei* and human dignity. The Japanese concept of *kyosei* means living and working together for the common good—enabling cooperation and mutual prosperity to coexist with healthy and fair competition. 'Human dignity' refers to the sacredness or value of each person as an end, not simply as a means to the fulfilment of others' purposes or even majority prescription.

The general principles in section 2 seek to clarify the spirit of *kyosei* and 'human dignity', while the specific stakeholder principles in section 3 are concerned with their practical application.

In its language and form, the document

owes a substantial debt to the Minnesota principles, a statement of business behaviour developed by the Minnesota Center for Corporate Responsibility. The Center hosted and chaired the drafting committee, which included Japanese, European, and US representatives.

Business behaviour can affect relationships among nations and the prosperity and well-being of us all. Business is often the first contact between nations and, by the way in which it causes social and economic changes, has a significant impact on the level of fear or confidence felt by people worldwide. Members of the Caux Round Table place their first emphasis on putting one's own house in order, and on seeking to establish what is right rather than who is right.

Section 1. Preamble

The mobility of employment, capital, products and technology is making business increasingly global in its transaction and its effects.

Laws and market forces are necessary but insufficient guides for conduct.

Responsibility for the policies and actions of business and respect for the dignity and interests of its stakeholders are fundamental.

Shared values, including a commitment to shared prosperity, are as important for a global community as for communities of smaller scale.

For these reasons, and because business can be a powerful agent of positive social change, we offer the following principles as a foundation for dialogue and action by business leaders in search of business responsibility. In so doing, we affirm the necessity for moral values in business decision making. Without them, stable business relationships and a sustainable world community are impossible.

Section 2. General principles

Principle 1. The responsibilities of business: beyond shareholders toward stakeholders

The value of a business to society is the wealth and employment it creates and the marketable products and services it provides to consumers at a reasonable price commensurate with quality. To create such value, a business must maintain its own economic health and viability, but survival is not a sufficient goal.

Businesses have a role to play in improving the lives of all their customers, employees, and shareholders by sharing with them the wealth they have created. Suppliers and competitors as well should expect businesses to honor their obligations in a spirit of honesty and fairness. As responsible citizens of the local, national, regional and global communities in which they operate, businesses share a part in shaping the future of those communities.

Principle 2. The economic and social impact of

business: towards innovation, justice and world community

Businesses established in foreign countries to develop, produce or sell should also contribute to the social advancement of those countries by creating productive employment and helping to raise the purchasing power of their citizens. Businesses also should contribute to human rights, education, welfare, and vitalization of the countries in which they operate.

Businesses should contribute to economic and social development not only in the countries in which they operate, but also in the world community at large, through effective and prudent use of resources, free and fair competition, and emphasis upon innovation in technology, production methods, marketing and communications.

Principle 3. Business behaviour: beyond the letter of law towards a spirit of trust

While accepting the legitimacy of trade secrets, businesses should recognize that sincerity, candour, truthfulness, the keeping of promises, and transparency contribute not only to their own credibility and stability but also to the smoothness and efficiency of business transactions, particularly on the international level.

Principle 4. Respect for rules

To avoid trade frictions and to promote freer trade, equal conditions for competition, and fair and equitable treatment for all participants, businesses should respect international and domestic rules. In addition, they should recognize that some behaviour, although legal, may still have adverse consequences.

Principle 5. Support for multilateral trade

Business should support the multilateral trade systems of the GATT/World Trade Organization and similar international agreements. They should cooperate in efforts to promote the progressive and judicious liberalization of trade and to relax those domestic measures that unreasonably hinder global commerce, while giving due respect to national policy objectives.

Principle 6. Respect for the environment

A business should protect and, where possible, improve the environment, promote sustainable development, and prevent the wasteful use of natural resources.

Principle 7. Avoidance of illicit operations

A business should not participate in or condone bribery, money laundering, or other corrupt practices: indeed, it should seek cooperation with others to eliminate them. It should not trade in arms or other materials used for terrorist activities, drug traffic or other organized crime.

Section 3. Stakeholder principles

Customers

We believe in treating all customers with dignity, irrespective of whether they purchase our products and services directly from us or otherwise acquire them in the market. We therefore have a responsibility to:

- provide our customers with the highest quality products and services consistent with their requirements;
- treat our customers fairly in all aspects of our business transactions, including a high level of service and remedies for their dissatisfaction;
- make every effort to ensure that the health and safety of our customers, as well as the quality of their environment, will be sustained or enhanced by our products and services;
- assure respect for human dignity in products offered, marketing, and advertising; and
- respect the integrity of the culture of our customers.

Employees

We believe in the dignity of every employee and in taking employee interests seriously. We therefore have a responsibility to:

- provide jobs and compensation that improve workers' living conditions;
- provide working conditions that respect each employee's health and dignity;
- be honest in communications with employees and open in sharing information, limited only by legal and competitive constraints;
- listen to and, where possible, act on employee suggestions, ideas, requests and complaints;
- engage in good faith negotiations when conflict arises;
- avoid discriminatory practices and guarantee equal treatment and opportunity in areas such as gender, age, race and religion;
- promote in the business itself the employment of differently abled people in places of work where they can be genuinely useful;
- protect employees from avoidable injury and illness in the workplace;
- encourage and assist employees in developing relevant and transferable skills and knowledge; and
- be sensitive to the serious unemployment problems frequently associated with business decision, and work with governments, employee groups, other agencies and each other in addressing these dislocations.

Owners/investors

We believe in honouring the trust our investors place in us. We therefore have a responsibility to:

- apply professional and diligent management in order to secure a fair and competitive return on our owners' investment;
- disclose relevant information to owners/ investors subject only to legal requirements and competitive constraints;
- conserve, protect and increase the owners/ investors' assets; and
- respect owners/investors' requests, suggestions, complaints, and formal resolutions.

Suppliers

Our relationship with suppliers and subcontractors must be based on mutual respect. We therefore have a responsibility to:

- seek fairness and truthfulness in all our activities, including pricing, licensing, and rights to sell;
- ensure that our business activities are free from coercion and unnecessary litigation;
- foster long-term stability in the supplier relationship in return for value, quality, competitiveness and reliability;
- share information with suppliers and integrate them into our planning processes;
- pay suppliers on time and in accordance with agreed terms of trade; and
- seek, encourage and prefer suppliers and subcontractors whose employment practices respect human dignity.

Competitors

We believe that fair economic competition is one of the basic requirements for increasing the wealth of nations and ultimately for making possible the just distribution of goods and services. We therefore have a responsibility to:

- foster open markets for trade and investment;
- promote competitive behaviour that is socially and environmentally beneficial and demonstrates mutual respect among competitors;
- refrain from either seeking or participating in questionable payments or favours to secure competitive advantages;
- respect both tangible and intellectual property rights; and
- refuse to acquire commercial information by dishonest or unethical means, such as industrial espionage.

Communities

We believe that as global corporate citizens we can contribute to such forces of reform and human rights as we are at work in the communities in which we operate. We therefore have a responsibility in the communities to:

- support peace, security, diversity and social integration;

- respect the integrity of local cultures; and
- be a good corporate citizen through charitable donations, educational and cultural contributions, and employee participation in community and civic affairs.

Caux Round Table Steering Committee

Friedrich Baur, President, MST GmbH, Germany; John Charlton, Managing Director, The Chase Manhattan Bank, USA; Nivelli Cooper, Chairman, The Top Management Partnership, Ltd, UK; Charles M Denny, Jr, Formerly Chairman and CEO, ADC Telecommunications, Inc, USA; Jean-Loup Dherse, (Chairman, CRT) Consultant, Formerly Vice President, World Bank, France; Walter E Hoadley, Senior Research Fellow, Hoover Institution, USA; Ryuzaburo Kaku, Chairman, Canon Inc, Japan; Morihisa Kaneko, Assistant Senior Counsellor, Matsushita Electric Industrial Co Ltd, Japan; Toshiaki Ogasawara, President Nifco, Inc, Japan.

Information:—For copies of the Principles for Business or further information, please contact the Caux Round Table Secretariat, 1156 Fifteenth Street NW, Suite 910, Washington, DC 20005-1704, USA (Tel: +1 202 872 9077; fax: +1 202 872 9137).

The CERES Principles

By adopting these Principles, we publicly affirm our belief that corporations have a responsibility for the environment, and must conduct all aspects of their business as responsible stewards of the environment in a manner that protects the Earth. We believe that corporations must not compromise the ability of future generations to sustain themselves. We will update our practices constantly in light of advances in technology and new understandings in health and environmental science. In collaboration with CERES, we will promote a dynamic process to ensure that the Principles are interpreted in a way that accommodates changing technologies and environmental realities. We intend to make consistent, measurable progress in implementing these Principles and to apply them to all aspects of our operations throughout the world.

Protection of the biosphere

We will reduce and make continual progress towards eliminating the release of any substance that may cause environmental damage to the air, water, or the earth or its inhabitants. We will safeguard all habitats affected by our operations and will protect open spaces and wilderness, while preserving biodiversity.

Sustainable use of natural resources

We will make sustainable use of renewable natural resources, such as water, soils and forests. We will conserve non-renewable natural resources through efficient use and careful planning.

Reduction and disposal of wastes

We will reduce and where possible eliminate waste through source reduction and recycling. All waste will be handled and disposed of through safe and responsible methods.

Energy conservation

We will conserve energy and improve the energy efficiency of our internal operations and of the goods and services we sell. We will make every effort to use environmentally safe and sustainable energy sources.

Risk reduction

We will strive to minimize the environmental, health and safety risks to 'our employees and the communities in which we operate through safe technologies, facilities and operating procedures, and by being prepared for emergencies.

Safe products and services

We will reduce and where possible eliminate the use, manufacture or sale of products and services that cause environmental damage or health or safety hazards. We will inform our customers of the environmental impacts of our products or services and try to correct unsafe use.

Environmental restoration

We will promptly and responsibly correct conditions we have caused that endanger health, safety or the environment. To the extent feasible, we will redress injuries we have caused to persons or damage we have caused to the environment and will restore the environment.

Informing the public

We will inform in a timely manner everyone who may be affected by conditions caused by our company that might endanger health, safety or the environment. We will regularly seek advice and counsel through dialogue with persons in communities near our facilities. We will not take any action against employees for reporting dangerous incidents or conditions to management or to appropriate authorities.

Management commitment

We will implement these Principles and sustain a process that ensures that the Board of Directors and Chief Executive Officer are fully informed about pertinent environmental issues and are fully responsible for environmental policy. In selecting our Board of Directors, we will consider demonstrated environmental commitment as a factor.

Audits and reports

We will conduct an annual self-evaluation of our progress in implementing these Principles. We will support the timely creation of generally accepted environmental audit procedures. We will annually complete the CERES Report, which will be made available to the public.

Disclaimer

These Principles establish an environmental ethic with criteria by which investors and others can assess the environmental performance of companies. Companies that endorse these Principles pledge to go voluntarily beyond the requirements of the law. The terms 'may' and 'might' in Principles one and eight are not meant to encompass every imaginable consequence, no matter how remote. Rather, these Principles obligate endorsers to behave as prudent persons who are not governed by conflicting interests and who possess a strong commitment to environmental excellence and to human health and safety. These Principles are not intended to create new legal liabilities, expand existing rights or obligations, waive legal defences, or otherwise affect the legal position of any endorsing company, and are not intended to be used against an endorser in any legal proceeding for any purpose.

CHARTER OF THE GLOBAL COMMISSION TO FUND THE UNITED NATIONS

An independent international organization, *The Global Commision To Fund The United Nations* ("the Commission"), was organized in August of 1994 by persons concerned with and knowledgeable about the United Nations and its needs for sources of funds to meet current and future daily operating requirements, beyond the current systems of dues and assessments of member nations.

The United Nations is a unique global organization performing indispensable services for member governments and the world's people. Its current funding from member countries' dues is inadequate and unpredictable. Dependable new income, even through new public/private partnerships, is needed if the United Nations is to take on additional assignments to solve global problems that individual nations cannot solve alone and which no other entity can be realistically expected to address effectively. The Commission will also take into account the importance of the growing global civil society of nongovernmental scientific, social welfare, professional, environmental and business associations in a world now dominated by nation states and international corporations. The 50th Anniversary of the United Nations in 1995 makes the work of the Commission particularly timely. Its initial report and findings were presented at the UN World Summit on Social Development in Copenhagen, March, 1995.

Commissioners and members of the Advisory Council to the Commission are experts or knowledgeable about, and can gain ready access to others expert in United Nations operations, budgets, and practices; international monetary and fiscal policies and practices; global geopolitics and governance issues; international activities such as air travel, arms sales and transfers, currency and international securities trading, insurance, military issues; and global environmental pollution, resource protection, and sustainable development. The Commission's high-level, internationally recognized persons are balanced geographically and by expertise, viewpoint, gender, etc. with a broad range of practical financial, business, academic, government, and nongovernmental experience. The Commission's Advisory Council is composed of high-level, academic and technical experts in the specific issue areas of the Charter.

The Commission is studying and developing workable plans for realizing one or more of various means that have been or may be proposed to fund the United Nations particularly its peacemaking, humanitarian, health, education, and sustainable development activities in a businesslike, fully accountable manner, including but not limited to:

      – UN members required to pay interest on unpaid dues and assessments to buttress this bedrock financing system.

    User-fees, royalties, fines or taxation of international activities, including:

      – International arms sales and transfers,

- International currency and derivatives trading,
- Dumping of toxic wastes in international waters,
- Global carbon combustion emissions crossing national borders,
- International air travel and freight,
- Use of global commons such as oceans, space, and electro-magnetic spectrum.

Fees-for-service, barter, or service exchanges:

- Facilities, equipment, supplies, weapons and training for peace keeping/making forces.

- Insurance for peace-keeping operations, such as those under written by a proposed public/private partnership: the United Nations Security Insurance Agency (UNSIA), which will contractually guarantee and underwrite UN peacekeeping support to nations which agree to pay an annual premium for a defined degree of support with security risk assessment performed by insurance industry, military, and financial professionals employed by or cooperating with UNSIA.

- Other such innovative proposals that may be brought to the commission.

The Commission develops and assesses viable, alternative plans to fund the United Nations that can be as widely and deeply supported as possible. In the process, the Commission obtains funds for its own work and seeks input and support from a broad range of constituencies. The Commission's plans will contain pro forma estimates of reasonable and acceptable levels and rates of taxation and/or fees; the methods and costs of collection and enforcement, including the roles of member-states and of UN staff; the expected revenues from and market acceptance of services offered and taxes assessed; the requirements of member-states and the United Nations as a whole for restricting and for empowering the use of received funds; the costs and compensation to member states, including those with deregulated financial markets who need to recoup tax losses, and to those in the private sector providing services that produce the UN revenues; and all start-up considerations relevant thereto.

The Commission operates as a non-partisan, non-sectarian, non-profit organization and has U.S. 501C3 tax exempt status for contributions. Committees of Commissioners interested in specific issue areas covered by the Charter include: 1) Global Financial Markets, 2) UNSIA and Peace-Keeping, and 3) Corporate Codes of Conduct. Consensus is sought among Commissioners co-authoring reports, while still reasonably representing diverse viewpoints within the Commission. Commission reports, while appropriately crediting all contributions, make clear that individual Commissioners bear no responsibility for report contents which they have not approved or authorized.

For information, write to:
Diane E. Sherwood, Director
Global Commission to Fund the UN,
1511 K St., NW, #1120, Washington, DC 20005
Phone: 202/639-9460; Fax: 202/639-9459